THE
Fight
IS FOR
Democracy

THE
Fight
IS FOR
Democracy

*Winning the War of Ideas
in America and the World*

EDITED AND WITH AN INTRODUCTION
BY GEORGE PACKER

Perennial
An Imprint of HarperCollinsPublishers

FIRST EDITION

Designed by Jamie Kerner-Scott

Library of Congress Cataloging-in-Publication Data

The fight is for democracy : winning the war of ideas in America and the world / edited with an introduction by George Packer.—1st ed.
  p. cm.
  ISBN 0-06-053249-1
  1. Democracy—United States. 2. National characteristics, American. 3. Anti-Americanism. 4. United States—Foreign public opinion. I. Packer, George, 1960–

JK1764.F5 2003
320.973—dc21

2003042983

03 04 05 06 07 WB/RRD 10 9 8 7 6 5 4 3 2 1

ACKNOWLEDGMENTS

The editor would like to thank Stephen Heintz, Priscilla Lewis, Benjamin Shute Jr., and the Rockefeller Brothers Fund for convening this book's contributors at the Fund's Pocantico Conference Center in August 2002. Our two-day discussion, which dovetailed with the Fund's new program on democracy and responsible U.S. global engagement, gave us a wonderful opportunity to hear one another's ideas before the essays were written. Thanks are also due to Kathleen Anderson of Anderson-Grinberg Literary Management, who placed this book with an enthusiastic publisher; to Terry Karten of HarperCollins Publishers, who backed it with editorial acumen and moral passion; and to Andrew Proctor of HarperCollins Publishers, who saw it through to publication.

CONTENTS

THE
Fight
IS FOR
Democracy

GEORGE PACKER

Introduction

Living Up to It

I.

IN THE MINUTES AFTER THE SOUTH TOWER FELL on September 11, 2001, an investment banker had an epiphany. Having escaped with his life just ahead of the collapse, he wandered through the smoke and confusion of lower Manhattan until he found himself in a church in Greenwich Village. Alone at the altar, covered in ash and dust, he began to shake and sob. Feeling a hand on his shoulder, he looked up. It was a policeman.

"Don't worry," the cop said, "you're in shock."

"I'm *not* in shock," the investment banker answered. "I like this state. I've never been more cognizant in my life."

The idea for this book—barely more than a sensation—came that morning around the same time that the banker noticed his changed consciousness. I thought, or felt, because there were really no words yet: Maybe this will make us better. That was all; I didn't know what it meant. The feeling made me ashamed because it seemed insufficiently horror-stricken. But like any repressed feeling, it continued to lurk. And in the hours and days that followed, it seemed to be borne out on the streets of New York.

I spent most of two days sitting on a sidewalk in downtown Brooklyn, waiting to give blood with hundreds of other people. I had long conversations with those near me, in the temporary intimacy between strangers that kept breaking out all over the city. There was Matthew Timms, a twenty-eight-year-old unemployed video producer who had tried to film the attacks from across the East River in Williamsburg, only to find his camera battery had gone dead. His own detachment, he said—which extended to his whole life—so disturbed him that he wanted his blood drawn in order to overcome it. "I volunteered so I could be a part of something," he said. "All over the world people do something for an ideal. I've been at no point in my life when I could say something I've done has affected mankind. Like when the news was on, I was thinking, What if there was a draft? Would I go? I think I would." Lauren Moynihan, a lawyer in her thirties, had traveled all over the city pleading with hospitals and emergency centers to take her blood and been turned away by all of them. As a "civilian," without skills, she felt useless. "This is like a little bit short of volunteering to go for the French Foreign Legion," said Dave Lampe, a computer technician from Jersey City who was wearing suspenders decorated with brightly colored workman's tools. A sixteen-year-old girl named Amalia della Paolera, passing out juice and cookies along the line, said, "This is the time when we need to be, like, pulling together and doing as much as we can for each other and not, like, sitting at home watching it on TV and saying, like, 'Oh, there's another bomb.'"

Everyone wanted to be of use and no one knew how, as if citizenship were a skilled position for which none of us had the right experience and qualifications. People seemed to be feeling the same thing: They had not been living as they would have liked; the horrors of the day before had woken them up; they wanted to change. So they had come to stand in line, and they continued to wait long after it became clear that no blood was going to be needed.

The mood that came over New York after September 11—for

me it will always be tied to the "Missing" picture posted at my subway stop of a young woman named Gennie Gambale, and then all the other pictures that appeared overnight around the city; the flags sprouting in shop windows; the clots of melted candle wax on sidewalks; the bitter smell of smoke from lower Manhattan; the clusters of people gathering in the Brooklyn Heights Promenade or Union Square to sing or write messages or read them; the kindness on the subway; the constant wail of sirens for no obvious purpose; the firemen outside a station house in midtown accepting flowers at midnight; the rescue workers at the end of their shift trudging up West Street with gray dust coating their faces and clothes; the people waiting at barricades on Canal Street with pots of foil-covered food; the garrulousness of strangers; the sleeplessness, the sense of being on alert all the time and yet useless—this mood broke over the city like a storm at the end of a season of languid days stretching back longer than anyone could remember. People became aware, as if for the first time, that they were not merely individuals with private ends. Whitman's spirit walked down every street: "What is more subtle than this which ties me to the woman or man that looks in my face?" The embarrassment of strong emotions felt by sophisticated people in peaceful times dropped away, and strangers looked at one another differently. We became citizens.

This mood lasted around two weeks, then it began to fade. The cleanup was taken out of the hands of volunteers and entrusted to experts with heavy machinery. Elected officials told the public to resume normal life as quickly as possible. Average people could show they cared by going out to dinner and holding on to stocks. Then came the anthrax scare, which created more panic than the air attacks had, replacing solidarity with hysteria; and then the Afghanistan war, which signaled the return of the familiar, since the public in whose name it was fought had no more to do with it than with other recent wars. By now, it's hard to believe that anything as profound as the banker's epiphany really happened at all.

I thought that the attacks and the response would puncture a bloated era in American history and mark the start of a different, more attractive era. I thought that without some such change we would not be able to win this new war—that the crisis that mattered most was internal. One undercurrent of the mood of those days was a sense of shame: We had had it too good, had gotten away with it for too long. In the weeks afterward, W. H. Auden's poem "September 1, 1939" kept appearing in E-mails and Web sites and on subway walls, with its suddenly apt first stanza:

> *I sit in one of the dives*
> *On Fifty-second Street*
> *Uncertain and afraid*
> *As the clever hopes expire*
> *Of a low dishonest decade:*
> *Waves of anger and fear*
> *Circulate over the bright*
> *And darkened lands of the earth,*
> *Obsessing our private lives;*
> *The unmentionable odour of death*
> *Offends the September night.*

For at least a low dishonest decade, large numbers of Americans had been living in an untenable state, a kind of complacent fantasy in which the dollar is always strong; the stock market keeps going up; investments always provide a handsome return; wars are fought by other people, end quickly, and can be won with no tax increases, no civilian sacrifices, and few if any American casualties; global dominance is maintained on the strength of technological and economic success without the taint or burden of an occupying empire; power and wealth demand no responsibility; and history leaves Americans alone. It didn't matter whether a Democrat or a Republican was in the White House, or whether we were bombing some foreign country or not. Public concerns had nothing to do with politics or citizenship, those relics of the eighteenth century, and everything to do with the market—"Where," Auden wrote, "blind skyscrapers use/Their full height to proclaim/The strength of Collective Man."

This fantasy took on its most lavish and triumphant expression in New York, and it was frozen in place there when the towers fell. Several weeks later, a journalist wandered into the ghostly executive dining room of Deutsche Bank, across Liberty Street from where the South Tower had stood, and noted the breakfast menu for September 11: smoked-salmon omelettes and chocolate-filled pancakes. The remains of a meal for two—half-drunk juice turning dark, a mostly eaten omelette, withering fruit—sat abandoned on a table. The whole scene was finely coated in the ubiquitous gray dust and ash, like the tableaux of Romans caught eating and sleeping by the lava of Vesuvius; except that Pompeii was entirely destroyed, whereas the American civilization at which the nineteen radical Islamist hijackers aimed passenger planes still persists in roughly its old shape, though ragged at the edges and shaky in the nerves.

Political predictions usually come true when reality and wish coincide, and as it turned out, I was wrong. September 11 has not ushered in an era of reform. It has not made America or Americans very much better, more civic-minded. It has not replaced market values with democratic values. It has not transformed America from the world's overwhelming economic and military power into what it has often been in the past—a light of freedom and equality unto the nations. None of this has happened, because America is currently governed by bad leaders, because the opposition is weak, because our wealth and power remain so enormous that even an event as dramatic as the terrorist attacks can't fully penetrate them, because a crisis doesn't automatically bring down the curtain on an era, because change usually comes in the manner of a corkscrew rather than a hammer.

Yet my first response on the morning of September 11 still seems the one worth holding on to. The investment banker jerked awake, the aspirations up and down the line of those wanting to give blood, revealed something about the moral condition of Americans at this moment in our history. Like any crisis, the attacks brought buried feelings to the surface and showed our society in a collective mirror. That day changed America less than most people anticipated, but it made Americans think about change—not just as individuals, but as a country.

2.

THE HIJACKERS BELIEVED THEY were striking a blow at a decadent civilization, and they were partly right. Islamic terrorists had been trying for years to make Americans aware of their implacable hostility. In 1996 Osama bin Laden declared war on American interests in the Arab world, and in 1998 he extended it to American and Jewish civilians everywhere, telling a reporter that he had learned from Somalia that Americans were too soft and cowardly to fight back. No one here noticed. Only a deeply insular, perpetually distracted people with a short memory, a vague notion of the rest of the world, and no firsthand experience of tyranny could have absorbed all the blows of the past decade without understanding that a serious movement wanted to destroy us. Imagine what the hijackers saw in their last days on earth—a society so capacious and free that it opened itself wide to the agents of its own destruction and gave them the tools to do it. The soulless motels and parking lots of small towns from Florida to Maine, the promiscuous street mix of colors and sexes and faiths, the lack of prayer, the half-dressed women, the fat people in tight clothes, the world empty of Allah, the supreme thrill of knowing in advance what every ignorant idiot around them did not, the endless stock-market news on airport lounge televisions, the drowsy security guards, and finally the towers coming into view, thrusting up out of the clear blue sky in their dazzling white arrogance. The hijackers would have seen, and hated, both America's best and its worst—the rowdy polychrome energy, the moral emptiness of wealth and power.

To imagine a new, and a better, American response—which, in one way or another, is the purpose of all the essays in this book—it's necessary to look hard at where we are now and how we got here. One of the features of American life that had fallen into decay by September 11, 2001, was our democracy. The reasons are numerous and have a complex history, but I want to discuss three. The first has to do with government, and with ancient (and more recent) American attitudes toward it. The second has to do with money, and how it's distributed in American society. The third has to do with an idea, which I will call liberalism, and the people whose business is ideas, who are called intellectuals.

Suspicion of government was seared into Americans' minds before there was a United States. But the Enlightenment pamphleteers and politicians—Thomas Paine, Thomas Jefferson, and others—distrusted government in a way almost opposite that of modern people. The eighteenth-century mind that gave birth to the new republic believed human beings to be rational creatures with a nearly limitless capacity for finding happiness if only they are free. "Government in a well-constituted republic," Paine wrote in *The Rights of Man,* his scathing response to Edmund Burke's *Reflections on the*

Revolution in France, the founding document of conservatism, "requires no belief in man beyond what his reason can give." In this sense all men are indeed created equal—endowed not just with rights but with reason. Liberal government, of which America gave the world the first example, was government based on reason rather than tradition (or ignorance, as Paine would have it; or faith, in the Islamists' terms). This confidence in the human mind to work out its own destiny meant that government, set up by consent to limit freedom only enough to ensure the public good, should remain small. If it got too big, it would concentrate too much power in privileged hands and turn back toward favoritism and distinctions, and against freedom and its rational use. Limited government, then, was a means, not an end; the end was human happiness, best achieved when men are free.

Individualism is part of our national character—the most famous part. But so is moralism, and this, too, goes back several centuries. The utopian fantasies of the pilgrims were submerged under the commercial practices of republican society, but they were never completely buried. The main theme of American history since independence has been the cheerful, vulgar, brutal, wantonly innocent pursuit of happiness, from the frontiersman to the venture capitalist. But a minor theme keeps recurring, a moralism so rigid that it baffles Europeans—from John Brown to Kenneth Starr. Just as American individualism can appear either healthy and dynamic or blindly selfish, American moralism swings wildly between high-minded idealism and hysterical intolerance. At certain moments— our entry into World War I was one—the transformation happens almost overnight: The muckraker gave way to the night rider, the progressive city commission to the Red Scare, without any letup in the sense of a national crusade.

The most potent political idea of my lifetime has been hostility to government—from Goldwater's crankish "extremism in the defense of liberty," to Reagan's triumphant "government isn't the solution to the problem; government is the problem," to Clinton's final tactical surrender: "The era of big government is over." In this thinking, the government doesn't embody the will of the people—in fact, it's something alien, and a threat to their well-being. The creed reached a reductio ad absurdum in the last days of the 2000 campaign, when George W. Bush proclaimed that the Democrats "want the federal government controlling the Social Security like it's some kind of federal program. We understand differently, though. You see, it's your money, not the government's money." The superficial similarity of modern conservatism to the language of the founders is misleading. Jefferson and his generation saw *democratic* government—a new beginning of human history—as the collective embodiment of rational man. It served the public good. Conservatives today have no concept of the public good. They see Americans as investors and consumers, not citizens.

Like most victorious ideologies, antigovernment conservatism grew as complacent as the welfare-state liberalism it replaced—and far more extreme. The thinking of Timothy McVeigh wasn't far from the core of the "respectable" American right in the 1990s. The doctrinal rigidity hardened to the point where, in the absence of government interventions, untreated problems, from the health-care system to the electoral system, continued to fester, and still do. Among other things, September 11 reminded Americans that they need a government: Inside the towers, public employees were going up while private ones went down.

One of the strangest things about the antigovernment era is that it coincided with the first prolonged drop in wages in American history. While free-market thinking was reigning triumphant, the middle class was contracting; even the brief pause during Clinton's second term turned out to be riding on a mountain of personal debt and a stock-market bubble that had to burst. So why was there no protest movement, not even a moderate legislative program, against the concentration of 50 percent of the nation's wealth among 1 percent of its people, the lopsided effects of tax cuts, the massive economic dislocations caused by deindustrialization and globalization? When you come to think of it, less calamitous forces sparked the American Revolution.

But the change from an industrial to a high-tech economy, along with the movement of jobs and investment around the world, has been too incremental and various and complex to arouse any focused resistance. Most of the influential voices in society—the politicians, scholars, and journalists who, along with other professional classes, seemed to do better and better—said that the change was inevitable and ultimately beneficial, and the public believed them. Meanwhile, the money kept adding up in the winners' column, staggering amounts that no longer meant anything—$150 million compensation packages for a CEO having a subpar year. This money bought unprecedented political power. Some businessmen spent their fortunes running for office; others paid for their influence indirectly.

The relationship between democracy and economic inequality—the subject of Jeff Madrick's essay—creates a kind of self-perpetuating cycle: The people hold government in low esteem; public power shrinks against the awesome might of corporations and rich individuals; money and its influence claim a greater and greater share of political power; and the public, priced out of the democratic game, grows ever more cynical about politics and puts more of its energy into private ends. Far from creating a surge of reform, the erosion of the middle class has only deepened the disenchantment.

For thirty years or more the musculature of democracy has atrophied, culminating in 2000 with a stolen presidential election.

For the past century, the political philosophy of collective action on behalf of freedom and justice has been liberalism. For most of that time, it was an expansive, self-confident philosophy, and history was on its side. Since around 1968, liberalism has been an active participant in its own decline. A creed that once spoke on behalf of the desire of millions of Americans for a decent life and a place in the sun shrank to a set of rigid pieties preached on college campuses and in eccentric big-city enclaves. It turned insular, defensive, fragmented, and pessimistic. The phenomenon of political correctness, which for a period during the 1980s and early '90s became the most visible expression of liberalism, amounted to a desire to control reality by purifying language and thought, to make the world better by changing a syllabus, or a name, or a word. It was a kind of cargo cult. At bottom, it represented a retreat from politics.

During these years, the energy that had once gone into struggles for justice under the heading of labor or civil rights balkanized and propelled narrower causes, defined not by any universal principles but along the lines of identity. This turned liberalism's original project on its head: Two centuries ago, and up until the late 1960s, it was conservatives who argued for the importance of tradition, tribe, culture, for all the things given, while liberals put their faith in the free individual, who transcended any specificities of time and place, and whose rights were universal, by virtue of being human. Rhetorically, at least, all of that changed in the past few decades. The right took up the universalist language of reason, freedom, and truth, while multiculturalism spoke for group grievances based on the accident of birth. Many of them were real and redress was long overdue, but the idea of social justice ended up being someone else's business.

While liberalism slept, the country became more corporate, less democratic, less equal, more complacent. Liberalism has been a kind of enzyme in America's democratic system, periodically catalyzing reactions, speeding up change, making the organism more vital. Without it, our democracy tends to get fat and sluggish, as the pursuit of happiness guaranteed in the Declaration of Independence becomes a wholly private matter. In the tension between individual and community that every democracy has to negotiate, what we saw in America in the years leading up to September 11 was the triumph of market individualism, without commitments. The polis was routed. As Todd Gitlin argues in his essay, the sense of civic responsibility died on both the left and the right. Instead, they offered a choice of hedonisms.

Dissatisfaction with the condition of democracy isn't new. It recurs among writers and intellectuals throughout American history, almost always couched in images of rot or decay or slackness, as periods of intense civic activism give way to ages of business dominance. The republicans of the Revolutionary era saw their new country release the massive energy of a free people into the getting of wealth, and it was not the republic for which men had pledged their lives, their fortunes, and their sacred honor. By 1809 Philip Freneau, a Jeffersonian poet and journalist, beheld his countrymen "besotted by prosperity, corrupted by avarice, abject from luxury," and in 1812 he proposed another war against the British as a dubious restoration of the spirit of '76. After the supreme sacrifices of the Civil War, Walt Whitman began to wonder what the fighting had all been for— whether making America safe for Jay Gould and John D. Rockefeller and a victorious people "with hearts of rags and souls of chalk" had merited Gettysburg's last full measure of devotion. "Is not Democracy of human rights humbug after all?" Whitman asked. In his 1949 book *The Vital Center*, Arthur Schlesinger Jr. tried to suck new life into the lungs of the New Deal and antitotalitarianism as the stagnant waters of the television era started to rise around him: "Why does not democracy believe in itself with passion? Why is freedom not a fighting faith?" Democracy, it turns out, is a muscle that needs more frequent exercise than Americans have generally been interested in mustering.

In our own gilded age—whose obituary some commentators wrote after September 11—intellectuals played a curiously muted role. Who will be regarded as the Freneau, the Whitman, or the Schlesinger of the Nasdaq era? There was no convincing critique, no passionate dissent, no partisan literature that moved significant numbers of people and stands a chance of being read in ten years. The reasons for this intellectual vacuum are many (and Susie Linfield explores them in her essay). Academic thinking, infatuated with postmodernist theory, has satisfied itself with a fake-specialist jargon and a coy relativism that prefers dancing circles around important questions to the risk of trying to answer them. Political dissidence suffers, as it has in this country at least since Thoreau, from a sneering contempt for average American life and a sentimental insistence that reality simply fall in line behind enlightened feelings. The best imaginative writers withdrew into the inner life and its discontents, or else wrote about American society with such compulsive irony that nothing could be affirmed beyond a style of narrative brilliance. There is also the possibility that most intellectuals, in universities and think tanks and journals, have no authentic quarrel with American life. Seduction by iced latte, mutual fund, and *The Sopranos* is a slow, nearly invisible disease; it can happen without leaving a trace in print, yet at some point the organism has lost the impulse to object. An opposition that is financially secure, mentally insincere, and generally ignored isn't likely to produce *Common Sense* or *Democratic Vistas*. Very few intellectuals today— and this goes for conservatives as well, including those who have made careers out of loudly claiming otherwise—feel a strong enough attachment to their country to want to change it. The idea that anything of great consequence depends on the condition of America's democracy sounds quaint.

This is the landscape on which the sun rose that late-summer Tuesday morning, as the polls opened in New York for a primary election that bored everyone, and the bankers rode the escalator toward their smoked-salmon omelettes. Then out of the blue sky came what Hannah Arendt called a new thing in the world. It was the worst thing most Americans alive today have ever known. And the task was now ours to understand how the world was, and was not, new.

3.

THE NINE ESSAYS IN THIS BOOK deal with the question of what American democracy stands for after September 11. They come in a variety of styles and voices, and there are disagreements between them. What they have in common is an attachment to the ideals of American democracy, a dissatisfaction with its current practice, and a belief that we are engaged in a war for world opinion, a war of ideas. No one should doubt that we are losing it—and that this has something to do with the condition of American democracy. Our leaders have failed to articulate what we are fighting for beyond our own security and the assertion of our power around the world; and the failure is no accident or "missed opportunity." It comes from the fact that they themselves have no ardor for democracy. The ideals of freedom and equality, secularism, tolerance, and critical inquiry that have lain at the heart of the American experiment from the beginning get lip service from those in power; much of the world, with some reason, sees America's commitment to them as shallow and hypocritical.

The fight against political Islam isn't a clash of civilizations, and it isn't an imperialist campaign. As Paul Berman writes, it is a conflict of ideologies and they come down to the century-old struggle between totalitarianism and liberal democracy. There is no possibility of a negotiated peace, because the ideologies are incompatible—they can't coexist. "Between democracy and totalitarianism there can be no compromise," said an authority on the subject, Benito Mussolini. Leaving aside the implacable foes who want us dead, America has to persuade people around the world that this is their fight, too; that the side of liberal democracy is where their hope lies.

In the war on terror, the ultimate enemy isn't a method, even one as apocalyptically menacing as al-Qaeda–style terrorism. It's the outlook that produced al-Qaeda—in this case, political Islam, but at bottom the view of all people who fear and hate the modern democratic world, with its fluidity, its openness, its assertion of the individual's freedom and of human equality. America is the most vibrant example. America is also the world's leading power, constantly racking up resentments. It's this combination of facts that makes our situation as complex and delicate as it is.

America is seen by much of the world as an empire without actual colonies, perhaps the most dominant since Rome. To Americans this view is bewildering. Unlike the British or the French, Americans have never had an interest in empire building. They elect presidents who have barely traveled abroad, eliminate the U.S. Information Service and shut down cultural centers in foreign capitals, resent being "the world's policeman," and pride themselves on their ignorance of other countries. Throughout the decade after the Cold War ended, American military action and inaction, corporate dominance, and cultural influence were making us the object of hope and confusion and anger among hundreds of millions of people, from Kigali to Jakarta. Meanwhile, it's difficult to think of a period when Americans showed less interest in the rest of the world. Genocide, famine, plague, economic upheaval, filthy wars on every continent, and, of course, international terrorism—an incredibly tumultuous period (at what was supposed to be the end of history), but citizens of the world's superpower largely succeeded in not paying attention. While we were absorbed with Internet chat rooms and a blue Gap dress, power and resentment accumulated in front of our noses or behind our backs. Even the battle over multiculturalism turned out to have nothing to teach us about anyone else—it was an internal fight and a ritualized one, the narcissism of small differences. September 11 came as an immense slap to this immense complacency.

The real question is not whether America is an empire, but what to do with the power we have. It's a question with which Americans are instinctively uncomfortable, none more than those who think of themselves as liberals. Much of what made up liberal thinking in the past few decades will be of no help from now on. The reluctance to make judgments, the finely ironic habits of thought, the reflexive contempt for patriotism, the suspicion of uniforms and military qualities, the sentimentality about oppressed peoples, the irresponsibility about hard choices, the embarrassment with phrases like "democratic values" and "Western civilization"—the softheadedness into which liberalism sank after the 1960s seems as useless today as isolationism in 1941 or compromise in 1861. If there is any guide to this strange new era in our recent past, it could be the liberal anti-Communism of the postwar period (discussed by Michael Tomasky), which confidently defended democracy in the face of totalitarianism but also took economic justice and nation building seriously. It was both tough and wise; it had a decent respect for the opinion of mankind; it understood the struggle against Communism to be a struggle for hearts and minds.

So is the current conflict. Kanan Makiya's essay looks at the political psychology of his native Iraq and, more broadly, that region where democracy has been slowest to take hold. Breaking the seal of tyranny in the Arab world and letting in fresh liberal air is a matter of our security as much as their freedom. But the ultimate audience for this fight is neither in the West nor in the Arab countries, but among the vast majority of the world's poor. Beyond the struggle to survive—to avoid disease, find enough to eat, educate their children, stay out of the way of men with guns—people in Asia and Africa and Latin America increasingly wonder whether the modern world holds a place for them, whether dignity and a decent life and a sense of identity are possible. This is an economic problem, but not only that—it's also cultural and, in a way, existential. Globalization—the subject of William Finnegan's essay—didn't lose its importance on September 11. Just the opposite: It underlies everything else, and the shape it takes in the new century will determine whether the world's poor see America as a beacon or a blackmailer.

Without a vibrant, hardheaded liberalism in America, the era that began on September 11, 2001, will continue in the direction that we now see: narrow, defensive, chauvinistic, an American war for American security that leaves the rest of the world feeling ignored or threatened. The title of a conservative manifesto proclaimed *Why We Fight: Moral Clarity and the War on Terrorism*. Moral clarity is not why we should fight; it is why the other side fights. What the title of Vijay Seshadri's essay calls our "idea of transcendence" is secular and democratic—an idea of human possibility, not fixed and eternal truth. Beyond sheer physical survival, a liberal civilization like ours should fight for the ability to remain open to what's foreign or unknown, tell leaders what they don't want to hear, tolerate moral uncertainty, act in spite of self-criticism, and ask questions like: Can a civilization remain liberal when it's as heavily armed as ours? Can a fight for democracy be led by the world's greatest power?

As Laura Secor discusses in her essay, liberals have an uneasy relationship with force. Force has no sense of complexity. It reduces everything to the elemental level where thinking is trampled underfoot. When America entered World War I, an argument broke out among the first generation of Americans to call themselves liberals. On one side, people like the editors of *The New Republic* saw the war as an international extension of progressive reform. In language as exalted as their hero Woodrow Wilson's, they proclaimed the world's first humanitarian war. On the other side stood skeptics like *The New Republic*'s own young contributor Randolph Bourne. To him, liberal intellectuals urging war were like children who imagined they could control a wild elephant by riding on its back. "Willing war means willing all the evils that are organically bound up with it," he wrote (but not in *The New Republic*, which banned his criticism). "A good many people still seem to believe in a peculiar kind of democratic and antiseptic war. The pacifists opposed the war because they knew this was an illusion, and because of the myriad hurts they knew war would do the promise of democracy at home. For once the babes and sucklings seem to have been wiser than the children of light." Intellectuals like John Dewey, Bourne said, were too rational to understand war. On airships of idealism, they unleashed a barrage of violence that fell on American towns as well as the trenches in France. The war whipped up a frenzy of intolerance all over the country that destroyed what was left of the progressive era, mocked Wilson's vision of a just new world order, and produced a backlash against reform lasting for the next decade.

Liberalism has a tendency to respond to its doubts by overreaching. There are good reasons in history and principle—Vietnam is one—to keep Randolph Bourne's warning in mind. But there are equally good reasons—the war against fascism—to imagine exceptions. We have to answer the demands of our own age. And what we need today is more, not less, confidence in liberal democracy. America has always swung feverishly between its individualism and its moralism—between periods of business dominance, when the rest of the world can go to hell, and bursts of reformist zeal, when America shines a light unto the nations. September 11 was a hinge between two such eras—and our current conservative leadership wants to take the country into one without leaving the other. It wants to wage war on terrorism and still preserve all the privileges and injustices of a low dishonest age. It wants lockstep unity and unequal sacrifice.

Citizens of a democracy need to know what they're fighting for, and to believe in it. We are fighting the wrong fight if corporations can move offshore to avoid taxes while the working poor get audited; if the vice president's former company profiteers off the war while Americans taking care of old people make $6 an hour; if millionaires buy elections here while generals win them by fraud and force overseas; if security becomes an excuse for taking away some liberties while self-censorship removes others; if Saudi oil princes are coddled while Muslim students can't get U.S. visas; if Afghan warlords are left in power while returning refugees are allowed to starve. In the long run we will lose if this fight isn't for something. It ought to be for democracy.

Michael Tomasky

Between Cheney and Chomsky

Making a Domestic Case for a New Liberal Foreign Policy

Publicly, in the late spring of 1964, Lyndon Johnson was about as hawkish on the Vietnam War as it was possible to be. The Gulf of Tonkin "incident," which we now know to have been at best half an incident, was three months away yet, and the first large-scale commitment of American troops to the region nearly a year distant. Nevertheless, even at this early interval, the public Johnson spoke bullishly on the need to defend America's interests and to beat back the Red wedge.

The private Johnson that spring spoke quite differently, according to transcripts of Oval Office meetings and telephone conversations that were made public in 1997. Confiding to an old friend and mentor, Georgia Democratic senator Richard Russell, in May 1964, LBJ agonized over the impending conflict in Southeast Asia as "the damnedest worst mess I ever saw. . . . I do not see how we are ever going to get out of it without getting in a major war with the Chinese and all of them down there in those rice paddies and jungles." That same month he spoke similarly to McGeorge Bundy, his national security adviser: "I stayed awake at night worrying about this thing, and the more I think about it, I don't know what in the hell . . . It looks to me like we're getting into another Korea. It just worries the hell out of me. . . . I don't think it's worth fighting for and I don't think we can get out, and it's just the biggest damn mess."

Why the two Johnsons? Well, we understand the answer to that. Politicians often have to say one thing in public while believing another in private—it buys them time to try to work behind the scenes to move public opinion in their direction. But Johnson failed to do this, of course, so the more compelling, and tragic, question is: Why did the public Johnson never act on the private Johnson's intuitions and beliefs? Why, in more blunt words, were fifty-eight thousand Americans sent to their deaths *even though* their commander in chief knew as he was signing their deployment orders that the United States' first-ever military defeat would be the almost inevitable result? Johnson's biographers have chiefly sought to explain the ghastly contradiction in terms of a great Shakespearean personal flaw. No doubt that was the case. It has proven an especially alluring analysis in light of Johnson's unprecedented courage on social policy: How could a man so willing, even determined, to take political risks on domestic questions have been such a coward on foreign affairs? But ultimately, the fatal-flaw theory is more a literary explanation— conducive as it is to the dramatic narrative arc that is a necessity of great biography—or, alternatively, a characterological one. It is not a *political* explanation. And when we're talking about politics, it is political explanations first and foremost that we should seek.

The main reason, then, that Johnson pursued the war? Without question, it was the domestic political pressure he felt to do so. Consider another snippet of that conversation with Senator Russell, as described by Robert Scheer in the *Los Angeles Times* in 1997:

> But [Johnson] did agree that the status quo in Vietnam was untenable; the choice was withdrawal or escalation. And he

*chose the latter because to do otherwise would endanger his
chances for victory in the election that fall. "The Republicans are going to make a political issue out of it," warned
Russell. "It's the only issue that they've got."*

Johnson concurred. He was particularly concerned about the
prospect that Henry Cabot Lodge Jr., then the U.S. ambassador to
Vietnam, might return to America to take a place on the GOP ticket
that fall. Though a moderate, Lodge was a Vietnam hawk who was
urging the administration to act with force and even, to Johnson's
eyes, turning the embassy in Saigon into his own little freelancing
fief. Johnson disdained Lodge's ambassadorship, but he knew, too,
that Lodge would have made an attractive running mate for either
fellow moderate Nelson Rockefeller or perhaps especially for conservative Barry Goldwater—and indeed, Lodge's political strength
had been made clear on March 10, 1964, when, in the New Hampshire GOP presidential primary, he defeated both front-runners by
collecting 33,007 votes *as a write-in*. One can easily imagine how that
showing must have impressed, not to say scared, Johnson. And so,
much as the president might have liked to recall Lodge, he dared
not, because "he'd be back home campaigning against us every day."

But the political cost that Johnson calculated of withdrawal was
not limited to having to endure the surly arraignments of a bother-
some vice presidential nominee from the other side. This former
senator, who had lived through the loyalty oaths and the McCarthy
era and the tumultuous debates over the loss of China and the
Korean War and so much else domestic turmoil around foreign-
policy questions, felt that his experience had led him to conclude
that there was only one way Congress would deal in an election year
with a president who withdrew from Vietnam: "Well," he asked

Russell, "they would impeach a president that would run out, wouldn't they?"

WOULD THEY? IN RETROSPECT, it sounds extreme; Democrats did control both houses of Congress at the time, and the America of 1964 was a nation where civic faith in the leaders and institutions was still strong enough that the idea of impeaching a president was something most Americans couldn't comprehend. On the other hand, Johnson's acumen in such matters is not to be shrugged off. He was nothing, after all, if not one of the great vote-counters in American political history. We should not doubt that he was doing the roll call in his head as he spoke the words, and that he understood the stakes with a bookmaker's precision.

But the hypothetical question about Johnson's fate isn't the point. The point, instead, is that Johnson believed he had no way to counter this pressure, and no public case to make against it. Here was a president wrestling with vital questions, questions of the gravest historical importance imaginable—about whether containment policy, which had been initially conceived to apply to Europe only, should pertain to Southeast Asia in either a strategic or a moral sense; about whether what was happening in Vietnam (and so many other places at the time) was better understood as a war of Communist machination or a struggle for national liberation; about which side of history a military intervention would land the United States on (the wrong one, James Forrestal, a China specialist on the National Security Council, bluntly warned in a May 1964 paper arguing against engagement). The loftiest questions a president can face, questions that plead to be answered on their own merit. But domestic political pressure—small, straightforward, vulgar— trumped them all.

Johnson was not facing a problem that was merely political in that summer of 1964. It was surely that, but it was more: He was facing a philosophical problem that strikes at the very center of liberalism's relationship to popular democracy. In a democracy, the first principle is that the majority rules; but liberalism has often depended for its strength and successes on a corollary principle of democracy— namely, that constraints are placed on the majority so that it doesn't become a mob. The noblest concerns of post–civil rights era social liberalism—civil liberties, especially for those most likely to be denied them; equality under the law; support from the state for those with the least political and economic power—are not those that a majority in this country has usually been inclined to endorse, except under particular and unique historical circumstances. Whatever liberalism's political fate at any given moment, certain safeguards have existed—the Bill of Rights, the Fourteenth Amendment, the federal courts—to help ensure that those constraints survive to one degree or another. Their existence has generally—by no means always, but generally— tilted events in liberalism's favor (it wasn't majority opinion, for example, that got James Meredith enrolled at the University of Mississippi).

But where questions of foreign policy are involved, few if any such constraints are in place. Manipulation of public opinion—of the majority—is what usually decides matters. This may seem paradoxical: It is often argued that foreign-policy making, the province of a handful of men (and just lately women) from rarefied backgrounds, is abstracted from the coarse push-and-pull of domestic politics, and in some important ways this is the case. A president can make many determinations by fiat, without consulting Congress or the public at all, and many other decisions are made within agencies that operate either without the same kind of congressional review that domestic agencies face or with virtually no review. But as Johnson learned, the major presidential decisions and broad policy initiatives—questions of war and peace, of alliance and agreement—are always taken within the bounds of what public and congressional opinion permits (or, sometimes, forces). Johnson could not fight that opinion in 1964 and 1965. Franklin Delano Roosevelt had to wait for it to coalesce behind him, in December 1941, to engage in the fight against fascism. And so, making foreign policy in this country has almost always meant doing whatever it took to agitate the public into accepting the desired point of view—by setting up phony attacks like Tonkin, by inflating some wretched Marxist tin pot into a grave threat to national security, or simply by making arguments to the people that were, in Dean Acheson's famous phrase with regard to the Truman Doctrine, "clearer than truth."

Conservatives have understood and exploited this far better than liberals* have. And they have driven foreign policy for the better part, really, of the last fifty years. For the last two decades especially, conservatism has dominated the domestic argument over foreign policy. Conservatism has disposed, while liberalism has reacted. And if this was true before the September 11 attacks, it has been, to steal from Acheson, more than true since. It was on extravagant display during the 2002 midterm elections, when George W. Bush and

---

*For simplicity's sake, this essay uses "liberals" and "Democrats" more or less interchangeably. I understand that there may be reasons not to do this: Connecticut senator Joe Lieberman is a Democrat who would not call himself a liberal, at least openly, and Vermont senator Jim Jeffords is a liberal who does not call himself a Democrat. More than that, there is, of course, a pretty dramatic schism within the Democratic Party between the centrists and the more traditional liberals. But the usage is justifiable here in this sense. Broadly speaking, the Democratic Party is the liberal party in America. That the nature of that liberalism may have changed from period to period, a reality this essay acknowledges and discusses, does not change the core fact that the Democrats have generally represented the liberal worldview, distinguishable both from the conservative view, expressed in the Republican Party, and the views of the far left, which has no mass-membership party per se and no real influence on the larger American public, but nevertheless has an influence beyond its numbers among intellectuals (and has very different ideas about the world, and about American power, than does liberalism).

the Republican Party ran circles around the Democrats on foreign policy questions, to such an extent that even an idea that began as a Democratic one—the creation of a Department of Homeland Security, proposed first by Senator Joe Lieberman, a Democrat—became solidly identified with the Republican president in the public mind, while the Democrats came to be seen as obstructing its passage because they were taking orders from the unions. That issue, and the GOP rout in those elections, showed a public whose lack of confidence in Democrats' ability to lead on foreign-policy questions verged on contempt. And no wonder: The Democrats showed, during the 2002 campaigning, that their only foreign-policy problem was that they didn't have one.

There are many reasons for this conservative domination of the foreign-policy debate, and they are generally well understood. Emotionally, they can be reduced to the notion that conservative arguments for a dominant America, continually outspending and checkmating the enemy, be he in Moscow or Baghdad, are just more appealing to a public not generally all that interested in foreign affairs or the world's complexities. And while American public opinion may have a strong isolationist streak, isolationism does not mean weakness; a desire to stay out of fights doesn't translate into a desire to be unprepared for them should they arise. And so telling people, "Our nation must be the strongest in the world!" has made for an easier sale than adding the "yes, but . . ." part that has been liberalism's dolorous burden.

The conservatives' arguments were dead wrong in 1964 and 1965; they forced us into a war we shouldn't have fought. (If such a thing were possible in this world, America should have erected statues to two actual heroes of the Vietnam War: Senators Wayne Morse and Ernest Gruening, who had the wisdom and courage to vote against the Gulf of Tonkin resolution.) And they led to the one period in our recent history in which the conservative argument fell out of favor, and liberals, and the Democratic Party, had won the foreign-policy debate. The years 1968 to 1978 or so constituted one of those rare intervals when a majority of public opinion gathered behind liberal foreign-policy arguments. For reasons we'll shortly get to, this era turns out to be bane today to liberalism; its guiding principles, while appropriate and morally essential at the time, have now calcified into a reflexive anti-interventionist posture that doesn't necessarily apply to today's crises and that, to return to this essay's theme, cost Democrats dearly in terms of the battle for public opinion. But at the time, those principles were anything but costly: On a range of fronts liberalism was ascendant. Majorities consistently opposed or were uncertain about the war in Vietnam and demanded a new phase of detente and arms negotiations. Richard Nixon, who rose to fame as a ferocious anti-Communist, won the presidency in 1968 only by announcing that he had a "secret plan" to end the fighting. He was even forced to respond to domestic liberal pressure by unveiling, in the fall of 1969, his "Vietnamization" policy, whereby he gradually reduced U.S. troop commitments and turned the fighting over to the Vietnamese (except in Cambodia and Laos, but that's another story).

The skepticism about American power outlived Nixon. Gerald Ford faced intense domestic pressure to bring the last troops home from Vietnam. The America of 1976—even the Republican Party of 1976—was not quite yet ready for the blunt remonstrances of a Ronald Reagan, who could not wrest the party's nomination for president that year. In 1975 and 1976, the congressional committees chaired by Frank Church and Otis Pike exposed the nefarious doings of American intelligence agencies in a series of astonishing hearings: Church even poked around in the influence large banks, rich from oil profits, had over U.S. foreign policy (imagine the reaction if someone called for an investigation like that today). In 1978 Jimmy Carter managed the passage, with gallant assists in the Senate from Church and from West Virginia Democrat Robert Byrd, of the Panama Canal treaty, and introduced human-rights concerns as one criterion on which American foreign-policy decisions should be hinged. Thus, the America of early 1979: leery of military power, antihegemonic, even, however haltingly, edging toward a foreign policy based more on humanitarian concerns.

It's very much worth mentioning that this was also a period when liberals came quite close to enacting domestic legislation that is unthinkable now. The two facts—liberal ascendance on foreign-policy and domestic questions—are not unrelated: Now that liberals weren't in their usual defensive posture about foreign policy, they were able to present their notions of equity and social justice at home more boldly. Some of that legislation undoubtedly smacked of too much social engineering (any movement enjoying a winning streak will overreach). But consider the legislation that passed— rafts of environmental and consumer legislation that have saved or improved many thousands of lives and were possible, arguably, only at that exact moment in history. More breathtaking in a way are the bills that nearly passed, which today would be shoved back down their sponsors' throats by Republicans and their corporate under-writers with the butt-end of a pitchfork. A guaranteed minimum family income—championed by Nixon—was narrowly defeated. A national health bill nearly made it out of committee in the Senate. A bill to break up the oil companies barely lost in the Senate. (Imagine telling Birch Bayh or John Culver, two redoubtable liberal senators of the day, that one generation on, not only would this legislation never have been reconsidered, but that Exxon and Mobil would merge!) The Humphrey-Hawkins legislation guaranteeing full employment nearly passed as well. To the extent that these measures failed, it was due only to the lobbies. Public opinion backed them all.

Then how quickly it all collapsed. The Iranian hostage crisis; the Soviet occupation of Afghanistan; the rise of Reagan. There are some reasons it deserved to collapse—Carter's paralysis over Iran *was* humiliating. Ascendant conservatives and neoconservatives made short work of converting Carter's failure into a symbol of American anemia. And opposition to the Vietnam War met the same fate: A position most Americans had agreed on just a few years prior was suddenly anathematized by a rebuttal that managed to blame a proper and morally sound opposition for a defeat that happened for other reasons entirely, reasons foreseen by virtually every expert a decade before. Liberals still fought Reagan, and sometimes there were even victories—occasional defeats of contra-aid votes, or divestiture pressure with regard to South Africa. But the larger public argument was lost. Most liberal Democrats in Washington opposed the Persian Gulf war but were terrified of standing against it on anything resembling a principle and instead came up with the tactical argument, not so appealing in retrospect, that intervention would surely lead to another Vietnam-like quagmire.

But by this time, it was already becoming clear that the era of liberalism's triumph contained the lineaments of its demise. Liberals, in arguing against the first Gulf War, relied on the Vietnam-era belief (by now encoded in the genes of liberalism itself) that American intervention could come to no good, with ominous warnings about quagmires and returning body bags and questions about whether what was proposed was worth that price. But there was no quagmire. Only 148 body bags came home (the number killed in action; nearly as many, 145, died in accidents). Saddam Hussein was chased from Kuwait and weakened. Civilian deaths in Iraq occurred, to be sure, somewhere between 1,000 and 3,500, according to various pro- and antiwar estimates; but there was no napalming of villages. The intervention worked.

Its success left a liberalism that was still raising specters about quagmires stuck in the mud itself—ironically, by arguing "no quagmires," it got trapped in its own, a rhetorical one that was losing credibility with American public opinion. And anyway, the argument was a misinterpretation of what had been noble about liberalism's opposition to Vietnam to begin with—men like Morse and Gruening didn't oppose Vietnam because it might become a quagmire; they opposed it on principle, whether fifty-eight thousand died or fifty-eight. What had been the only noble position in the 1960s was becoming harder and harder to defend. Bill Clinton understood this reality and, from time to time, fought it: His insistence on using U.S. troops to reinstall Jean-Bertrand Aristide as president of Haiti and his administration's determination (exasperatingly late, but nevertheless) to do what the European powers had failed to do and beat back Serbian pan-nationalism serve as examples of liberal interventionism that stand outside the usual post-Vietnam parameters of unwillingness to use military power. But these moves never seemed part of a broader vision about the world and America's role in it. History will applaud Clinton's attempts to bring the United States more fully into the world community: the Kyoto environmental accords, the International Criminal Court, various new regulations on offshore banking and money laundering that his administration was working out with the European Union when he left office (and which George W. Bush's administration promptly canceled). And his central foreign-policy argument, for globalism, was a mixed bag. It did teach Americans to think about their connectedness to the rest of the world. But globalism had the distinct downside of too often sounding like cover for American corporate power, reminding us of another central truth of American foreign policy, the amazingly coincidental ways in which it serves the interests of American business. Granted, Clinton faced domestic political pressure—hatred, really—unlike any president in history. Granted also, it was a time of confusion in general, so soon after the Soviet Union's collapse; many thinkers offered definitions of what exactly had replaced the bipolar world to which we'd become accustomed, but since there was no consensus on what that world was, none of them took. It was all but inevitable that the Clinton era would reflect this lack of consensus.

Through all these years, liberal ideas about foreign policy were characterized chiefly by a crippling loss of nerve. And the loss of nerve has led to a lack of ideas. Liberals essentially have no foreign-policy argument. They have generalities, about multilateralism and international agreement and so on, that can serve them passably well in peace time. But those generalities sound evasive to many Americans; too much blather about multilateralism just makes people think that the person doing the blathering isn't quite serious about the problem. It has left liberalism without a vision for American leadership that a majority of citizens feels it can rely on in a time of crisis.

THEN, OF COURSE, the crisis came. The first reaction to September 11 was easy, at least for everyone this side of Noam Chomsky. A country is not only justified in answering such an attack but has a moral obligation to do so. Public opinion, and the vast majority of liberal opinion, recognized this and cheered the response.

It seemed, for a brief time, that a reasonable consensus on fighting terrorism, and on America's leadership in the world, might have a chance to emerge. The space between the parties closed for a while, as did the space between the United States and Europe, which the Bush administration, before September 11, had gone out of its way to widen. This same Europe, or at least those nations that are North Atlantic Treaty Organization (NATO) members, had chosen to overlook Bush's belligerence in the wake of the attacks and invoked its Article V, asserting that an attack on one nation was an attack on all, for the first time in its history. All that happened before the fires at the World Trade Center site had burned themselves out. But as the weeks and months wore on, and the post–September 11 unanimity of purpose retreated, if one looked under the rosy overlay of tributes to fallen heroes and flags in shop windows, a less cheerful image could be made out.

The administration, far from working with Democrats, ostracized and insulted them, and its ideological stooges took to producing leaflets claiming that Senate Majority Leader Tom Daschle was more dangerous than "American Taliban" John Walker Lindh. This particular broadside, from a GOP political action committee, was never repudiated by the White House—nor, it's worth pointing out, did spineless Democrats make much of a fuss about it. In April 2002, the administration boycotted the ceremonies marking the creation—something that took fifty years for the nations of the world to achieve—of the International Criminal Court, announcing that the ICC would have no jurisdiction over Americans that the Bush team would recognize. Indeed, the administration threatened to quash the court by withdrawing all its funds for UN peacekeeping. Then came the bullying of Europe, chiefly, but of the world body at large, to join the anti-Iraq coalition on U.S. terms and only those terms. The result, as Michael Ignatieff wrote in *The Financial Times* around the first anniversary of the attacks, was that "Europe and the U.S. no longer understand the event in the same way. . . . On the first anniversary of a day of infamy, Americans might have expected to have more friends than ever. The surprise is that they have fewer." Ignatieff partially blamed the European Left for this state of affairs, and it deserves a share of blame for reverting to reflexive and sometimes shameful anti-American and anti-Israel broadsides. But the European Left doesn't run the most powerful country in the world, and it wasn't the European Left that pulled out of Kyoto and the ICC. The Bush administration welcomed Europe's scorn and indeed, emotionally, seemed to invite it, even pray for it.

The Bush administration's first instinct was to repudiate everyone—U.S. allies, the United Nations, the loyal opposition. When it turned its attention from the war in Afghanistan to a potential war in Iraq, it did so with a schoolboy swagger and in a nakedly political context, during the heat of the 2002 midterm elections. It did the minimum necessary to answer its critics—Bush's speech at the United Nations, for example. But its basic message was clear: We're going to do what we're going to do, and if you happen to be in our way when we do it, well, we warned you.

And the Democrats? Without a coherently articulated foreign policy of their own, they were all over the lot and again had nothing to say. There were some exceptions. The same Robert Byrd who had defended the Panama Canal treaty became something of a national hero to foes of the administration in October 2002, when he eloquently riposted that the administration had embarked upon a path of "presidential hubris" that he found "breathtaking." But a majority of his fellow Senate Democrats, twenty-nine out of fifty, went the other way.

Like virtually every liberal in America, I admire what Byrd did. But I admire it more for the simple fact that one Democrat had the guts to step up and say things about the administration that the conventional wisdom disapproved of than for anything positive it had to say about what path ought to be pursued instead. About this even Byrd didn't have a great deal to say, and neither did Al Gore in a September 22, 2002, address to the Commonwealth Club of San

Francisco—again, a credible critique of the Bush administration's global aims, but one that didn't really offer an alternative vision of what the place and role of the United States in the world should be. Yet this is what the Democrats urgently need to do. To be convincing, they first have to understand—and have the mettle to explain to the American people—the real aims of the Bush administration.

I LISTENED TO OR READ the floor speeches of most of the twenty-one Senate Democrats who voted against Bush's war resolution on Iraq. I heard (or read) lots of arguments, about how the vote had been overtly politicized by the administration and about waiting for the United Nations to act, which obviously came in at number one on their pollsters' hit parade. But I hardly heard a word that cut to the core, which has to do with the administration's real motive for going into Iraq, a motive the administration advertised on September 20, just days before the vote, with the release of a thirty-one-page paper called the National Security Strategy.

Before I get to the contents of the NSS, it's worth taking a few paragraphs to discuss its provenance. The goals for America, made explicit in the NSS of 2002, were first broadcast in a document dating to early 1992, when Dick Cheney was still the secretary of defense (a job he fully expected to be holding for the next four years), called the Defense Planning Guidance (DPG). The drafting of the 1992 DPG was overseen by Paul Wolfowitz, who was then the undersecretary for policy at the Pentagon. Arriving as it did right after the end of Cold War hostilities, the DPG sought first and foremost to throw cold water on any notion that the United States might now trim its defense budget and stand down anywhere in the world: The base force of 1.6 million men would stay in place, and defense spending would not decrease. Its salient points regarding the post–Cold War world, and the place of the United States in it, consisted of the following syllogism:

- *The main goal of the United States would be to ensure that no rival superpower could emerge—or even think about emerging—anywhere (the United States, Colin Powell said at the time, must be "the bully on the block").*

- *Maintaining that preeminence would require that the United States act wholly in its own strategic interests.*

- *Therefore, the United States should reject collective internationalism—permanent alliances (NATO partially excepted) would be frowned upon, and future coalitions would consist of "ad hoc assemblies, often not lasting beyond the crisis being confronted, and in many cases carrying only agreement over the objectives to be accomplished."*

- *Finally, maintaining this world order would require, possibly, preventive military action on a variety of fronts, for a variety of reasons: a defense of Poland and Lithuania from attack by Russia; smaller-scale interventions in Panama and the Philippines; invasions to halt the proliferation of weapons of mass destruction in such places as North Korea and Iraq.*

The DPG implicitly rejected the concepts of deterrence and containment, but it said even more: In sum, it argued that the United States had to reject or at least subordinate longstanding collective security arrangements that dated to the post–World War II period and assume its position as the world's lone great economic and military superpower, and that perceived threats to that hegemony had to be stopped cold. "Anticipatory action to defend ourselves" was a key phrase. At first blush, it sounds benign enough; who, after all, could argue with defending ourselves? But one need read only a few such papers to get the hang of their lingua franca, which consists of implication, emphasis, tone, and those things left unsaid. In this light the phrase, when placed alongside many others like it, expressed an entirely new definition of what the U.S. world posture should be, based on a quite expansive interpretation of what "to defend ourselves" means.

The document was leaked to the *New York Times*'s Patrick E. Tyler by "an official who believes this post-cold-war strategy debate should be carried out in the public domain." (Imagine!) Tyler published its contents on March 8, 1992. A hailstorm of protest ensued—from Europe, where leaders read the DPG as a warning against Europe's initiating any collective security agreements without the U.S. imprimatur, and from liberals and Democrats at home (Byrd called it "myopic, shallow, and disappointing"). Even some who supported the basic premises were alarmed by the rambunctiousness of tone. Indeed, the Bush I administration found the paper bellicose and danced away from this vision quickly and furiously; three days after his initial report, Tyler filed a story in which senior White House and State Department officials called the DPG "a dumb report" that "in no way or shape represents U.S. policy." When the DPG was officially released in late May of 1992, it was much watered down; the essential points were still in there, but the rhetorical emphasis was on collective security now, and the United States was positioned more firmly as one actor, albeit the lead one, among many on the stage of world security.

But that was then. The current Bush regime assumed power, and the DPG's intellectual fathers climbed the ladder. Cheney became vice president, Wolfowitz took the number-two slot at the Pentagon (under a number one, Donald Rumsfeld, who endorsed the DPG's worldview); other officials who were fringe stars under the first Bush—I. Lewis "Scooter" Libby, then a Defense Department deputy, later Cheney's national security adviser and chief of staff—grew into supernovas. Now there were no countervailing pressures from moderates, no pesky leakers who cared about the disinfecting sunlight of public debate. The DPG that was rejected by one Republican president as inflammatory in 1992 was becoming policy under another Republican president, his son, nine years later. As David Armstrong put it in the October 2002 issue of *Harper's,* Cheney's patience had established him as a surefooted Babe Ruth of geopolitics: "He pointed to center field ten years ago, and now the ball is sailing over the fence."

But even so, enthusiasm outside the administration and right-wing circles for the "American colossus" approach laid out in the DPG was, in the early days of Bush II, scant. Then September 11 happened. On the one hand, it has to be acknowledged that the DPG foresaw the possibility, indeed probability, of such unpredictable threats. It was prescient in that regard, and right to draw attention to the need to answer such threats and the need to do so unilaterally if circumstances warranted. At the same time, though, it seems clear in retrospect that in one regard September 11 came to the Bush II hawks as a gift (I do not mean, obviously, to allege that any of them welcomed the attacks in any way). Dick Cheney, in a speech to the Council on Foreign Relations in February 2002, made the point:

> *When America's great enemy suddenly disappeared, many wondered what new direction our foreign policy would take. . . . There was no simple, immediate, global threat that*

any roomful of experts could agree upon. All of that changed five months ago. The threat is known and our role is clear now.

With America reeling from having been ambushed in such a manner, now, surely, if ever there was a context in which expert, congressional, *and* public opinion would coalesce behind such a plan, it was this. The iron could never be hotter.

How clear, in light of this, and how entirely explicable, was Rumsfeld's gut reaction to the September 11 attacks, delivered within hours of the strikes on the towers and the Pentagon: "Best info fast. Judge whether good enough to hit S.H."—meaning Saddam Hussein—"at same time as UBL" (Osama bin Laden). Well, of course: Launching a preventive strike against Hussein had been the policy of Cheney, Wolfowitz, et al., since 1992. And, of course, the administration tried to peddle a story, apparently untrue, that al-Qaeda operatives had met with Hussein attachés in Prague; there was a hunger to find a quick and unassailable justification for a strike. And, of course, Bush named his "axis of evil" of Iraq, Iran, and North Korea in his 2002 State of the Union address; they had all been identified as such, albeit without the snappy fillip appended by Bush II speechwriter David Frum, a decade before.

Thus, the history of the 1992 DPG. A new Bush II DPG was leaked in July 2002 to the *Los Angeles Times*—like attentive defense lawyers on appeal, the Bushies sought a change of venue—which retained the basic arguments of its predecessor but now, with September 11 as cover, added a few new twists, such as a justification for the preemptive use of earth-boring nuclear weapons that would strike at "hardened and deeply buried targets." Then, finally, on September 20, in the midst of the heat of debate over Iraq, came the

NSS. If anything, the NSS states matters even more directly: Rejection of deterrence was not implicit but explicit ("traditional concepts of deterrence will not work"). The cards of preemptive war are laid more openly on the table: The phrase "anticipatory action to defend ourselves" is reused and amplified. (Such action will occur "even if uncertainty remains as to the time and place of the enemy's attack . . . The U.S. will, if necessary, act preemptively.") Now, a first strike was the goal.

What once represented the wish list of the right-most fringe of respectable opinion is now the policy of this country. It is a prescription for empire. A plan, as Jay Bookman wrote in the *Atlanta Journal-Constitution* in the best piece of newspaper journalism to appear on the topic, "for permanent U.S. military and economic domination of every region on the globe, unfettered by international treaty or concern." True, a reader of any or all of these documents will find plenty of rhetorical lip service paid to international arrangements and coalitions, but the language on those varies here and there and comes across as pro forma, the honey with which the medicine is to be administered. And the medicine, the points on which the language is constant, is an unchallenged and unchallengeable—even by its allies—America, which will use its might to advance its interests, period. The world's other nations will be traded around like baseball cards, added to the collection or discarded as needed. Little will be asked of them; the phrase "in many cases carrying only agreement over the objectives to be accomplished" with regard to the ad hoc coalitions we will form to advance our interests surely brings smiles to the faces of our Pakistani and Egyptian and Saudi Arabian "friends." It means we will basically keep quiet about their al-Qaeda links, their political prisoners, their antidemocratic practices, and their enslaved women (in "advanced" Egypt, some 85 percent of all women undergo clitoridectomies) so long as they get with the program on Iraq. And so long as they keep sending us oil. The Pax Americana will be thirsty.

ALL OF THIS REPRESENTS a much harder line toward the world than any American administration has taken since World War II. Compared with his son, George H. W. Bush, who took care in the fall of 1990 to assemble an international coalition against Iraq and who refused to press for a politicized war-resolution vote in the heat of that year's midterm elections, practically looks like George McGovern, or at least Hubert Humphrey. And here, perhaps, the current administration has created an opening for a liberal counter-argument that can persuade American public opinion over time.

The counterargument is essentially a simple one: America is not an empire, it is a democracy. A democracy leads the world, but it does not seek to rule it. The Cheneyites want to rule the world. There is certainly an American tradition to support their point of view, but it is not one most Americans are especially proud of: Even the right wing doesn't openly invoke the occupation of the Philippines after the Spanish-American War or the repeated invasions of Latin America in the early twentieth century as being among our greatest hits. Instead we celebrate those instances that are more expressive of our democratic values: the defeat of fascism, the Berlin Airlift, Kennedy's nimble diplomacy during the Cuban missile crisis, when he acted against the aggressive advice of the Wolfowitzes of his day.

Democratic politicians have to have the courage to fight the Cheney-Wolfowitz argument head-on. As I write these words, no Democrat, with the partial exceptions of Byrd and Michigan Senator Carl Levin, has had the backbone to lay out the Bush administration's global designs in anything approaching the way I just did above. They're afraid. Their fear may be understandable, but it represents exactly a continuance of the failure of nerve that has typified liberalism for years. The time has come to have this argument openly, and the fact that the administration has never wanted to have it openly, instead hiding behind its inconsistent excuses for moving against Iraq, should be enough by itself to tell us that the liberal counterargument has a chance. We shouldn't underestimate Americans' susceptibility—or the mainstream media's—to tough-guy rhetoric; nevertheless, it's hard to imagine that 51 percent of Americans really want their country to bestride the world as some sort of quasi-Victorian empire on which the sun never sets. A very vocal and powerful and well-financed right wing does, but there are signs that the American public wants the United States to act within multilateral norms (for example, the insistence of public opinion throughout the fall of 2002 and into 2003 that Bush win UN approval for moving against Iraq and that he act multilaterally).

The above constitutes mostly critique of the Republicans, and critique, of course, is the easy part. The hard part is backing up the critique with an alternative vision. That, too, should be simple, and for consistency's sake it should follow from the critique: The world's leading democracy should support . . . democracy. The Cold War is over; the twentieth century, the century in which all the "isms" became "wasms," to borrow a phrase, is over; it's the twenty-first century; the United States should declare it to be—American liberals should declare it to be—the century of democracy. Free elections, civil liberties, freedom of speech and of the press, basic judicial rights, equal rights for women, rights for religious and ethnic minorities—these and other freedoms have been laid out and enumerated a thousand times over, but they've been ignored by autocrats and totalitarians, and sometimes by us, when expediency demanded. That must start to change, and Democrats have to do it.

Obviously, this won't be easy; it will take generations, and there will surely be inconsistencies and even hypocrisies, as there always are. The worst ones are likely to occur not in the Middle East but, in keeping with our history, in Latin America, where the principle I'm laying out would require a Democratic U.S. president to give American banks less say in how the nations of Latin America govern themselves, which no politician of either party is in much of a hurry to do. But just starting the process, emphasizing the problem, making democratic values a real priority in the world, could initiate dramatic change over time. Picture a Democratic president, or even a presidential candidate, making such a case forcefully on the world stage; for the purposes of showing he (or she) *really* means business, he (or she) might choose one test case that highlights some outrage to which the United States has heretofore turned a blind eye—the plight of the Kurds in Turkey, or, better still for the purposes of domestic political consumption, oppression of women in Saudi Arabia. There will be initial resistance, but ultimately, who can afford to buck the United States? The world will start, in its lumbering petulant way, to change.

This is what the Democrats should be: the party of world democracy—encouraged and, when needed, enforced by the United States and its democratic allies acting together to do three things: to spread democratic values and freedoms; to surround and neutralize terror and the fundamentalism from which it grows; to make the world a more hospitable place. Democrats should have a ten- or fourteen-point program for fighting terror and safeguarding collective world security. They should offer specific legislation for a massive aid package for the Arab world that would be intended as a bulwark against terrorism and fundamentalism—with specific and credible dollar amounts, and with the money tied to specific and measurable democratic reforms that countries would have to undertake to qualify. Perhaps such an aid program could even be done multilaterally, a sort of international version of the Marshall Plan. The Democrats have to come forward with a dramatic plan for cutting energy consumption and developing alternative energy sources that could free us from our dependence on foreign oil. The simple act of issuing such proposals would proclaim that at least someone was taking a stab at expressing a vision for the world; it would work wonders, too, in terms of building a larger popular base for liberalism. Finally, with regard to foreign policy, liberals would have something to be *for,* and Americans who identify as neither liberal nor conservative would have something positive to associate with liberalism—which, with regard to foreign policy, hasn't been the case, well, pretty much since the Marshall Plan.

While doing the above to contend against Cheneyism, liberals must make a clear break with Chomskyism as well. Many liberals still cling to the leftish worldview of 1968–78, the last period of liberal foreign-policy regnancy. In 1968 it was easy for liberals to see little Vietnam as the victim and the United States as the actor in bad faith; today, it's hard to see Iraq and North Korea and Egypt and Iran and Saudi Arabia as anything other than what they are. And certainly, al-Qaeda is no plucky little Vietnam. Applying the old Vietnam-era schema to these situations makes no sense, and rejecting such a worldview is not a matter of moving to the right, as some would have it; it's a matter of adapting to the world as it now is.

So liberals must separate themselves explicitly and conclusively from the Left, and from those vestiges of the liberal foreign-policy argument that suggest equivocation about America's capacity as a moral force. Liberalism needs to assert anew that American power can be employed to good ends, and indeed that American power must be used wherever needed around the globe to support the principles to which liberalism is dedicated. During the Cold War,

American power was used, whether offensively or defensively, chiefly in opposition to an idea (the threat of Communism). Now that power can be and should be marshaled in support of the advance of democratic values. There is nothing inconsistent about using power toward democratic ends. In this context there was a liberal case for invading Iraq, which has nothing to do with trumped-up arguments about Saddam's nuclear capability and everything to do with the suffering of the Iraqi people—that is, it has to do with free elections, freedom of assembly and speech, equality under the law, everything we say we hold dear and need to be willing to support, even militarily if it becomes necessary.

A liberal affirmation of these broad principles—forcefully offering an alternative to the Right's argument for America as empire on the one hand, while repudiating the Left's view of a malign America that cannot be a force for good in the world with equal zest—is one that can hold its own in the domestic political arena. The first half of the proposition exposes the Right's agenda as something that's more aggressive and unilateral than most Americans want, and, harnessed to some specific positive proposals, it presents the kind of competing vision liberalism hasn't offered in generations. Such an affirmation also squares with the tenets of liberal democracy that liberalism has to defend if it is to be worth fighting for. The second half implicitly rejects "Vietnam syndrome" and insulates liberalism from the usual right-wing critiques about weakness and lack of vision.

Doing all of this will take more courage than Democrats have shown. But more than courage, constructing these arguments will require vision and imagination; for that, today's Democrats should look to their predecessors who reshaped the world after World War II. This advice undoubtedly sounds shocking or repugnant to some liberals. History—at least, post-Vietnam history—has not been kind to the Cold Warriors, to say the least. To be sure, there were good aspects and bad to the world the Cold Warriors made, and the bad should never be ignored. The Truman Doctrine made an important statement about the defense of free societies, and it probably did save Greece from becoming a Communist state, which was handy for Americans and rather more than that for the Greeks. But at the same time, it was the overly broad rhetoric of the doctrine—rhetoric pressed upon Truman by Secretary of State Dean Acheson and Arthur Vandenberg, chairman of the Senate Committee on Foreign Affairs, for the purpose of persuading public and congressional opinion to support it—that committed the United States to the defense of any "free people" fighting subjugation anytime, anywhere. It was that rhetoric, in other words, that committed us to Vietnam.

But the Cold Warriors at least did this: Confronted with a new world, an unprecedented global situation, they devised the schemes and policies and institutions and international organizations that met the situation in ways that were visionary and imaginative. They constructed a new liberalism that accomplished many salutary things. It rebuilt Europe (most conservatives were keenly suspicious of the Marshall Plan) and Japan, it slowly began to move away from colonialism, it fed the starving masses of Berlin, it created a democratic Jewish state, it set up and funded nongovernmental organizations devoted to health care and agriculture and economic development, it placed at least some of its faith in a United Nations and a World Court. All of which is to say: It contained an idea about liberal democracy that was grounded in Enlightenment principles and tried to bring those principles to life in the institutions it built. This vision didn't always succeed; it clearly had its baleful cousin in the form of the CIA and the coups; it was based on certain assumptions—about the virtue of progress, say, or about the moral appeal of universalism over particularism—that in the intervening years have faced a deserved critique and reexamination. But to state these points does not nullify the fact that this vision had accomplishments that today's and tomorrow's liberal democrats (and Democrats) can build on.

The Wise Men may have been only half-wise, with one foot planted in the old sod of imperial power and hegemony and the other in the virgin soil of spreading the principles of liberal democracy around the world. But leave it to the Left to catalog their defects and to argue with cool dialectical precision that even their benevolent decisions were nothing more than stalking horses for dominion. Contemporary liberalism should see the late 1940s through a more optimistic lens, as the beginning (fitful and compromised, but a beginning nevertheless) of a struggle in behalf of defending and spreading the values of democracy.

That struggle is what it's all about, isn't it? It is what the United States is supposed to do. The struggle is also, in the context of the whole course of human history, remarkably young. It began, arguably, in September 1939, when Hitler struck Poland (or perhaps for U.S. purposes in December 1941); it entered a second and equally precipitous phase in 1947, when the Cold War started; we might think of Vietnam as a quasi-Thermidorean third phase, the only phase during which the United States stood clearly and tragically against the cause of liberation; the fourth phase, relaxed but confused, began when the Soviet bloc collapsed in 1989 and 1991; and September 11 marked the commencement of its fifth phase—maybe not its most dangerous, all things considered, but already the one that has struck closer to the American bone than the others managed to do.

Liberalism, and the Democratic Party, must respond to the new phase in the right way. Vietnam-era bromides and reflexes won't do.

Indeed, of the above five phases, ours resembles the second most closely, and the third perhaps least of all. Talking to the people of the United States and all nations, seriously and in good faith, about the work the nations of the world need to do—together—to get there from here, will be at least a start. I believe most Americans want to get there from here, if only someone will bother to show them the way.

LAURA SECOR

The Giant in the House

Mitrovica was a good place not to go in the summer of 2000, and I had every intention of not going there. But Virtyt, my translator, was driving. It had been almost exactly a year since NATO bombers liberated Kosovo's Albanians from Serbian misrule, inaugurating an era of lawlessness and reverse ethnic cleansing aimed at Kosovo's Serbs and Roma. Mitrovica, a sizable mining town near the Serbian border, was the most volatile flashpoint for this reversal of fortunes. Crowded on the north bank of the Ibar River, a population of radicalized Serbs formed a tense and snarling fortress. Across a bridge that had become a kind of perilous postwar no-man's-land, the south side of Mitrovica, still scarred from wartime Serbian assaults, lay in Albanian hands.

"We hate the French," Virtyt told me—speaking of himself and his friends, a circle of educated, young Albanians—"because they divided the city of Mitrovica." What would have happened if they hadn't? I asked. Virtyt smiled. The answer was casual and effortless: "There would be no Serbs in Mitrovica."

Later, when I saw my photographs from that day, I was struck by the natural beauty of the landscape we passed through—watercolor hues, a sweep of open land, arid and still. But during that drive

I was transfixed by the white cement skeletons of houses clustered along the roadside. Village after village gone, frames still standing, grass grown inside—like a graveyard, weather-beaten and silent. Meanwhile, nearby Pristina, where I was staying, had swollen to three times its prewar population. Mounds of garbage festered on street corners, awaiting an infrastructure that never came. What little decent real estate existed in Pristina was occupied by the "internationals": that polyglot band of some sixty-five thousand aid workers, bureaucrats, and diplomats who, together with the multinational military force known as KFOR, had suddenly made former Yugoslavia's most isolated ghetto town one of the most cosmopolitan cities in the world.

From Mitrovica itself, I remember only a few things. The bridge, after all I'd read about it and the stone-throwing mobs bristling along its banks, seemed diminutive and prosaic. Barbed wire, asphalt, impassive Polish troops—an ugly "security zone" that looked more like a parking lot. We ventured into it for only a moment. And then we turned around and headed for a nearby café.

Should we have been nervous, so close to the river? An hour later, we would learn that as we sat in that café just south of the bridge, Serbs were torching UN vehicles on the north side, and peacekeepers had fired warning shots that killed and injured several Serbs. It was after that incident that the United Nations declared it would no longer bring relief to Mitrovica's Serbs north of the Ibar. And that, in turn, led to a flurry of Serbian accusations of UN bias.

Why didn't I hear those gunshots? Or was there a moment when something sounded like thunder and we cast a glance above for rain? What I remember, instead, is this. A little boy in shorts sat on the railing that surrounded the café's patch of sidewalk. He was by himself, maybe eight years old, with short hair and grubby knees, holding a cardboard box of chewing gum and cigarettes he meant to sell. But he was watching us, or specifically, watching me. He caught my translator's eye and asked a question. "He wants to know if you're Albanian," Virtyt told me.

For a moment, to my shame, I was afraid. Did the boy think I was a Serb from north of the river? Would there be time to clear up the misunderstanding before he announced it to the café?

"She's American," Virtyt told the boy in Albanian.

The boy grinned, beaming at me with wide eyes. And I'm not kidding. What he said next, in English, was this:

"America good."

IT IS AN UNCOMFORTABLE MOMENT for a traveler. A mood of menace dissolves into welcome, based on nothing but the accident of your birth. Can you accept this as yours? It comes, in a place like Kosovo, with a powerful tug of conscience. Whatever evil happened here, the United States had the power to stop it. Whatever the United States accomplished here, all parties knew it would be definitive—down to the last omission, the last unintended consequence. It's a weight that fell on American shoulders with particular gravity when the Cold War ended. Ever since then, foreign policy thinkers and journalists across the ideological spectrum have wrestled with the question of uncontested power and the boundless responsibility it entails. How can we act? How can we not act?

That sense of responsibility was a complicated one in postwar Kosovo, where American action had accomplished an enormous good in liberating a threatened people but did not prevent subsequent evils, such as the returnees' brutal treatment of Serbs and especially Roma, or the spread of Albanian nationalist militancy to neighboring countries. The question was still more complicated in Serbia that summer. Arriving in Kosovo, as I did, directly from Belgrade was like barreling through a looking glass.

In June of 2000 Serbia looked for all the world like a ruined country. NATO's 1999 bombardment had set back what little was left of Serbia's industrial and public infrastructure, and it had terrified a great many ordinary Serbs, who found themselves on the wrong side of a quarrel between their government and the world's mightiest air force. Over the course of a decade, Milosevic had corrupted his country's economy and culture to the core. Many of the Serbs trapped in his jailhouse felt that the West was to blame for his continued hold on power. When would Western governments start engaging with the Serbian opposition, instead of pursuing a purely punitive tack aimed at their oppressor but ultimately visited upon them?

A brutal mafia dominated virtually every aspect of Serbian life. The entire economy under sanctions was an illegal one; the education system had become a narcissistic propaganda machine; shanty towns of battered Serbian refugees from Croatia ringed Belgrade, ostracized and festering with neglect. Belgrade's streets were squalid, buildings crumbling, water and electricity arbitrarily cut for several hours each day. Filthy old buses lurched down potholed boulevards, an impossible number of arms and faces pressed against streaked windows. Sputtering Yugos belched black-market petrol fumes into the soot-filled air. Hardly anyone was employed; the country had produced nothing in ten years. Hospitals had no bandages, no thread for stitches. But music pulsed from swank bars favored by the criminal elite and guarded by men in black jeans and leather jackets. A bedraggled band of fifteen to twenty protesters gathered every night on the pedestrian thoroughfare in the heart of

Belgrade, accompanied by stray dogs and police. More than a year of these nightly protests passed. Nothing changed, but the streets grew quieter.

The bombing left a Westward-looking opposition exhausted and, in some cases, betrayed. Milosevic seized gleefully on popular anti-Americanism, portraying the antiregime student movement as a quisling army. Posters depicting Madeleine Albright with fistfuls of dollars suggested that the United States lay behind the opposition's activities, luring Serbs to the enemy's breast. Twice, old women on buses cowered from me upon learning that I was an American. I was a CIA agent, they were convinced; to one such woman, it clearly followed that I would steal her jewelry. Cabdrivers inquired into my views on the bombing, and a waiter lectured me about the evils of American materialism.

At a gathering in a smoky apartment in the city center, a young father—we will call him Mladjan—told me of the fear he'd felt for his family during the war. Because his passport had expired, he'd been unable to join his wife and daughter when they fled the country. Instead, he followed the news helplessly the day his young family crossed a bridge just two hours before it was blown up from the air. The night I met him, he was red-faced and angry. "You have to think about what your country did in your name!" he shouted at me.

I had come to Belgrade determined to listen rather than to demand a moral accounting from civilians who had neither supported nor fought in Milosevic's wars. And I suspected that few Serbs would be willing to discuss Kosovar suffering with an American until they'd discussed their own. But at that moment with Mladjan, I found myself torn among complicated feelings. "*You* have to think about what your country has done in your name," I wanted to say. God knows, didn't he? But wasn't this a kind of deflection, on my part?

I held my tongue, but that proved harder the next day, when I met with Stasa Babic, an archaeology professor and opposition activist. Stasa told me that the American intellectuals who greeted NATO's surgical bombardment of Serbia as a just war were no better than the Serbs who cheered Milosevic's tanks as they left to flatten Vukovar in 1992. "Are you going to compare bodies and bodies?" she spat. "Just because Vukovar is destroyed, and Belgrade is *sort of* still standing?"

To Stasa, the bombing—and the widespread support it enjoyed in Europe and the United States—was all but a personal betrayal. For a decade, she had instructed her students to look to the West for humane values, liberal politics, and deliverance from Serbia's deepening nightmare. What was she to tell them when the West delivered not help but violence? What moral high ground could she now claim for NATO in the eyes of young people, who had neither elected Milosevic nor fought in his wars, but who saw their own futures foreshortened by sanctions and now bombs, and who saw even the West settling Balkan problems with military might? She told me bitterly of graffiti she saw in Belgrade during the war: "NATO in the sky, Milosevic on the ground. Where is god?"

We were only three months away from the nonviolent revolution—heavily funded and actively organized by Western governments, as it turned out—that would topple Milosevic. But we did not know it then. Serbs and outside experts predicted that the summer would end with a bloody civil war, most likely in the streets of Belgrade.

TRAVELING IN THE SMALL COUNTRIES the United States has prodded with its enormous fingers, it's not hard to imagine that the world's sole superpower behaves like a giant arranging the affairs of a doll's house. Setting a lamp upright, it knocks over a sofa. Everything it brushes past, in even the most noncommittal way, it alters permanently. More often than not, the miniature world is too intricate and too distant to capture the giant's eye at all—unless it happens to be in flames.

The territory of the former Yugoslavia was such a place in 1991. Its political structure was extremely complex; its economy was unique in the world; it was home to at least seven nationalisms at cross-purposes, and to political strains ranging from the authoritarian to the decidedly liberal. Its very history was contested among its citizens, and it boasted a rich and diverse civil society with a welter of competing post–Cold War ambitions. Once defined by its nonalignment, like a taut thread stretched between NATO and the Warsaw pact, Yugoslavia went slack when the bipolar world crumbled. It was a country that could go in any number of directions. Who in Washington had time for all that?

When Yugoslavia became the scene of a new European genocide and a rolling quake of wars and secessions, time would be made. But by then, arguably, the moment for the most constructive possible engagement had passed. The world's great powers chose among evils, shrugging as they explained that they'd done the best they could under circumstances that offered no options.

The debate over humanitarian intervention, which emerged as the major foreign policy challenge of the 1990s, centered on this foreshortened field, and though it centered on the Balkans, it was not centrally about the Balkans. It was about the United States' role in the post–Cold War world. The people of the former Yugoslavia were incidental to this discussion; they lived in its interstices. A few American liberals concerned themselves with the potential future of homegrown democracies in the ashes of Yugoslavia—civic, universalist states that would have human rights and equality built into their cores, and that would bode well for the long term stability of the region. More liberals pitched themselves into a U.S. foreign policy debate that was abstract, global, moral, military, and strategic; the one with the drama and the clarity and the universal applications. It was the same one, ultimately, that found itself choosing among Balkan nationalisms, often to the despair of those Yugoslav democrats, human rights activists, antinationalists, and humanists—a small but courageous band that existed in all of the former Yugoslav republics—who had hoped for something better.

Participating in the larger-scale discussions is, to some extent, the duty of American intellectuals and policy makers. No other country in the world carries so much at stake in its self-conception and in its attitude toward foreign affairs. The United States is, in point of fact, a giant, and as such it is obligated to contemplate the outsized consequences of its actions. At the same time, however, the world is not a doll's house. The United States is but one citizen of the so-called international community; and as such, it is obliged to know not only its strength but its singularity, its limits. The infamous American arrogance stems from the tendency to see the former and not the latter—to understand the United States only as a function of its power, and the world only as a screen for grand projections.

In the 1990s the Balkans were the major theater for the projection of three distinct American foreign policy positions. Most significant was the rise of a muscular, interventionist liberal idealism that was forcefully articulated in the pages of *The New Republic*, among other places. The sheer extent of U.S. power carried a nearly universal obligation, the liberal internationalists argued. Wherever innocent people were victimized, particularly in cases of genocide, the United States, which had the means to protect them, could not escape responsibility. Military action was not only justified in such cases; it was a moral requirement.

This was a liberal internationalism that had broken with the pacifism of the Vietnam era and the so-called Third Worldism of the Cold War era. Even more radical was its condemnation of state sovereignty, long fundamental to international law, as a reactionary notion that protected brutal regimes at the expense of their citizens. Sovereignty necessarily accrued to the members of the Security Council; but elsewhere in the world, the internationalists saw it as a fluid concept, one that could be granted and revoked on the basis of a state's behavior, and at the behest of the sole superpower and its allies. By the summer of 2002, advocates of this position had gone so far as to reclaim the idea of imperialism, as Michael Ignatieff did in his July 28, 2002, *New York Times Magazine* article, "How to Keep Afghanistan from Falling Apart: The Case for a Committed American Imperialism." American domination of other countries and peoples was not in itself a bad thing—not, at least, if it became the vehicle for the distribution of American wealth and freedoms to the formerly oppressed. The job of the liberal elite was then to pressure not against empire building but for the building of a committed, benevolent empire that would disseminate American goods and democratic values.

This sort of thinking was anathema to most of the foreign policy establishment prior to the Clinton era. The conservative realist tradition views military engagements with great caution, sanctioning them only in cases where strategic, security, or economic interests are distinctly imperiled, and even then only rarely. Because realists view the world in terms of interests rather than values, they are capable of expressing a chilling disinterest in the suffering of others, so long as it does not touch Washington's strategic plans. At their worst, realists unflinchingly lend U.S. support to tyrants and war-lords where doing so may prove expedient. At their best, realists envision the United States as the first among equals rather than as the global enforcer of universal values or as a missionary bent on reforming the world in its image. But because they act not on moral values, which are static and universal, but on interests, which are mutable, their respect for things like sovereignty and human rights is situational. When allies like Manuel Noriega and Saddam Hussein are suddenly demonized as enemies, critics from the Left decry realist hypocrisy. But they project a value system that does not concern realist policy makers. Alliances are not friendships, interests are not commitments, and the greatest good for the greatest number is not a national interest; foreign policy is a game of strategic survival. Former Secretary of State James Baker succinctly articulated the realist view of the Balkans when he declared of Bosnia, "We don't have a dog in that fight." Intervene? What's in it for us?

If the liberal interventionists meant to challenge a cynically realist foreign-policy establishment, the more vocal response they received was from a third position, and one with considerably less influence in the halls of power. Left anti-imperialists object to the notion of an unrestrained right of intervention as fiercely as they object to the self-interested pursuit of power. They uphold sovereignty as a bulwark against the disempowerment of the world's small nations, viewing with mounting concern the extension of American hegemony and the presumption of its benevolence. They greet humanitarian alibis with particular suspicion, charging liberal interventionists with knowingly or unknowingly furnishing a fig leaf for wars of venal self-interest or imperial domination. With the possible and occasional exception of Bosnia, left anti-imperialists opposed all the U.S. wars of the 1990s and of the early 2000s, but few identified themselves as pacifists. As Noam Chomsky put it when he spoke to Harvard's Kennedy School recently, the burden of proof should fall on those who advocate violence. The result has often been a curiously conservative Left—one that cleaves to the status quo in foreign affairs, viewing even the most virulently oppressive foreign regimes as worth defending on the basis of sovereignty. To the liberal interventionists, this is a Left whose cynicism outstrips even that of the Right.

The grand foreign policy debate would undergo a tectonic shift after September 11, 2001. Humanitarian intervention was no longer the cause du jour, and the Balkans had all but vanished from the map. But the debate over intervention, and the larger debate about the responsible use of power, had entered a new phase. For the first time in living memory, U.S. civilians felt themselves in the sights of a foreign enemy—one that was faceless, possibly vast, and virtually invisible. Worse, some of the most toxic global conflicts had reached a boiling point, from Kashmir to the West Bank to the Korean peninsula. Each of these had implications for American security, as well as for the human rights and self-determination of the local peoples who might once have been the subject of moral concern. Had the time come for an uncompromising American military leadership that would enforce a desperately needed Pax Americana without apology? Or was this sort of American unilateralism and imperiousness precisely the catalyst that could set an already volatile world aflame?

As the left anti-imperialists feared they would, hawks of all stripes deftly adapted the morally appealing language of liberal interventionism to their own ends. The war in Afghanistan, which was unquestionably motivated by security interests, was all but sold to a jittery public as a campaign to liberate Afghan women and to end the Taliban's human-rights abuses. The word "intervention" slipped into popular parlance around U.S. war plans in both Iraq and Afghanistan, despite the fact that in neither case was there a domestic conflict in which the United States found itself called to "intervene"; rather, intervention had become a euphemism for war, and one that carried the comforting valence of altruism. The United States was not waging war on sovereign nations; it was interceding between innocents and their brutal governments. Given that both the Taliban and the Iraqi Baath were indeed brutal and largely hated by their people, the idea of U.S. "intervention" in these cases was not a pure fabrication. It was merely a substitution of secondary effects for primary goals.

Most interestingly, since the advent of the George W. Bush administration, a fourth foreign-policy position has assumed significant sway, and it is one from which liberal internationalists are at pains to differentiate their worldview. Within the Republican Party, realists have found themselves increasingly marginalized by the louder, more ethically compelling voices of neoconservative idealists like Paul Wolfowitz, Richard Perle, William Kristol, and Robert Kagan. These policy thinkers, like their counterparts in liberal circles, eschew the situational ethics of realism in favor of a campaign to extend American values throughout the world. They, too, have little truck with the sovereignty of small nations, but unlike most liberal idealists, they view the sovereignty of the United States as so inviolable that even the United Nations poses an unacceptable threat. And they share the belief that American military might can bring democracy, human rights, and prosperity to benighted corners of the globe, though they carry the mantle of empire less gingerly than their liberal counterparts.

Like realists, conservative idealists appeal to interests, but their solution to strategic concerns is visionary and global. American security and prosperity demand the extension of American power and the continuation of the United States' uncontested global pre-eminence. But these are also goods in themselves. Where liberal idealists tend to believe that given the extent of its power, the United States must strive to promote the good conservative idealists presume that in promoting itself, the United States *does* promote the good. And these idealists from the Right are willing to go out on a limb that many liberal interventionists still find far too shaky: They believe that even first-strike or pre-emptive wars can be legitimated if in the end they export democracy. For liberals who have argued that brutal regimes cannot hide behind the mantle of sovereignty, this has been a difficult call to answer. Where does the moral obligation to the constructive use of power end and a dangerous bellicosity begin?

DURING THE DEBATES AROUND THE BALKANS in the 1990s, the liberal interventionists took the classic moral questions of American oppositional politics and turned them on their head. They focused not on actions—what evil is our government doing abroad, and how can we stop it?—but on omissions. To what evils does our government acquiesce by its inaction? The result has been a destigmatization of warfare. Particularly following September 11, the burden of proof in liberal foreign policy debates has tended to fall not on those who advocate violence, but on those who advocate doing nothing in the face of violence.

The shift is undoubtedly a historic one. At the end of the Cold War, the United States found itself in a nearly unprecedented position in the world. It possessed a power so vast and so uncontested that it could, at least theoretically, impose its will anywhere on earth. The moral problem this presented was profound and insoluble.

Wherever there was evil or suffering, the action or inaction of the United States could be decisive. And so it followed that the United States bore a responsibility without end.

One response to this quandary was isolation—in the realist instance, from moral engagement, which was potentially infinite, but not from strategic engagement, which appeared to be bounded; in the anti-imperialist instance, the solution was to withdraw from both, with the understanding that the former was merely a guise for the latter.

Idealists instead called for the United States to engage the world on moral grounds, but it was an engagement that trended toward violence. And in that, for all their insurgent optimism, the interventionists lacked imagination, conceiving foreign policy as coextensive with military policy, and taking for a point of departure the point of no return. So it was that the exemplary instance of human rights–based liberal idealism became the Kosovo war—rather than, say, the intricate and precarious defusing of conflict in Macedonia, or the behind-the-scenes collaboration that enabled the Serbian opposition successfully to oust Milosevic.

It's a peculiarly American worldview that begins and ends its discussion of international engagement with force—the most spectacular, muscular, and unequivocal response to the internal troubles of distant states. We might hasten to add that the use of force is merely admissible, though still a province of last resort. But if we do so, we should see Kosovo not as the triumph of a salutary trend toward humanitarian intervention, but as the unfortunate consequence of a decade of failed policy.

Military intervention, after all, was never meant to be a broad strategy for engagement with the Balkans. It was crisis management. It was decisive, but it was also superficial, and it did nothing to resolve the problems that had produced the crisis in the first place—chief among them the continuing fragmentation along ethnic lines, and under ethnically charged leadership, of an extremely complex multiethnic society. In a region as diverse as the Balkans, ethnically defined states automatically create minorities. These minorities do not demand their human rights and cultural freedoms from the state, because the state is explicitly defined as belonging to others (the ethnic majority). Instead, minorities demand autonomy or independence—the way Albanians did in Kosovo and Serbs did in Croatia. Outside military intervention in the Balkans tended to reinforce those claims—certainly, it did so in Kosovo—despite the fact that the new ethnic states necessarily reproduced the conundrum of the old ones. The result has been long-term instability and human rights problems that are likely to change only under leadership that does not define itself in exclusionary ethnic terms.

To contend constructively with this problem would require something more shrewd and precise than a laser-guided missile. It would necessitate a respectful intimacy with the affected region—familiarity with its internal forces, long-term investment in its well-being, forethought, sustained attention, creativity. When the United States and its allies have put their minds to averting conflict or ousting tyrants without violence, they have been surprisingly effective. Take Macedonia, where war was averted for a decade through vigilant diplomacy and the first and only UN preventive deployment. When war finally did threaten this struggling country, whose ethnic divisions and historical fragility were actually more profound than Bosnia's were in 1992, it was defused diplomatically, not least because it was clear that no Western military support was forthcoming for either nationalist faction. A year later, one of the two ethnic blocs (ethnic Macedonians) voted its nationalists out of power. We have only to see Macedonia's Albanians follow that lead, and the country will have embarked, of its own volition, on a road, albeit a rutted and imperfect one, to something like civic democracy.

Consider, too, the transfer of power in Serbia, orchestrated by the opposition in that country with extensive Western backing and training. American-organized focus groups selected Vojislav Kostunica as the opposition's most viable presidential candidate; an American agent trained Serbia's student movement in methods of nonviolent resistance; and Western funds sustained the multitude of groups that engineered Milosevic's downfall. Ironically, the revolution propelled a staunchly anti-American Serb nationalist to power. But it also jump-started Serbia down the path of reform, through a revolution that was deeply felt to be local. In fact, it *was* local: The forces that toppled Milosevic were not, as much of the American press crowed at the time, NATO bombs. They were indigenous activists who accepted outside help but risked their own lives to oust a regime they despised.

In neither case did the United States remake a Balkan country in its image or bring about an immediate end to all human-rights abuses and suffering. Macedonia is recovering from its halting descent into warfare, but the country is wounded, impoverished, and divided. So long as the country's political units are defined ethnically, there is a risk that the country's Turks, Roma, Serbs, and other minorities could grow restive. Anti-Western sentiment remains powerful among ethnic Macedonians, many of whom blame NATO's intervention in Kosovo for setting off the conflict in the first place. Post-Milosevic Serbia, meanwhile, has suffered its share of turbulence and continues to wrestle with the legacy of national chauvinism. There, too, much of the suffering of the 1990s is laid at the feet of a West that is believed to pass unfair judgment on ordinary Serbs.

But in both cases, bloodshed has been minimal, and a foundation exists upon which citizens can erect more representative, peaceable, and durable structures. Croatia managed the painstaking transition from nationalist autocracy to a stumbling but promising new democracy; the same trajectory can reasonably be predicted for Serbia in the near future, now that its cultural and political life has the oxygen it has long needed to grow and change. The same cannot really be said of post-Dayton Bosnia or of postwar Kosovo, both of which are still administered by international troops to stave off the spiral into ultranationalist politics and ethnic violence. Nor could it have been said for Serbia prior to 2000, when the Milosevic regime, isolated and under sanctions, effectively crushed its even more isolated opposition.

Nonviolent conflict resolution rests on local political will. That's why it needs to happen early and to anticipate conflict before it erupts. It is not a substitute for forceful intervention in the case of wholesale slaughter. But it has the advantage of not requiring wholesale slaughter to take place before anything can be done. Crucially, because it rests on local political will, it is also a form of engagement that does not suggest that the United States abrogate the self-determination of small states or take sides in ethnic conflicts with no possible good end. Instead, it requires vigilance and foresight. It demands that we take an interest in complex political realities that lack the stark drama of violence.

Nonviolent intervention also requires compromise. In the best case scenario, Western diplomats and nongovernment organizations (NGOs) throw their weight behind the most responsible liberal forces—human-rights workers, liberal democrats, voices of conscience. But often, politics will require compromise and the knitting together of unlikely coalitions. Imagine if the United States had pursued this strategy not in devastated Serbia in the summer of

2000, but in both Serbia and Kosovo as early as 1996 or even 1992 (both years when the Serbian opposition was united and organized). Suppose the condition of Western support had been that the Albanian and Serbian oppositions find common cause and form a voting bloc. These would have made strange bedfellows—an Albanian opposition bent on independence, a Serbian opposition that included national chauvinists. But it might also have empowered different elements of both opposition factions, or provided an incentive for even mutually distrustful elements to find common ground. Together, anti-Milosevic Serbs and Albanians had more than the necessary numeric weight to oust Milosevic years before the Kosovo war. With Albanian involvement, that would surely have meant the end of apartheid in Kosovo, and the beginning of an entirely unprecedented era of interethnic political cooperation.

It sounds far-fetched, and indeed it might be. Such a strategy might have proved unacceptable to both sides, and a war very likely would still have been necessary by 1999. But NATO fought that war after having all but ignored Kosovo and Serbia for the four years after Dayton (and, for that matter, the five years before Dayton). During that time, Kosovo persisted in a state of apartheid, not civil war, and Serbia's dictatorship was both brittle and strangely permissive. This was not Iraq, where no form of oppositional organization has been possible for thirty years. There is no reason the Western allies couldn't have spent the post-Dayton period constructively engaging with indigenous forces for peace. If we'd done so and succeeded, we might have averted much bloodshed and destruction. If we'd done so and failed, we might truly have waged war in Yugoslavia as a last resort, when all other options were exhausted. The missed opportunities in Croatia and Bosnia, and for Yugoslavia as a whole, are too legion to enumerate, and still more tragic.

• • •

To THEIR CREDIT, the liberal interventionists of the 1990s raised a stark challenge to the paralysis and pacifism of colleagues to their left. For many of us, that pacifism is instinctual. Our political and human instincts lead us to abhor violence, recoil from militarism, and believe that the first obligation of a superpower is, as far as is possible, to do no harm. Interventionists insist that there are times when it is better to do some small harm in order to stave off a much greater harm. For many on the liberal Left, Afghanistan chipped still more pacifism away. There are times, liberals found themselves arguing, when the sorts of interests that move realists are not expendable.

How, then, do we reconcile these concerns with our values? Do we wholly jettison our aversion to violence? There have been times in the last decade, and especially following September 11, when interventionism seemed to tip toward militarism—when liberals seemed not just to accept warfare as a necessary evil but to romanticize it as the wings that would carry our missionaries to the dark reaches of the undemocratic world. To dare to criticize an American war marked one as a pacifist or an appeaser.

A dangerous solipsism lies down that road, and not only because it risks privileging military solutions to soluble conflicts. We may hope and imagine that the world associates with the United States the very best of its expressed values—that, like the little boy I met in Mitrovica, others identify this country with some larger, universal idea of the good. We would be boundlessly naive to think it so. The United States chooses action or inaction based on its own interests in every region of the world. In this it is not unusual. Most states for all of history have taken care of themselves first, others later if at all.

What's unusual is the expectation that it should be otherwise, and what seems like genuine American shock when we discover that others don't perceive our country as the guardian of the universal good.

The Balkan wars contributed something to this flattering self-perception. But as the journalist David Rieff has eloquently argued, NATO did not intervene in Kosovo solely on the basis of conscience, or because it had suddenly awakened to the moral imperative enshrined in the genocide convention. NATO had geopolitical concerns about the stability of the region, the outflow of refugees, and its own credibility as a military alliance centered on European security. These coincided with moral concerns, and with the success of the liberal interventionists in raising the stakes of inaction. According to Samantha Power's *"A Problem from Hell": America in the Age of Genocide,* the Clinton administration genuinely feared the domestic political fallout of another Serbian genocide on its watch.

This tells us several things. First, and crucially, it reminds us that realism is a flexible creed to the extent that interests are themselves flexibly defined. The stakes of ignoring genocide, for example, are only as high as the American polity raises them. There are all kinds of possibilities for political pressure here. Isn't it in the American interest to promote democracy in the Middle East? To help stabilize the Balkans? To make the United States the ally and benefactor of democratic movements in parts of the world it considers strategically vital?

The question remains, of course: What of the parts of the world that are not considered strategically vital, or where American interests lie with repressive governments rather than with their peoples? Though they are not mutually exclusive, interests and values should not be mistaken for one another. The 1990s did not give us a revolutionary interventionism that would prod NATO to the aid of Chechens or Turkish Kurds, for example, or any number of other threatened peoples isolated from Western moral concern by the strictures of realpolitik. In Kosovo, NATO did not inaugurate an era of genocide protection for the world; it did, however, draw a line at genocide committed by weak, intransigent European states without allies and with histories of bloody regional aggression.

It is the nature of international politics that the right thing is rarely done for the right reasons. If we were to insist on purity of intentions in international affairs, we would be left altogether without recourse. I raise this issue not to condemn the Kosovo intervention as selfish, nor to call for intervention in Chechnya. I do not think that charges of hypocrisy should paralyze foreign policy; consistency is not in itself a virtue, especially if it mandates holding fast to a pattern of inaction in cases of dire need. But I do think that the interventionism of the 1990s ignored the question of interests at its peril. It is not only unrealistic to imagine that the world's most powerful nation will assume the mantle of protector to the world's least powerful peoples. It is a potentially dangerous delusion.

Outside our borders, the United States is seen—rightly—as one nation among nations, not as an abstract and universal moral authority. As we well know, the American foreign-policy establishment has gone to great lengths to redefine the term "genocide" in order to avoid deploying it in situations where it would not be in the American interest to intercede. If we really care, then, about genocide, we ought not to leave it to one self-interested power to declare when it is committed and when not. If we believe, with the liberal interventionists, that some acts of violence transcend politics, we ought not to leave their definition to one nation with alliances to maintain and enemies to rebuke. What is at stake here, rightly or wrongly, is moral authority. By its very nature, moral authority is not ad hoc. It suffers no exceptions. It does not envision separate justices for separate peoples.

The ad hoc criminal tribunals for the former Yugoslavia and Rwanda have been justly commended as a giant step forward in the quest for international justice. But there is much to be learned from their experience about the necessity of a true International Criminal Court with genuinely universal jurisdiction. The International Criminal Tribunal for Yugoslavia (ICTY) at the Hague was imposed by the Security Council on the countries of former Yugoslavia. To most of us in the West, it represents the will of international justice enacted upon a region rent by cruelty and bloodshed. Why, then, do we hear that many Serbs scoff at its legitimacy, and should we care that they do? These Serbs, including Vojislav Kostunica himself, dismiss the ICTY as a political instrument. The trouble is that it is difficult to argue otherwise: The ICTY is a court imposed exclusively on small, weak countries by large, powerful ones that exempt themselves from the reach of international law. Even those of us who heartily support the Hague, and who dismiss Serb grievances as so much recalcitrance and denial, are hard-pressed to counter the impression that the tribunal is at its core political. We may be wholly confident that our politics are far and away the right ones. But what we will want from an International Criminal Court, eventually, is not righteousness but justice.

I am reminded of a joke that was making the rounds when I returned to Belgrade in the summer of 2001, just a week before Milosevic was finally surrendered to the Hague. In it, Slobodan Milosevic begins his day by walking out onto the balcony of his suburban Belgrade mansion. He gazes up into the sky and demands, "Sun, who am I?"

"You are the hero of your people," the sun replies, "and the defender of small nations against the crushing force of empire. You are the true leader of all Serbs, and beloved by them. Your leadership is an example to the world's independent nations. Your wife is beautiful and brilliant. You have two lovely, successful children."

Milosevic puffs up with pleasure and returns indoors, where he goes about his daily business. It is nearing dusk when he remembers his fine morning moment, and he pulls his wife aside.

"Mira," he says, "come out onto the balcony. You have to hear what the sun has to say."

They go outside, where again Milosevic demands, "Sun, who am I?"

"You are the butcher of the Balkans," the sun replies. "You are a gangster and a war criminal, the perpetrator of genocide. You've robbed your people and starved them. You're loathed by all Serbs. Your wife is ugly and cruel. Your children are thugs and psychopaths."

"But sun," Milosevic sputters. "I don't understand. That's not what you said this morning."

"Ah," says the sun. "In the morning I was in the East. Now, I'm in the West."

SOME JUSTICE IS BETTER THAN NO JUSTICE. Better to have ad hoc interventions and ad hoc war crimes tribunals than none at all. Better to bring some vindication, however small or symbolic, to the victims of the Bosnian war than to win an argument in Belgrade. The interventionism of the 1990s has gone a long way toward international justice, and it has raised a vital challenge to the cynicism of the realists and the quietism of the left.

Nonetheless, in the long run, we must be careful where we invest our hopes. If we imagine that the United States is exceptional, that it represents universal interests, behaves altruistically, or commands an unrestrained right to intervene in the affairs of other states, we run the risk of deceiving ourselves, but we are unlikely to deceive anyone else. We may mistake what is at its best enlightened self-interest for an unbounded moral warrant for waging war. Moral authority cannot be arrogated on the basis of might, nor even of good intentions. The U.S. government justifiably declares Saddam Hussein a menace and Slobodan Milosevic a war criminal. But these claims and the equally justifiable ones that no American government will ever make will always be open to political challenge, because they spring from a political source. That does not mean that our government should stop making such claims. But it does mean that as critical observers of our country's foreign policy, we cannot calibrate our moral compasses to that of the Pentagon.

The world lacks institutions that stand outside of all geopolitics and command a genuinely universal moral authority. But the closest we have are the United Nations and its related organs of international law. Because these institutions are imperfect, American liberals have chosen to place their hope instead in the United States military. But it is precisely American disengagement that erodes the legitimacy of the international institutions our unilateralists of all political stripes have come to shun. The United States needs to get behind international law and its institutions. Otherwise, no one will—not just because the United States leads the world with its soft and its hard power, but because so long as these laws and institutions apply to everyone but the United States, they, too, lack moral authority.

The fact that the American populace requires the tug of conscience in order to accept military action is in itself a fascinating phenomenon, reflective of what's best and worst about our political culture—its beneficence and its narcissism. And it may be why American liberals do not possess a clear foreign-policy creed. We want so badly to be good that we cannot bear to look with clear eyes upon the exigencies of strategy and interest. There was a moment after September 11 when it was obvious that to ignore questions of security was to place the American citizenry at an unconscionable risk. Security threats had always seemed like conservative bogeymen. Suddenly, they mattered gravely. But to our dismay, we were left with the Bush administration's framing of the issues, because we lacked one of our own—one that would take security seriously but maintain respect for civil liberties, human rights, and the self-determination of distant peoples.

One way to develop an alternative framework is to broaden our thinking about engagement abroad. If we do not insist on exhausting all nonviolent alternatives to conflict resolution, and on working respectfully with indigenous forces for democracy in countries where human rights and freedoms are threatened, who in our political culture is going to place their emphasis there? Similarly, it has fallen now to liberals to defend the international system the United States has spent this century reluctantly putting into place. But we need to do more than defend it. We need to reenvision it, with an eye toward as universal and multilateral a justice as it is possible to imagine.

Who knows for how long our "unipolar" system will endure? Some political scientists have speculated about the rise of China or Europe; realist travel writer Robert Kaplan has predicted a global splintering into premodern anarchy. But by far the majority of international relations experts insist that any real challenge to American world hegemony is a long way off. Power on this scale coerces with even its gentlest touch. For that reason, it is vital to regard such power with skepticism, and to insist that it tread lightly but purposefully through a delicate world.

I RETURNED TO BELGRADE in November 2000, just a month after euphoric demonstrators had set the Yugoslav parliament on fire, watched police officers and soldiers defect in droves, and threatened those who remained with bulldozers driven all the way from small rural municipalities like Cacak, a hard peasant town in Serbia's north. The butcher of the Balkans had been defeated without a drop of blood.

Nonetheless, November found Belgrade sober and reckoning. Many Serbs were reckoning not with war crimes in Bosnia, unfortunately, but with the strange provenance of the revolution just passed: Suddenly, there was open discussion of the torrent of Western funding that had sustained much of the opposition movement through the U.S. Agency for International Development (USAID) and third party foundations like the National Endowment for Democracy and the Charles Mott Foundation. No one regretted the passage of Milosevic, though many of the most principled opposition figures had serious qualms about the new president, nationalist legal scholar Vojislav Kostunica. What was at issue was the relationship with the West. Did Western interference compromise the integrity of the supposedly indigenous democratic revolution? Did the funding of nationalists, ex-generals, and mafiosi compromise the integrity of the West?

The United States and Serbia were antagonists, after all. They had severed diplomatic ties in 1999; the average American had been taught that Serbs were bloodthirsty chauvinists, while the average Serb viewed the United States as a distant oppressor that sought to homogenize the world, and which had made common cause with Serbia's enemies. How were we to make sense of the intimacy of our relationship—Serbian nationalists and American intelligence operatives, Serbian pro-democracy revolutionaries and American training and funds?

That relationship was an open secret in Belgrade, but one that groups like Otpor, the celebrated student movement that was the catalyst for Milosevic's overthrow, carried close to the vest. "It is very important that the people see us as a people's movement," said one

Otpor activist, Marko Djuric, when I questioned him about outside funding that November.

Branko Ilic, another Otpor activist I'd met with in June and looked up again in November, had a different take. He would like to have his Western contacts come to Belgrade, he told me; he would stand with them and introduce them to the populace as Otpor's allies. If the Serbian public was pleased with Otpor's actions, it should also accept the partnership of Otpor's American friends. Maybe that would go some way toward a new mutual understanding. (I don't think that ever happened. And as for mutual understanding, a deputy of Kostunica's called on the Serbian public on September 11, 2001, to "please put aside your feelings" and try to find sympathy for the American people. New York's loss on that date was greater than most estimates of the casualty toll in Serbia from three months of heavy bombing.)

My host in Belgrade was Obrad Savic, an antinationalist NGO leader who found himself looking with cynicism on the Serbian revolution. "It's the final victory of Serbian nationalism," he told me bleakly, as the old nationalist clergy and intellectuals closed ranks with the new president. And with all that Western funding, could we really trust that a genuine repudiation of Milosevic lay at the popular movement's base? "The American dream was to kill Milosevic," he recalled. And with the Serbian economy in ruins, "they realized they could buy it for two hundred deutsche marks for every person on the street." Obrad never accepted funds from a foreign government. But American diplomats and operatives would ask him to approve lists of potential recipients, many of whom Obrad reviled as nationalists. "Look, Obrad," he recalls one American diplomat telling him. "We know only one percent of Serbs think like you. Serbs are nationalists. We've chosen to work with these people." Just before Milosevic fell, Obrad had made public statements in support of the Hague and began receiving anonymous death threats, along with summonses to appear before the police.

By the time of my next visit to Belgrade half a year later, the discomfort with American intervention seemed somehow both more complex and less pervasive. It was an eventful visit: Milosevic was shipped off to the Hague on June 28, 2001—Vidovdan, a Serbian national holiday that also happened to be the date Serbian nationalist Gavrilo Princip assassinated Archduke Franz Ferdinand in Sarajevo in 1914. Conveniently, a refrigerator truck full of slaughtered Kosovar Albanians had been dredged from the Danube in time for the new Serbian government to make the case for extradition. Not, of course, that the case was made with unanimity: Kostunica opposed extradition and was essentially steamrolled by his prime minister, the late pro-Western reformer Zoran Djindjic.

Now that Serbia had complied with the West's most urgent demand, diplomatic relations would soon be restored between the United States and this pariah nation that had occupied so many American resources, military and otherwise. William Montgomery, recently the American ambassador to Bulgaria and Croatia, would be the new ambassador to Yugoslavia. Excitement attended this appointment: Where Montgomery was posted, some Serbian NGO leaders informed me, democracy soon followed. On July 4, 2001, he reopened the American ambassador's residence with a Fourth of July barbecue on its ample grounds.

The residence sits on a winding street in the Belgrade suburb of Dedinje, just across from one of Tito's former palaces where Milosevic had sheltered before his extradition. Now the Serbian riot police I remembered from the bedraggled demonstrations a year before lined the road to protect Montgomery and his guests. A crowd of Serbian notables snaked down the road, waiting to have invitations checked at the gate. Obrad was particularly impatient. He'd just returned from a conference in Kosovo, where he and another Serbian delegate had to be escorted to the conference center by a military convoy, and where he had unwittingly provoked a furor among his Albanian colleagues by sipping bottled water with a Serbian label. Were Belgraders going to start behaving like Americans now—too squeamish to drink the local water? On his way home from Pristina, Obrad gave his embarrassingly conspicuous KFOR convoy the slip.

At the ambassador's reception, Obrad plucked a small American flag from a buffet table and perched it in his buttonhole. Waiters plied the crowd with platters of *cevapcici,* traditional Balkan meatballs. And the yard overflowed with the onetime Serbian underground: human-rights workers, civil society leaders, intellectuals, and activists who had repaired to the "NGO scene" philanthropist George Soros had long cultivated here and throughout Eastern Europe. I'd spoken to a lot of these NGO leaders in their hushed offices during the Milosevic era; the shades were drawn, important papers secreted to the homes of friends for fear of raids by the secret police. Now some of them told me of their new governmental posts. Others spoke openly of their past activities for the first time. "I've been working for the CIA for ten years, and I'm proud of it," one gentleman with the Helsinki Committee for Human Rights in Serbia informed me.

Could the United States have done better, sooner, in Yugoslavia? What avenues did we fail to explore? What other outcomes were possible, both for the region Serbia menaced, and for Serbia itself, as it struggled under a genocidal leadership that corrupted everything it touched? Was there a solution to the Yugoslav crisis that would have prevented the region's explosion into exclusionary nationalist states?

These are questions we forget to ask when we are busy congratulating ourselves on military successes. They are difficult and knotty, counterfactual and burdened with hindsight. But as we find ourselves embroiled in the complexities of the Middle East, we'd do well to think in such terms now, instead of later. If we are really interested in morality in foreign affairs, why not start here? Start not with ourselves looking outward, but with the world looking in.

Ideas of Transcendence

T HE OLD MAN'S NAME WAS SARFRAZ, but he was always addressed or referred to honorifically as "Sarfraz sahib." When, in 1989, while in Pakistan on a fellowship to study Urdu, I rented a room in the rooftop courtyard of his house in Lahore, calling him "sahib" (pronounced in Urdu and Hindustani exactly like the name of the Swedish automaker) gave me a pleasure that was incommensurate and slightly absurd. I called him sahib whenever I could, dropping his name in conversations for no other reason than to attach the word "sahib" to it, and using it in ways that were unidiomatic and reminiscent of the painstaking pedagogic explicitness of a reader for four-year-old Urdu speakers.

"*Sarfraz sahib ḳaha(n) haī?*" (Where's Sarfraz sahib?), his daughter Nusrat would ask me.

"*Sarfraz sahib chatt par haī.*" (Sarfraz sahib is on the roof.)

"*Kyaa soe hue haī?*" (Is he sleeping?)

"*Sarfraz sahib so rahe nahī. Sarfraz sahib parh rahe haī.*" (Sarfraz sahib is not sleeping. Sarfraz sahib is reading.)

The word "sahib" means "master of the house." The house Sarfraz sahib was the master of sat at the end of a little cul-de-sac near Shah Alami gate, in the *purani shehr*—the old city, the medieval quarter—of Lahore. The sprawling, deteriorating mud-walled house, the alley where stray goats and the occasional chicken promenaded, and the thousand-year-old old city itself were appropriately picturesque, but I didn't appreciate this the day I went to meet the family and look at my room. I was still jet-lagged from my flight from New York and dazed by the massive, unblinking late-summer heat. I found the exoticism of the world around me oppressive rather than charming. My Urdu was awful, and left me feeling embarrassed. I was already experiencing intestinal distress.

I remember acquiescing, finally, to my new reality when I encountered Sarfraz sahib, who had a large, mild brown face—the immemorial agriculturalist face of Punjab and the North Indian plains—and an instinctive, reassuring delicacy in his interactions with other human beings. I remember, as well, the satisfaction—the first satisfaction of my time in Pakistan, and one that was, improbably, political—that I got from employing the old honorific. Loaded as the word "sahib" is with British imperial echoes and associations, with the trace memories of the Nicholson sahibs and the memsahib Mrs. Hauksbees of the long years when Britain siphoned off the surplus wealth of what would become India and Pakistan, using it to modify the being of my prospective South Asian landlord made me feel as if I were participating, however belatedly and inconsequentially, in the enterprise of restoring the Indian independence movement, that I was reenacting in a small way something large by returning the word to its rightful owner and semantic terrain.

Though it was primitive, this mind game comforted me and gave at least a little reason and meaning to my first weeks in Pakistan. I was careful, therefore, about ignoring its latent ironies and historical imprecision. Pakistan was a big proposition for me, and the religion of the Muslims, the force by which the country knew itself as a country, even bigger. A vague desire to understand the conditions and circumstances of India; an even vaguer desire to involve myself in what I saw as some of the real problems of the world; and a sharp, secret urge to take the measure of Islam itself had led me to the study of South Asia. But, though going to Pakistan would help me progress in that study immeasurably, and was understood as a desideratum by the people who ran the graduate program I was enrolled in, none of this added up for me to a year in Lahore. While preparing for the trip, I'd had the feeling that I'd gone out on a limb, that I was getting in over my head. I began to see myself, to use a word familiar to readers of V. S. Naipaul, as "vulnerable," particularly to underlying racial and social insecurities. Weren't these the real reasons I had decided to study the history and literature of Islam in India, instead of, say, Shakespeare or abstract expressionism? I knew my Naipaul. I'd published an essay about him, and had crawled a little in the process of writing it under his examination of such insecurities and of the consequences of indulging them. Nothing could have appealed to me less than imagining myself in a version of one of his Third-World romances, as a hapless, insufficiently self-aware figure trapped between cultures that simultaneously collide and diverge, between a past that can only provoke regret and a future that can only induce dread. But that was the way, in the absence of an overarching motivation, I was beginning to see myself.

I'd felt some minor apprehensions about going to South Asia. The thought of getting sick, for example, worried me. The obligatory inoculations—for illnesses that included bacterial meningitis (a terrible disease, because it can kill so quickly and unexpectedly) and cholera—intensified rather than assuaged my fears of the local microscopic fauna. I was worried, too, about Pakistan itself, about how the Pakistanis would take to me, someone they would conclude was an Indian, obviously, and a Hindu besides, however insistently I waved my passport and my impeccable Americanization at them. And my Lahore wouldn't be the Lahore of the Gulberg district and the English-speaking middle and upper-middle classes but the Punjabi- and Urdu-speaking old city. Its markets and alleys would be brimming with people who had found—in the face of a modern world largely inimical to themselves, in the face of the failures of their political institutions and their own constricted and arduous lives—a revitalized sense of their worth as individuals through their religion, and who were asserting themselves, in Pakistan and across the Muslim world, in ways that were unaccountable and politically charged and, as many were saying even then and had been saying since the Iranian revolution, ominous.

What worried me the most, though, was that I had no consciousness to speak of about where I was going, and no reasons solid enough to make myself enthusiastic about going, though what I was embarking on was sufficiently against the grain to require reasons and an explanation, to myself and to my intimates. Some of them had already told me that my going to Lahore instead of an Urdu-speaking Indian city, like Lucknow, to study the language was another example of my perverseness. Why Pakistan? my father had asked me. Not wanting to reveal my misgivings and worry him, I'd told him that Gandhi was on his way there when he was assassinated, and I thought I'd go in his place. Dumbfounded at my blasphemy, he had made that little retroflex click—effected by a slight explosion of the tongue after it is placed on the lower palate, and so satisfying to its author—by which South Asians vocalize exasperation and disdain.

If I'd thought of it at the time, I could have responded to my father's little click by laying the blame for my growing anxiety about the enterprise I was undertaking at his feet. He was, and remains, a living refutation of W. H. Auden's claim that emigrants don't know what they want, only what they don't want. When he left India for America in the mid-1950s to get his Ph.D. in physical chemistry—in an era when only a scant handful of Indians made what was then a formidable journey—he never looked back. He knew exactly what he wanted. He came to America not for money but for science. He wanted the secular, experimental, positivistic world, which in the India of his time was still notional, embryonic. He wanted to breathe the air of the Enlightenment. Progressive, relentlessly empirical—Robert Frost's "The fact is the sweetest dream that labor knows" is his favorite line of poetry—horrified by generalities, antipathetic to tradition and custom and ancient and oppressive social orders, possessed by the faith, touchingly common in his gen-eration of Third-World intellectuals (who brought to progressive ideas none of the ironies of their brethren in the West) that science and technology would eventually solve all human problems, he was made for America. And America, or, at least, *an* America, the best America, was made for him—the America of the Tennessee Valley Authority and the Argonne National Labs and rural electrification; the America of munificently endowed land-grant research universi-ties determined to educate everyone (he taught chemistry at one of these); the America of the civil-rights movement, which for him, newly emerged from India's caste system and the racial regimes of the British, was a confirmation of American success rather than a revelation of American failure; and, most important, the America of natural, as opposed to divine, law, of inalienable rights, which enshrine, instead of an economic class (disagreeable to him) or a theophany (even more disagreeable), the human individual at the center of political life: the America, in short, of Locke and Jefferson, which it is the peculiar privilege of the immigrant to discern in a way that, perhaps, no native-born American can. When my son was learning to read, my father presented him with an expensive facsimile copy of the Declaration of Independence (an absurd enough gift for a four-year-old, I thought at the time).

One of the consequences for me, though, of my father's deep satisfaction with America was my own deracination, so thoroughgoing that it "problematized" (as they say) my imminent departure. I grew up with no experience of India and therefore couldn't anticipate what my experience of Pakistan might be. Not only did my father never take us back, he seemed oblivious to the country of his birth. He never talked about it except when he referred to Indian scientists. He didn't go back to visit until the 1970s, when he returned, briefly, to take care of family business after his mother's death. Apart from six weeks in the mid-1960s, when my mother had taken my sister and me to see her father, who was ill with diabetes, I hadn't set foot in that part of the world for thirty years. And this lack of experience inevitably reinforced my feelings of intellectual uncertainty about my trip to Pakistan. I'd been studying Islam, Indian history, Persian, Urdu, and Urdu poetry for the previous two years—it seemed as if I'd done nothing else—and for much of that time I'd meditated, under the influence of a variety of critical theories, on the niceties of interpretation. But I had no interpretation. I'd picked my way through "Allegories of Reading" and "Morphology of the Folktale," but I didn't have narratives to either allegorize or morphologize, and certainly none, devised by myself or invented by others, that could accommodate me, except for the stark ones I found in Forster and Naipaul and others of the Westernized Indian bouncing between the new world and the old and unable to live in either. Those narratives made no sense to me and wouldn't make me happy, let alone functional, in an environment that would require me to commit all my imaginative and physical energy.

The feeling that I had no consciousness, no reliable subjectivity, began growing on me in the cab from my house in Brooklyn to JFK Airport. The estrangement from the familiar that characterizes the beginning of a journey, when the world that has surrounded us, which we've assumed is inevitable, suddenly looks accidental, tacked-on, an afterthought scribbled on the body of reality—an estrangement that in the past I'd always enjoyed in a melancholy, de Chirico–like way—now seemed symptomatic and sinister. My unease got worse and worse as New York fell away from the plane, and by the time we reached Frankfurt for a two-hour stopover, I was in a state of dread. Walking around the Frankfurt airport, looking at all the things in the duty-free shops that money could buy and appreciating how beautifully institutions, machines, and people functioned, I began to feel that simply by going to South Asia I was compromising my American identity (which had been far more hard-won for me than my father's had been for him, lacking as I did his serene faith in science and progress). By doing nothing more than trying to reconnect myself to the places my people had come from, I was losing this West, in all its achieved glory, and running the risk of being absorbed by something that was—or, at least, so I imagined—the opposite.

The America I grew up in had been filled with impulses to transcendence. They had flowed for generations out of the Protestant insistence on an unmediated relationship between the individual and God. They ranged from born-again Christianity to a variety of Emersonianisms to meditation of every kind, yoga, nature worship, veganism, and soul travel. They encompassed a bewildering retooling of borrowed spiritual technologies. They allowed—they invited—the citizens of the republic to invent their own religion. But they all stressed one thing: the mystical and transformative power of positive thinking. I, though, had no positive thinking. I had no transcendental clarity. Even worse, I had no clear idea where I was going. I knew only where I wasn't going. I wasn't going to the pre-Partition Lahore, the cosmopolitan Hindu-Sikh-Muslim Lahore, which had harbored some of the most progressive Muslim intellectuals in the Islamic world. I wasn't going to Kipling's Lahore. I wasn't going to the city where Ranjit Singh established the Sikh *darbar* that ruled a kingdom stretching from the Sutlej River to Kabul; or to the city where Dara Shikoh translated the Upanishads into Persian while his austere and orthodox brother Aurangzeb plotted to rip the Mughal empire from his hands; or to the place of retirement of al-Hujwiri, the author of the most renowned handbook of Sufism, the Kashf al-Mahjub, the Unveiling of the Mystery, about whom scholars have inferred that he had a short and unpleasant married life; or to the pre-Islamic city that might or might not have been the home of the great Sanskrit grammarian Panini; or to the Sapta Sindhava of the Rig Veda, where the first (or maybe the second) poem known to humankind was written.

And about this place that was not all these places, I knew nothing of real usefulness. What knowledge I had of the region—apart from the two Dravidian languages, Tamil and Kannada, in which I had a domestic fluency—was entirely bookish. Almost all that knowledge had been recently acquired, from historians and scholars of literature and religion, all of whom came from the American heartland, and were the children of Congregational ministers and small-town Midwestern bankers. They had taught me about *wahadat al-wujud* and *viraha;* about the Simon Commission, the Rowlatt Acts, dyarchy, the Radcliffe Boundary Award; about *fana* and *baqa,* which are the last stages of the soul's long ascent to the Godhead. But they had failed to teach me—being rationalists, how could they not have failed?—about the Lahore that I now imagined myself on the way to. Lahore had been one of the central killing grounds of

Partition. Partition was what was in store for me; Partition, in which neighbor had turned on neighbor hundreds of thousands of times in inexhaustible hatred. In Frankfurt, the reality of Lahore seemed to me consumed by that fact. What, I wondered, could I learn there, except that man is a wolf to man, and that the purpose of human government is not to promote justice but to impose order, by force if necessary. And I hardly needed to go to Pakistan to learn that.

It took me awhile after I got to Lahore to work myself out of the Hobbesian frenzy I'd worked myself into in Frankfurt. Sarfraz sahib was the medium of my reconciliation. Not only was he old, he was ill, too. Illness had given him the ectomorphic, almost exoskeletal, look—the gaunt, undernourished bodily elongation—of the poorest South Asians. (Though his family wasn't starving—they owned a modest-sized house in the old city, which in that part of the world made them lucky—they were, in fact, poor enough; they badly needed the room-and-board money I gave them, and the food they served me, though nutritious, was small in portion and pretty much unspeakable.) On my first early mornings in his house, jet-lagged and not sleeping deeply, I would drift in and out of a semi-consciousness that was accompanied by the sound of his coughing rising from the lower rooms. Each morning, he coughed himself back into life in long, rattling convulsions that were punctuated by little groans and seemed as if they'd never stop. Each of these fits always sounded as if it would be his last, but by the time I'd got out of bed and washed and dressed, he would have worked his way back to the world and be on the roof, tending to his hibiscus plants, which were strewn along the perimeter in large earthenware pots.

I was interested in him from the first. It turned out that he was almost as interested in me. He wasn't a Punjabi. He came from Meerut, in what is now called Uttar Pradesh, in the Urdu- and Hindustani-speaking heartland of India. When the country was partitioned in 1947, he had made the two-hundred-mile journey to Lahore on foot, hiding out all the while from the outriding bands of Sikhs and Hindus who were killing any Muslim they could find. I wanted (and also didn't want) to know more about this journey than what I had been told by the people who had put me in touch with the family. But it was difficult for me, still a little discomfited by the feeling that there was something outlandish about my being in Lahore, to approach him in the beginning; and, though age and illness must have made him feel doubly shy (my Urdu should have made me shyer than I was), he was the one who broke the ice. We had exchanged distant pleasantries on encountering each other for about a week after I moved in. One afternoon, coming back home from a class and finding him on the roof, I greeted him with my customary formal heartiness (I wasn't fluent enough for emotions more complex than heartiness): *"Janab! Aap ki tabiyat kaise hai? Tiik hai? Aacha."* (Sir! How are you? Good? Good.) Sitting in the sun under the dovehouse wall, he responded by offering me a banana from a bunch he had on a plate in front of him. After I ate it, I said something idiotic about the bananas in Pakistan, about how really great they were, so sweet and flavorsome—an attempt, clumsy and obvious, on my part to continue developing the social opportunity while leaping on a chance to assure him that I wasn't implicated in the ancient and terrible grudge between the Hindus and the Muslims. I was startled by his reply.

"These are nothing compared to the bananas in India," he said.

Climate, overcrowding, and immemorial custom ensure that much of the domestic life in South Asian cities is lived on rooftops. The rooftops of Lahore's old city had for centuries been subject to home-improvement schemes. Rooms enclosing a central courtyard had been built on many of the flat roofs around us, and often these structures were large enough to support more rooms on top, and on top of these rooms, dovecotes or postage stamp–sized spaces furnished with rickety benches that looked as if they'd been retrieved from a midden. Running my eyes over these excavations of the air was a constant source of pleasure for me. I'd found when I arrived in Lahore that the Punjab landscape seemed flat to the point of unreality (the dreamlike impression I retain of the entire Pakistani and North Indian landscape, from the Hindu Kush and the Himalayas to the Vindhyas, in Madhya Pradesh, is of an impossible flatness, of a million square miles flatter than a playing field). I craved three-dimensionality and contour. Because I found them on the roof, I tended to be there when not attending classes. I would climb up to the highest aerie I could reach to study my idioms. It was late summer and early fall, and except for the midday hours, the sun and the monolithic sky could be withstood, and even enjoyed. The kites wheeled in the firmament; the bats came out to hunt in the twilight; and on certain moonless nights I could see the palatial arms of the Milky Way, a sight lost to inhabitants of Western cities, with their extravagant illumination, but still accessible in Lahore in the late summer, when the streets and the houses are dark at night and the winter fires aren't yet polluting the air.

It was on the roof that Sarfraz sahib and I forged our separate peace. I'd forged a different kind of peace with his grown-up daughters Ismat and Nusrat, and his son, Riyaaz. They were orthodox and pious Sunnis, about my age. They deplored the saint-worshiping and the charismatic and pantheistic impulses that have always crept into South Asian Islam. If they noticed my Indianness, they didn't mention it, and never alluded to India, a country riddled with these tendencies, which was only a dozen miles away as the crow flies. I had, though, a rapidly expanding knowledge of Islam, and an appreciation for it that wasn't just adapted to my circumstances. I admired Islam's intellectual rigor and internal consistency, its philosophical cleanliness, economy, and lucidity. I recognized and honored the tremendous commitment to social justice that marks the calling of the Prophet. To this, my sympathetic awareness, they responded with gratitude; they were so taken with it, in fact, that they began to develop a touching, and constricting, solicitude for my soul. When I went out into the bazaars with my tape recorder to record the itinerant singers who performed the ecstatic Punjabi devotional poetry of Bulhe Shah and Baba Farid, and received for their pains showers of rupees and praise and obeisance, they patiently explained to me on my return that this kind of passion for a performer of religious songs was *shirk,* the making of a companion to God by offering devotion appropriate only to Him to one of His creatures; that this was the most terrible of sins; and that I should henceforth avoid even the sight of it. One night I went to a Sufi *khanqah,* a gathering of mystics, and watched a puffy and slightly bedraggled *pir,* a Sufi elder, dance in what was assumed to be holy rapture. When I got back to the house, I was greeted with looks of fretful disappointment.

My relationship to Sarfraz sahib was free of these pressures. He had a real and deep feeling for India. It had survived Partition, three wars between India and Pakistan, and the Islamization of the Pakistani state, with all its attendant propaganda and determined forgetfulness of the common origins of the two peoples. He talked about Meerut, about his family members who still lived in Delhi, about Sikh and Hindu friends of his youth. When, as the weather got colder, I asked at what point the blankets would be put up to insulate the rooms that opened onto courtyards, he replied, *"Diwali ke bad"*—"after Diwali," the Hindu festival of lights, which takes place in October and marks the end of the harvest season; it is celebrated in India by all the religious communities, but had not been celebrated in Lahore for the forty-odd years he had lived there.

He was satisfying to contemplate; he both felt and provoked a bittersweet nostalgia for a vanished past. Through him, I began to imagine a contrafactual history—a secular Pakistan, at peace with India in the way he and I were at peace, with neither country wasting precious resources on armaments; or, even more inconceivable except in his presence, a subcontinent where Partition hadn't occurred at all, where the nightmare had been undone. He incited these kinds of fantasies in me. He was the product of what Nehru had lovingly called the "composite culture," the multilevel, multilingual, multireligious, overlapping eight-hundred-year-old culture of North India, which developed continually in the face of spasms of religious conflict and long periods of political chaos and imperial subjugation, and of which Lahore once had been one of the notable capitals. By occupation, he was a *katib,* a calligrapher, working in Nastaliq, the most widely disseminated of the major styles of Islamic calligraphy. His living had been made as a graphic artist, producing signs and circulars and advertisements, but he had an excellent traditional education, and he knew classical Urdu literature. One afternoon, I was on the roof toiling without much success over a translation of a simple ghazal by Mirza Ghalib, the last and greatest of the Urdu poets of Delhi. Sarfraz sahib came up to me and asked why I looked so unhappy.

"Koi uumid bar nahī ati; koi surat nazar nahī ati" (Hope remains unfulfilled; beauty remains unseen), I told him tragically, quoting the first couplet.

"Maut ka ek din muayyann hai; nind kyō rat bher nahī ati" (The day of your death has long been appointed; so why can't you sleep the night through), he responded antiphonally with the second couplet, and then reeled off several more.

Sarfraz sahib had an enormous number of ghazal verses committed to memory, not only Ghalib's but those of all the major Urdu poets of the classical era. From that day on, whenever I was around to listen to him recite, he did. His favorite lines were the famous trenchant or comic ones of Ghalib and Mir Taqi Mir (lines impossible to translate adequately into English) in which, in small, epigrammatic spaces, tragic irony, satire, and self-mockery are fused into a rhetoric of extraordinary power and lyrical balance: *"Ibtida-e-ishq hai, rota hai kyaa?; age, age dekhiye, hota hai kyaa"* (Love has just begun, and you're already weeping?; wait until you see what comes next); *"Yih masaial-e-tasavvuf, yih tera bayan, Ghalib; tujhe ham vali samajhte, jo nah badakhvar hota"* (These matters of Sufism, this eloquence of yours, Ghalib; if you weren't such a drunkard, we'd think you were a saint). What I persisted in seeing as his Indianness—wishfully, I suppose—made him appreciate the cunning blasphemies of Ghalib and Mir. He had the old sophistication, the ancient skeptical glimmer about religion, which, though not banished in the younger generation, seemed to have gone into hiding. He was too old to hide anything, and he was fond of subversion. He loved to tell the famous story of Ghalib during the rebellion of 1857. The British—or, rather, the Sikhs and other native units officered by the British—had retaken Delhi after having lost the city to the rebels, and British policy required savage reprisals for the atrocities committed upon the European population in Delhi and elsewhere, reprisals directed disproportionately at the Muslims, who were seen as the ringleaders of the rebellion and became the objects of relentless fury. British soldiers had strapped Muslims to cannons and blown them to bits. This was done so that when the body was resurrected on Judgment Day and called to confront its Maker there would be no body to answer the call. In this atmosphere of violence and vengeance, Ghalib, then an old man living on a small pension, had been brought before a British official. "Are you a Muslim?" the official asked Ghalib, who replied:

"Adha Musalman hū. Sharab pita hū, suar nahī khata." (I'm half a Muslim. I drink wine; I don't eat pork).

BEYOND THE BADSHAHI MOSQUE, the enormous sandstone exaggeration built by Aurangzeb to honor his piety and the grandeur of his orthodoxy, and on the nearside of the swarming road between the old city and the memorial park that commemorates the birth of Pakistan, there was written, on a long, low wall, a graffito in foothigh Nastaliq. The legend read, *"Pakistan ka matlab kyaa hai?: La illaha il-allahhu Muhammad ar-rasul illah"* (What is the meaning of Pakistan?: There is no God but God, and Muhammad is His prophet). Pakistan was Islam, and Islam was Pakistan, or so the writer of the legend would have it. All human space—public, private, interior—belonged to God, and He had insisted upon this to Muhammad again and again. There was no place He was not, and, after all, how could there be? For a decade and a half, the country's politicians had constantly played the religious card: first, in the 1970s, to boost morale after the humiliating defeat at the hands of India in the Bangladesh war, and then because a method by which social solidarity could be imposed so easily in a country so essentially fractious—both the Indians and the Pakistanis have a predilection to anarchism as deep as that of the Spaniards—proved impossible to resist. Five times a day, the *azan*, the call to prayer, would be sounded from loudspeakers all over the city. Five times a day, not all but a decisive majority of the male population would stop whatever they were doing and turn to Mecca. Often during the *azan*, the shopkeeper with whom I was haggling over the price of a pomegranate would turn abruptly away from me, roll out his prayer rug, and prostrate himself. The ricksha wallah who was driving me home would veer over to the margin of the road the moment he heard *"Allah u Akbar,"* turn his engine off, and roll his prayer rug out on the shoulder. Henry James has a beautiful phrase: "the publicity implied by such privacies." At moments like this, while waiting for everyday living to resume, I would wonder what the privacies could be that such publicity, such an open and continual confession of faith, implied.

Wahadat al-wujud—the unity of being, which confirms that all human action is indistinguishable from the ineffable transparency of God. "There is no God but God"—the awesome Islamic tautology, so subtle and far-reaching, which furnishes the believer with the definitive response to all the other testaments of human faith. The Sunna—the actions of the Prophet of God, Qur'anic and extra-Qur'anic, which are the models of human behavior. Shariah—the path that leads to the water, the legal code, normative Islam, Islam par excellence, derived from the Sunna and the Qur'an. Hadith—the extra-Qur'anic traditions of the Prophet, which are carefully classified by the relative strength of their attestations, and which confirm the Sunna and lend support and credence to the Shariah. The Qur'an itself—not an account of God but His very Word, spoken in Arabic, His cherished language, and transcribed by His messenger, Muhammad, of the tribe of Quaraysh, the Prophet of God, the seal of the prophets, who came to notify the citizens of Mecca and Medina and the world that *al-sa'at*, the Hour, the Day of Judgment, is at hand. And, finally, God—that interesting figure, who in the Qur'an manifests Himself with a vividness, complexity, versatility, compassion, disdain, and ambiguity equaled in the two other Semitic traditions in only certain moments in Genesis and Exodus and certain passages of the Book of Job.

These were all important things. They were changing the world, and in Pakistan in 1989 you could watch the changes happening. Increasingly, as fall began to wear into winter, I left my rooftop fastness and went down into the old city to see these changes more clearly. I did this with a certain reluctance. While trading Urdu couplets with Sarfraz sahib on the roof I'd found something that satisfied me and justified my coming to Lahore. But that something was India, not Pakistan; the composite culture, not the Islamic republic; secularism, not theocracy. To just linger in my satisfaction would have been nice. It would also have been a disservice to the people who were funding me, who expected me to acquire some new knowledge (secularism, the composite culture, and India being old and harmless knowledge). And as the weather got colder Sarfraz sahib appeared less and less on the roof, and had to be searched out in front of the TV downstairs, where, huddled in a coarse wool blanket, he would watch Pakistani soap operas or Indian films beamed into Lahore from Amritsar, just across the border.

So I began spending my free time exploring the old city. What I discovered there, though, while shopping at the sweetmeat stalls or looking curiously at the people in the shuttered, secretive red-light district, wasn't what I thought I would discover—something about Islam or about the conflict between India and Pakistan and the possibilities for peace therein. What I discovered in Mughal Lahore was America, and it was America that answered, finally, the crisis of consciousness I'd experienced on my way to Pakistan. In America, I never thought about the country, except to deplore, occasionally, its materialism and to condemn, more than occasionally and for very good reasons, its foreign policy. In Lahore, I began to see America the way my father saw the country because I began to understand a little the real nature of what he had liberated himself from. All around me was the Islamic insistence that the human will submit to God. In my head, though, I heard, more clearly than I ever had before, the American invitation to self-invention, which I recognized now as a product not of the accidental prosperity of the country but of its essential character and vitality. This, not my Indianness, was what made Pakistan possible for me—for an Indian proper, even if he or she is a Muslim, Pakistan can never quite be possible. America had given me an imaginative freedom so expansive, so without restriction and condition, that I'd imagined I could take on Islam itself. The idea was ridiculous, certainly, but the responsibility for that was mine, not America's.

And America had given me not only the freedom to take on Islam but the intellectual resources to carry the adventure to at least a partial resolution. I was free of the paralyzing fatalism so common to Third-World intellectuals. I might be naive, but the corrective to that could never be despair, simply because the kind of mental freedom I'd been offered precluded it. The real American freedom was benignly indifferent to the burning question of who created the world, and why. It offered nothing more than a negative capability; it asked nothing more than an awareness of the world's multiplicity. The implications of American ideas were open-ended; the social and personal responsibility they demanded was partial, pragmatic, voluntary. They were ideas that could be easily trivialized and abused, and they were trivialized and abused all the time. But they'd been born out of a bitter, profound, and accurate wisdom about the limits of human understanding and the dangers of centralized power, religious and political. In Pakistan, confronted with the certitude and forbidding completeness of Islam, these ideas began to take on uncanny qualities for me. Incited by the religious assertion in which I was immersed, I started seeing American ideas and the individualism they promoted as not just a convenience for the

American economic system but as a revelation—something I could never have done in America—and as equal in metaphysical substance and grandeur to Islam itself. They, too, were transcendental, and, more important, they worked. They were capacious; they located responsibility, spiritual and temporal, where it belonged, within the self; they could accommodate anything. They could even accommodate Islam. Islam, though, still struggled to accommodate them. The Muslim world had wrestled with similar ideas many times, and had yet to find a synthesis. *"An al-haq"* (I am the Truth)—al-Hallaj, the great Sufi mystic, proclaimed in the tenth century, prefiguring Whitman, and was forthwith hanged by the clerics of Baghdad.

AMONG PEOPLE WHO STUDY the conflict between India and Pakistan and the history of the Muslims of the subcontinent, it's commonplace to remark on the fatality that brought Islam, the most resolutely monotheistic, creedal, historicizing, and chiliastic product of the human religious genius, face-to-face with vegetative, syncretistic, polymorphic, sensual Hinduism, with its proliferating gods and myths, its atheistic philosophical offshoots (Vedanta and Buddhism), its cyclical notion of time, and its subversive tolerance (the bigoted Hindu nationalism of the party currently ruling India is a cultural, not a religious, phenomenon), which suggests, ultimately, that human life, though often terrible, is not quite serious. The struggle between these radically opposed visions of reality lasted many centuries, and wasn't at all unfruitful. What remains of that conflict, though, is just politics now, and the most woebegone remnant is Kashmir, the bloody, unfinished, seemingly unfinishable stepchild of Partition.

I had only one conversation about politics when I was in Pakistan, and that was an argument about Kashmir. It wouldn't have been unusual in most years in Pakistan never to encounter, in ordinary social life, a political discussion that went beyond gossip about the foibles and corruptions of politicians. In a country where serious, and sometimes violent, political crises are frequent, and where the expression of political opinion has often proved to be dangerous, it makes sense that people would talk about other things. But 1989 was not an ordinary year. While I was in Lahore, the Soviets were dismantling their empire; the Berlin Wall fell, an inconceivable event, about which I acquired an imperfect understanding through the Urdu newspapers (in an attempt to improve my language skills, I'd restricted myself to the vernacular press). And things were changing rapidly in Pakistan itself. The Soviets had withdrawn from Afghanistan earlier in the year—a triumph of sorts for American and Pakistani policy—and for a year the country had had an elected government, whose head of state, Benazir Bhutto, was the first woman to rule an Islamic nation. (I'd gone to hear her at a rally in the old city organized by her party, the Pakistan People's Party, and had almost been crushed to death in the crowd.)

By mid-December, I was eager to talk about these events, some of which were earthshaking, and to talk about them in English, so I could express without hesitation or fumbling the thoughts crowding my head. At about that time, I got what I imagined was a chance. In Ferozsons, the famous bookshop on Lahore's mall, I ran into a Pakistani whom I had known slightly in New York. I will call him Farrukh. Farrukh had graduated from college in America and had come back to Lahore to teach in one of the English-language schools that train the Pakistani elite. Though I'd hardly interacted with him in New York, I greeted him lavishly in Lahore. He seemed just as glad to see me, and we immediately started hatching plans for excursions—to Taxila, the ancient, ruined city down whose central thoroughfare Alexander had ridden mounted on an elephant; to Peshawar, to see the arms and opium bazaars; all the way to the wilds of Baluchistan. Farrukh came from one of the feudal landholding families who, along with the military, have ruled Pakistan with fitful incompetence for the past fifty years. He said he would take me hunting for game birds on his family's land. I said, Wonderful, I'd love to go, though I wouldn't shoot. It would be like Turgenev, though Pakistani.

We met for lunch a couple of days later in one of the fancy Chinese restaurants in the Gulberg district. While waiting for the dumplings to arrive, Farrukh pointed out some of the notables at the other tables—local politicians and businessmen, about whom he was trenchant and cynical, and an Afghan warlord who had played a major part, he said, in the resistance to the Soviets. Then, as the dishes were laid in front of us, he turned his attention to Kashmir. There had been major, continuous antigovernment demonstrations in Srinagar, the Kashmiri state capital, in recent weeks. The newspapers in Lahore had been full of accounts. Farrukh said he had gone the night before to hear a lecture by Khushwant Singh, the Indian writer, originally a Lahori, who had come to talk about Kashmir at the invitation of the local Muslim literati, among whom he had many friends from the old days. After telling me what Khushwant had said, Farrukh went on with the subject. The lecture must have been gnawing at him, enough to breach a serious social protocol: It's a given that the one thing never discussed directly between Indians and Pakistanis in a neutral social environment—such as a party in London or a Chinese restaurant anywhere in the world—is Kashmir. Farrukh said that nothing could happen between India and Pakistan, there could be no lessening of tension, until the Pakistani grievance over Kashmir was addressed. I responded in a way I thought was generous, and also merely descriptive and accurate. I said he was probably right, and that there was a chance that the Kashmiris could win their independence if they played their cards right. But, I added, there was no chance that the Indians would let them go to Pakistan. At this point, he grew incensed. What happened when Kashmir became a part of India instead of Pakistan was a crime, effected by a collusion among Nehru, Mountbatten, and Sheikh Abdullah, and there would be war, always, on the subcontinent until the consequences of this crime were erased. It was all well and good for someone like me to come to Lahore, but it really meant nothing, could mean nothing, until Kashmir was given to Pakistan. I became almost as angry as he was. I told him that what was happening in Srinagar now had nothing to do with Pakistan and little to do with Islam (which was true then but ceased to be true in the 1990s), that it was a product of the Kashmiri exasperation with the corruption and fraudulence of recent elections there, and why would the Kashmiris want to go to Pakistan, a state plunging into theocracy, when they could do so much better in India? We finished our Chinese food in bitter silence. I never did go hunting with him.

Soon after this lunch, with a month of free time on my hands because I was on an American academic schedule, I decided to go to India and see the sights and visit relatives scattered across the country. When I went to say good-bye to Sarfraz sahib, he recited one of Ghalib's most famous and characteristic couplets: *"Ishq se tabiyat ne zist ka maza paya; dard ki dava payi dard-e-bedava paya"* (Love gave my being a zest for life; I found a cure for pain and a pain beyond curing). I hitched a ride in the back of a truck to the checkpoint at Wagah and crossed over into Indian Punjab. In India, unsurprisingly, Kashmir was not only a bigger story than it had been in Pakistan but seemed to be the only story people were paying attention to. The fall of the Berlin Wall might as well have happened on another planet. A dramatic new incident was at the center of the news. The daughter of the Indian home minister, Mufti Muhammad Sayeed, a Kashmiri Muslim, had been abducted by militants in Srinagar. The government was employing all its resources to find her. India was shockingly modern after Pakistan. It was like Italy with huge numbers of poor people. The media coverage of the abduction had a contemporary and European flair. There were crisply edited shots of the worried minister and his tearful wife trailing a crowd of reporters in and out of government buildings. The anchors handled their duties with grave detachment and a faint, barely discernible superciliousness worthy of the BBC. India has arrived, I thought, while sitting in the house of family friends in Delhi watching the news. India has mastered television. The story stayed alive as I crisscrossed the country, visiting relatives, and eventually came to a satisfactory conclusion. When I was in Madhya Pradesh, staying with an uncle, the girl was released unharmed.

That story, though, wasn't the last brush I had with Kashmir in my time in India. When I got to Bangalore, where most of my relatives are clustered, the issue, the unbearable dilemma, came bouncing back. The aunts and uncles I was visiting were pious, orthodox Vaishnavites. They were very different from my father, who had left and never looked back. Looking back was something my aunts and uncles did often. They were scandalized that I had gone to Pakistan, and wanted to know nothing of my experience there. (Indians of their generation have historically dealt with Pakistan by pretending it doesn't exist.) My young cousins, on the other hand— hip, knowing, contemporary, and schooled in the new Indian sophistication—were eager to talk about Pakistan. Why did I go live there? I told them that I went to study Urdu poetry. Yes, Urdu poetry was very great, but the best Urdu poetry was in India, in Bombay and Delhi and Lucknow, and did I know that when India and Pakistan played cricket against each other, the Muslim students in their schools rooted for Pakistan?

I pointed out that many of the greatest Indian bowlers and batsmen were Muslim. They changed the subject. The Bharatiya Janata Party (BJP), the Hindu nationalist party, was at the beginning of its ascent to the national power it now holds. The issue the party elders had chosen as a vote-getter was the Babri *masjid,* a mosque in the North Indian town of Ayodhya, which had been built by a lieutenant of Babur, the first Mughal emperor, on what might or might not have been the foundations of a temple. The Babri *masjid* had been a source of low-level communal tension since the 1960s. The Hindu Right claimed that the mosque had been built on the birthplace of Rama, the hero of the Ramayana and an incarnation of God to believing Hindus. The mosque, they said, should be torn down and a temple to Rama built in its place. The mosque had been padlocked for a quarter century, and the claims, as well as the counterclaims by Muslims, had been in the courts for decades—the somewhat feckless strategy of successive provincial and central governments being to drown the dangerous controversy in legalism. But now the issue was out on the streets, exploited in dramatic ways by the BJP and other groups on the Hindu Right. In a piece of highly effective political theater, caravans had been sent all over the country to collect bricks—sanctified, holy bricks—to rebuild the temple of Rama at the place of his birth, which the BJP promised its faithful it would do.

My young cousins were supporters of this dreadful project. They'd gone to see the caravans and cheered them on. Did I know that the Muslims had destroyed the temple where Rama was born and put a mosque in its place? I told them I had heard something to that effect. Then I spent a half hour or so trying to get them to admit that Rama was a character in a piece of fiction, which they did, even-

tually, but grudgingly, as if out of politeness. After this, they began
chattering about other things. Look at the Japanese, how well they
had come up. If only India could do the same. All of them planned
to go into the small but growing private sector after they graduated
from college, rather than get government jobs. It was a risk, but
graduates they knew were making ten times more working for
companies than they would in the civil service. To work for the
government, as their parents had done, was to waste your life. Hear-
ing them trash not one but two of the central pillars of the Indian
republic—first secularism and then socialism, both of which had
been enshrined as the defining qualities of the Indian state in the
preamble to the Indian constitution—was a little disheartening. But
I couldn't argue very far with them. I was, after all, going back to
America, which was rich and advanced, while they, though they
were children of the Indian middle class, had tough choices to make
and difficult barriers to surmount. I nevertheless made one more
stab at them. As they were enthusing about the private sector, I
burst in.

"If you guys keep going on like this about the Babri *masjid*,
you're going to lose Kashmir."

The oldest of them, a fine-boned, loquacious, articulate girl,
gave me a distant and indulgent look.

"We will never lose Kashmir," she told me. "Kashmir is ours."

TODD GITLIN

Varieties of Patriotic Experience

1. Patriotism Out of the Blue

*T*O TELL THE TRUTH, the jolts of September 11, 2001, jammed my mental circuits, and I spent much of the ensuing year trying to get them unjammed. This was as much an intellectual as an emotional undertaking, if, indeed, it makes any sense to separate the two. To devote yourself to such a task, you must resist what is called "closure." You must open yourself to the shock, again and again, and refuse to let any ideology take possession of it. You must not shy from bewilderment, from unprecedented feelings and thoughts, neglected topics, whole shelves full of cans of worms. When you ask *What?* and *Why?* and *What follows?* and the subject under discussion is mass murder, you must not be satisfied to rummage through your mental file cabinet of prepackaged answers—not if you want to be alive to the shock, that is, to reality. You know that all the preprinted labels are wrong. You refuse to honor the shallow thought that the images of atrocity "looked like an action movie." You do not classify deliberate massacre as an "understandable" response to an objectionable foreign policy, or, for that matter, as a singular outburst of evil directed against a people innocent of evil. You do not try to dispel your immediate feelings, horror and astonishment, because your feelings are your links to reality, even if sometimes they throw you for a loop. It was through my emotions that I found myself in contact with—thinking about—questioning—and taken by—patriotism.

Proximity wasn't the cause. It wasn't that I or my family was in danger directly—we live a mile north of the ruins of the Twin Towers, a sizable distance, as these things go, though close enough to see and hear the second explosion. A day and a night later, and for weeks to come, we were breathing the World Trade Center, the tons of acrid smoke, the vaporized remnants of thousands of computers, copy machines, phones, glass and steel, carpets and desks, asbestos, God knows what—corpses, too, but it took time to realize that. But the fumes of catastrophe, however deeply they sink into your lungs, don't make you rethink your principles. Fear—fear that this one-time event might not turn out to be a onetime event—comes closer to accomplishing that. But fear was only one feeling and there were others, surprising ones. Love, for example.

Thinking about that crystalline, desperate morning forever enshrined by a number, I have tried to hold on to the astonishment and deepen it with reflection, not to flee from the downright shock. Experience that astonishes is not the sole truth but it is an indispensable truth—the truth of "wild history," in the historian Richard Slotkin's phrase, history that did not have to happen but that, once having happened, changes not only the future but the history that happened before. The risk of such an endeavor is that you become trapped in the trauma, fixated on the suppurating past. You can sink into a state of mental arrest, where trauma rivets you to memory, but memory is selective, and there is a danger that when you remember, you screen out the inconvenient stuff.

My memories are of strangers and their losses, but no less of solidarities. I think of a distraught young woman, red-haired, staggering up the sidewalk from the direction of the vanished Twin

Towers, a continuous cascade of tears flowing down her face. I think of the handbills posted everywhere in lower Manhattan, the photos of the missing, *Have you seen*————*?*, the desperate phone numbers to call, the candles burning on the sidewalks next to the fire stations, the hand-printed signs: THANK YOU TO OUR HEROIC FIRE-FIGHTERS. I recall a homeless woman on the subway declaring her sympathy for my wife, whose home, after all, was a mile from the rubble. Strangers wished each other good luck. It's not too much to say that I, and they, felt love for each other—love of a people who would continue. I think of mourners and mutual aid, in other words, not of the dead themselves. I also think of an open mike in Union Square where people already debated the American response, people who disagreed vehemently but were willing to hear each other out.

I did not, as they say, "lose anyone." But I hope it does not sound either callous or self-congratulatory to say that in those awful days I *found* people—a people to whom I belonged. Not the lost, but those who were working feverishly not only to repair losses but (in a phrase of James Baldwin's used by Richard Rorty to entitle his book about the patriotism of the Left) to "achieve our country." Around five o'clock on the afternoon of September 13, my wife and I walked down to the perimeter of the ruins along the West Side of lower Manhattan and fell in with a crowd that was greeting and applauding rescue workers—police, firemen, phone- and gas-company people, iron workers and welders, most driving slowly northward out of the smoking Ground Zero area as other trucks drove south, heading in. Some came trudging out of the zone, their boots caked in gray ash. Some people came around handing out pictures of loved, lost ones.

Out of the zone of ruins walked a man and woman in their early thirties, handsome, clear-eyed, wearing yellow slickers and boots.

They were trying to figure out how to get to the subway. We advised on directions and fell in with them. Mary and Dean had driven down from Syracuse, 250 miles away, to volunteer, and had just spent thirty-six hours in the belt of destruction, digging in rubble, dispersing whenever horns sounded to signal that buildings were in danger of collapse. They'd been directing themselves, more or less. Now the federal managers were coming in to take over.

They said it hadn't been easy to get into the damage zone; in fact, they'd had to trick their way in. They had reported to the main volunteer depot at the Javits Convention Center a mile and a half north. Mary, an image consultant at a cosmetics company, had some therapeutic experience and wanted to work with children. They found three hundred people lined up in front of them. So they attached themselves to an upstate fire company, got their yellow slickers, boots, and smoke-protection masks, and made their way to Ground Zero. They didn't know George W. Bush had made his appearance that afternoon (or that he'd been given a far less vigorous reception than Mayor Giuliani), nor were they impressed. At the time, they'd been catching a couple of hours' sleep. Soaked by the first rain in days, they'd gone first to the shell of a nearby hotel, but there was a stench, and somebody walked up and told them not to sleep near the bodies.

I asked Dean what he thought the United States ought to do now. "We have to do something," he said, "but it's not easy. We have to be careful about retaliating. We need diplomatic pressure. We can't go bomb a lot of innocent people. *Then we've done what they've done.*" That same week, I was also struck by a third-generation New Jersey flag factory owner, Gary Pontenzone, interviewed on ABC. He said that he sold twenty-seven thousand flags in a single day, adding: "It's not like the Gulf War. That was, 'Get 'em, get 'em.'

This is more solidarity. I'm very happy to see true patriotism. This is so much warmth."

I loved these strangers, and others I met in those days, and didn't feel mawkish about it—these new, less aggressive New Yorkers, speaking in hushed voices, or so it seemed, lining up to give blood at the local hospitals from day one, disappointed that no one was collecting it; the cabbies driving in unaccustomed silence, all the gratuitous horns silent; New Yorkers without their carapaces, stripped down to their unaccustomed cores, no longer islands unto themselves. I took inspiration from the patriotic activists who seem to have brought down Flight 93 over Pennsylvania and probably saved the White House. *They* hadn't waited for authorities to define their patriotism for them. They hadn't trifled with symbolic displays. It dawned on me that patriotism was the sum of such acts.

PATRIOTISM IS NOT ONLY a gift to others, it is a self-declaration: It affirms that who you are extends beyond—far beyond—yourself, or the limited being that you thought was yourself. You are not an isolate. Just as you have a given name and a family name, you also have a national name. It gives you a past and a future. You are in solidarity with strangers: Their losses are your own. One deep truth about September 11 is that a community was attacked, not an assortment of individuals. A second truth was that the community of survivors was a *political* community, a community where diversity is not a feel-good slogan and debate is lifeblood. At war, it is important to know what you are at war for, even when you are not the one declaring the war. The night of September 11, in search of clarity and shoring up, I reread George Orwell's 1945 essay, "Notes on Nationalism," wherein Orwell distinguishes between the English patriotism that he affirms in the name of the values of the Left and the bombastic nationalism that is the cowbird version. "By patriotism," he wrote, "I mean devotion to a particular place and a particular way of life, which one believes to be the best in the world but has no wish to force on other people. Patriotism is of its nature defensive, both militarily and culturally. . . . Nationalism, on the other hand, is inseparable from the desire for power." Orwell leaves some difficult questions in abeyance: Can you be patriotic if you don't think the place and the way of life you are devoted to are the best in the world? Can you think some aspects (democracy and human rights) are most definitely worth spreading, even at times by force, if it comes to that, and others most definitely are not? I'll come back to these difficulties later, but the important thing is that they complicated the devotional feeling I had but didn't erase it.

No surprise, a few days later, my wife and I decided to hang an American flag from our terrace. It was a straightforward household decision—hardly a decision at all, because no one in the house felt like debating it. We didn't send out a press release. There was no controversy and we didn't consult anyone. The flag was a plain affirmation of membership. We did not put it up to claim that the United States of America deserved to rule, or war on, anyone else. (As it happened, we supported the use of force against al-Qaeda and the Taliban in Afghanistan, though with plenty of worries about terrible consequences that might ensue, but the worries were neither here nor there.) A few days later, Clyde Haberman, a metropolitan columnist of the *New York Times,* called to round up a quote about flag-bearers, and when I told him that we had put up a flag, that we had never thought we would undertake such a display, that it was not meant as support for the policies of George W. Bush but as an affirmation of fellowship with an injured and resolute people, then our private fact was transformed into a news fact, and featured prominently in his column of September 19, whereupon a lot of friendly mail came my way, and some not so friendly: some tut-tuts, some insults. An appreciative friend—a human-rights activist, as it happens—who teaches at a prominent liberal arts college told me that he had mounted a flag on his office door, whereupon a student had complained to college authorities that this constituted an abuse of professorial authority. I heard later that on a couple of campuses, the fact that I had put up the American flag was cited as a reason why it was, at the very least, not forbidden for someone on the Left to fly an American flag.

But the interesting question is, Why this fervent debate in the first place? Why did left-wingers of my generation get into arguments with their children who wanted to fly flags from their windows? Why should the flying of the flag have been seen as a betrayal? What was it betraying?

2. What Patriotism Rubs Raw

A HISTORY, BUT ALSO A BELIEF.

If you belong to a certain class—call it the cosmopolitan class, middle to upper-middle in income, college-educated and beyond, university and culture-industry based—patriotism has been robbed of its allure. This history is connected to—in a single phrase—the "Vietnam generation," though Vietnam only launches the problem. But there are other factors that get in the way of patriotism, make it at the least weightless and irrelevant, or even more, laughable, demeaning, *embarrassing*, even infuriating. Why should this be?

To understand why patriotism is (or has been) tainted, it will help to consider the opposite concepts against which patriotism is counterposed, for they suggest what people think they are turning toward when they turn away from patriotism. One is individualism, the other, cosmopolitanism.

First of all, patriotism gets in the way of individualism, a declaration of identity that is as fundamental for critics of rugged individualism as it is for the most fervent advocates. For patriotism affirms that we are bounded, attached, unfree. It places value on a certain conformity. On this, Nietzsche called the shots when he associated patriotism with the herd instinct. We pride ourselves on being individuals, after all. This is an article of faith, our modern gift and glory. We are self-created (or trying to be). However and wherever we were born, with whatever roots and equipment, into whatever class, race, religion, region, or nationality, we insist that we remain free to choose the essentials of our lives, that our freedom is inalienable, that whoever tampers with it is our enemy. Choice is our mantra. As women and men with reproductive rights, we declare ourselves pro-choice. As voters, believers, advocates, consumers, we are nothing if not free—or so we firmly believe. Even as religious souls, Americans like to imagine that they are born-again, affirming a choice to *accept* Jesus Christ, something they can do or not, something that wasn't preordained by their parents.

But patriotism decrees that we are not free. We are obliged. Patriotism is sticky. It is imperious about its imperatives. It values a certain unfreedom, for it declares that in a crucial way we are not free to choose the condition we were born into. Unless we are naturalized citizens, we did not choose our obligation. We are free to imagine our country any way we like, but we are not free to deny that it *is* our country. In fact, American patriotism is an especially compelling and demanding sort of patriotism, because the American nation is founded on an idea, not on blood. The idea is an apparent paradox—that we are most ourselves when we affirm our roots, that we are free now because we are bound by the American past.

What we are loyal to is the condition of our freedom, and yet when we are loyal, we have renounced our freedom.

All of this is to say that if you believe that you are free and that it is important to be free, patriotism, to the degree that it claims your loyalty, is unnerving. The more insistent the claim, the more unnerving it is. One way to ward off the claim is with cosmopolitan disdain. Patriotism is parochial. The cosmopolitan impulse is to declare that patriotism is for other people—lesser people, really. Superpatriots, we call them. They are the herd of the weak. They live by cant. Why? How can they live that way, how can they talk the way they talk? They've been brainwashed. They've succumbed to propaganda. This is partly because they're surrounded by propaganda, but let's face it—it's only possible because their character is degraded. They're gullible, or stupid. Some of these attributes we infer but there are others that are highly visible. Patriots, to get down to it, are people of bad taste. Part of what marks our class is good taste, and we distinguish ourselves as people of good taste—we collect, confirm, and multiply our "cultural capital," to use the sociologist Pierre Bourdieu's phrase—by scorning people of bad taste. So patriotism is objectionable because it's tacky. It means vinyl and trailer parks. It means slogans and lapel pins. It means klutzy rituals at ball games and truculence in policy debates. It means bluster and sentimentality. It means myopia, willful ignorance. If we forgive the patriots flying their flags during the Gulf War or after September 11, 2001, in depressed areas like upstate New York, it is because patriots are pitiable. Let them have their flags if flags make them feel better. The nation is what they have—or fancy they have—when they don't have much else.

Worst of all, from this point of view, patriotism means obscuring the whole grisly truth of America under a polyurethane mask. It means covering over the Indians in their mass graves. It means covering over slavery. It means overlooking America's many imperial adventures—the Philippine, Cuban, and Nicaraguan occupations, among others, as well as abuses of power by corporations, international banks, and so on. It means disguising American privilege—even when America's good fortune was not directly purchased at the cost of the bad fortune of others, a debatable point. So from this point of view, patriotism betrays the truth. It's a story, all right, but a story in the sense of a lie. It can't help spilling over into what Orwell thought was the harsh, dangerous, and distinct phenomenon of nationalism, with its aggressive edge, its implication of superiority. Scrub up patriotism as you will, the cynic asserts, and nationalism, as the political theorist John H. Schaar put it in a prophetic (and for a man of the Left, courageous) 1973 essay, remains "patriotism's bloody brother." Was Orwell's heroic distinction not, in the end, a distinction without a difference? Didn't his patriotism, disdaining aggressiveness, still insist that the nation he affirmed was "the best in the world"? What if there is more than one feature of the American way of life that you do *not* believe to be "the best in the world"—the national bravado, the pride some Americans take in their ignorance, the overreach of the marketplace? The very emphasis on difference—I belong to *this* nation—might well be the door through which you march with the rest of the conformists to the beat of a national anthem.

So it follows that patriotism deserves to be unmasked. It is the recourse of scoundrels. It deceives. It masks interests. It defends privilege. It masks pettiness. So patriotism is for small people, not for the likes of you and me, reader, unless we submit to diminish ourselves. Patriotism's morality is bad faith, because it assigns to someone else the moral initiative that is properly mine; it beggars my freedom, alienates rights that are fundamentally inalienable.

Nietzsche made this point more than a century ago and it has lost none of its force.

But—so goes the complaint—patriotism betrays not only the small and the personal but the large and the impersonal. Affirming the larger unit, it picks the wrong one—it doesn't think big enough. The term "patriotism" is often paired off against "cosmopolitanism," which, by one definition in *The American Heritage Dictionary of the English Language*, means "so sophisticated as to be at home in all parts of the world." Cosmopolitanism embraces the cosmos, patriotism the parish—it is parochial. When the global environmentalist declares, "Think globally, act locally," the locality she has in mind is not the nation. It might be the county, perhaps, or the bioregion, or as far as the eye can see, but it is not the nation, let alone the state. The impulse to disdain the nation is a recognition of the arbitrariness and pettiness of the nation. If war is the health of the state, as Randolph Bourne wrote against the carnage that started the twentieth century off with a bang, then the rejection of the state (and therefore the nation that tags along with it) is the beginning of the end of war.

No surprise, then, that in the wake of the Vietnam War, a generation of post-Vietnam skeptics about the nation-state fell upon the work of the political anthropologist Benedict Anderson, who neatly argued in a book called *Imagined Communities* that that is what nations are, that they are not natural, organic, primordial, objective, or anything of that sort, but the creatures—"constructions"—of intellectuals and the stories they tell about history and culture. In the more vernacular rendition, a nation was an entity possessed of an army, a navy, and a dictionary. The implication that some readers drew was that nations, being constructed, were superficial, not deep, artificial, not natural, malleable, not traditional—and thus lacked moral standing. So patriotism seemed a presumption, an unearned imposition.

I have been making a case abstractly, on first principles, about a logic conducive to a culture clash that afflicted—was bound to afflict—those of us who value individualism and cosmopolitanism. But for a large bloc of Americans my age and younger, too young to remember World War II—the generation for whom "the war" meant Vietnam and possibly always would, to the end of our days— the case against patriotism was not an abstraction. There was a pow- erful experience underlying it: as powerful an eruption of our feelings as the experience of patriotism is supposed to be for patriots. Indeed, it could be said that in the course of our political history we experienced a very odd turnabout: The most powerful public emo- tion in our lives was *rejecting* patriotism.

3. Loving and Leaving

AMERICA IS A NATION that invites anxiety about what it means to belong, because the national boundary is ideological, hence dis- putable and porous. Part of what it has meant to be American has been to participate in a debate about what it means to be American. As the first constitutional republic, America has been not just a homeland but a land of ideas, of American*ism*. At its best, to affirm American*ism* has entailed affirming a lineage to 1776. Thus did Lincoln declare, on his way to take up office in the White House, "I have never had a feeling politically that did not spring from the sen- timents embodied in the Declaration of Independence." Later he refined this idea into the stark propositions of the Gettysburg Address. Lincoln was affirming what John H. Schaar, in the essay I have already referred to, called "covenanted patriotism"—as opposed to the blood-and-soil variety. But under stress, the covenant is prone to wear thin. Civic patriotism, which demands self-rule, collapses into the follow-the-leader principle. Under strain, authoritarians conclude that questioning authority is an unaffordable luxury. Like the citizens of race-based regimes, even citizens of the democratic American republic have been, from time to time, acutely vulnerable to the accusation that their membership is not authentic after all, and that by expounding the wrong ideas they have forfeited their membership. They are prone, in other words, to be accused of un-Americanism.

Astoundingly, the 1960s upended this accusation and turned it into a mass movement of pride. From membership and anger combined came a tradition of antitraditionalism. Most of the '60s, and frequently since, I have groped for words to express, in the right proportions, the membership and the anger at once—the anger deriving from the membership, of course, the membership an intimate fact, making it easy to feel that the nation, by acting contrary to justice, violates its very right to exist, and that this is a fact on which I am bound to act, for ultimately it is not anyone else's doing. I, as a citizen, cannot shake responsibility. If the covenant turns out shallow, if humanity is betrayed by those who would purport to be its saviors, there is no one to rectify the wrong but those of us who understand how deep the betrayal goes.

For me, the anger and the horror predated the Vietnam War. I launched into activism as a campaigner against the American nuclear-weapons stance in 1960, and only deepened my estrangement from national policies under the pressure of the Bay of Pigs invasion of Cuba, American collusion in South African apartheid, and most of all, the egregious war in Indochina. But for some reason, one particular moment in March of 1965 stands out. I was twenty-two, living among the Students for a Democratic Society

(SDS) circle in Ann Arbor, Michigan, helping organize the first national demonstration against the Vietnam War. The war was already a daily assault on brains and conscience, and so I could scarcely bear to watch the TV news. But one evening, for some reason, I turned on NBC News and saw pictures of American marines occupying Santo Domingo while young Dominicans protested. It was, on the scale of enormities, only a tiny exercise in old-fashioned imperialism, this expedition into the Caribbean to shore up a military regime blocking the restoration of an elected social-democratic government that it had deposed. There was no napalm, no white phosphorus, no strategic hamlets. I don't know why these particular pictures of young Dominicans resisting the Americans stirred me so deeply, but I know I identified with them. I don't know what I felt more keenly: horrified disbelief that my country could be waving the wrong flag, betraying its better self, or horrified belief that my country could only be doing something so appalling because it—not its policies, not this or that wretched decision, but it in the core of its dark heart—was committed to suppressing the rights of inconvenient peoples. Gunboat diplomacy, we learned to call this, in my high school history class. How do you reform a leviathan?

I remember writing a poem that night—not a good one, but a sincere one. I was a nonviolent twenty-two-year-old and I wanted to stand with the young anti-Americans in the Dominican Republic: The poem ended with a romantic line about "a rifle and a sad song." Another phrase I like better sticks out in my memory: "I would only curse America, like a drunkard his bottle." America, love it and leave it at once. A nice trick, though it may put a kink in your lower back.

I have felt such moments of horrified recognition countless times since, and devoted many waking hours to fighting against imperious American foreign policies. I am not speaking of my ideas here, but of feelings, deep feelings. In the second half of the '60s and early '70s, I was choking on the Vietnam War. It felt to me that the fight against the war had become my life. The war went on so long and so destructively, it felt like more than the consequence of a wrong-headed policy. My country must have been revealing some funda-mental core of wrongness by going on, and on, with an indefensible war. I was implicated because the terrible war was wrapped in my flag—or what had been my flag. Then why persist? Why not sur-render title, and good riddance? Right! The American flag did not feel like my flag, even though I could recognize—in the abstract—that it made sense for others to wave it in the antiwar cause.

I was a tactician. I could argue—I did argue—against waving the North Vietnamese flag or burning the Stars and Stripes. But the hatred of a bad war, in what was evidently a pattern of bad wars—though none so bad as Vietnam—turned us inside out. It inflamed our hearts. You can hate your country in such a way that the hatred becomes fundamental. A hatred so clear and intense came to feel like a cleansing flame. By the late '60s, this is what became of much of the New Left. Those of us who met with Vietnamese and Cuban Communists in those years were always being told that we had to learn to love our people. In my case, it was a Communist medical student in Cuba who delivered the message in 1967. Love our peo-ple! How were we supposed to do that, another SDSer and I argued back, when our people had committed genocide against the Indians, when the national history was enmeshed in slavery, when this expe-rience of historic original sin ran deeper than any class solidarity, when it was what it meant to *be* American? Lessons in patriotism taught by Communists—a definitive New Left experience drawn from the comedy of the late '60s. Well, we would try.

We would go looking for historical lessons, for one thing. Revisionist historians went looking for "history from the bottom up"—heroic seamen during the American Revolution, slaves in revolt, Native Americans, union organizers, jailed World War I socialists, Wobblies. But the America of Richard Nixon was not conducive to our invention of *this* tradition. The American flag did not feel any more congenial as Nixon widened the Vietnam War into Laos and Cambodia, and connived in the Pinochet coup; or in the '80s, as Reagan endorsed the Nicaraguan contras, the Salvadoran and Guatemalan death squads. To put it mildly, my generation of the New Left—a generation that grew as the war went on—relinquished any title to patriotism without much sense of loss, because it felt to us that the perpetrators of unjust war had run off with the patrium. The nation had congealed into an empire, whose logic was unwarranted power. All that was left to the Left was to unearth righteous traditions and cultivate them in universities. The much-mocked "political correctness" of the next academic generations was a consolation prize. We lost—we squandered—politics but won the textbooks.

Read history with open eyes and it is hard to overlook the American empire. Honest conservatives acknowledge imperial power, too—though enthusiastically. What is the idea of Manifest Destiny, the onward march westward, if not a robust defense of righteous empire? What was the one-time California Senator S. I. Hayakawa's brag about the Panama Canal, "we stole it fair and square," if not a sly recognition of the truth? You need not subscribe to the Left's grandest claims that America from its birth is essentially genocidal and indebted to slavery for much of its prosperity to acknowledge that white colonists took the land, traded in slaves, and profited immensely thereby; or that the United States later lorded it over Latin America (and other occasional properties, like the Philippines) to guarantee cheap resources and otherwise line American pockets; or that American-led corporations (among others) and financial agencies today systematically overlook or, worse, damage the freedoms of others. If all this lording over does not rise to the level of colonialism in the strict sense, and if it can be acknowledged that empires may have benign consequences, even for far-flung peoples far from the metropolitan core, then still, American wealth, resource access, military power, and unilateralism qualify as imperial reach. Add that America, counting less than 5 percent of world population, uses about one-quarter of the world's nonrenewable, environment-wrecking, fossil-fuel energy—and the Bush administration proposes to keep doing so as long as it pleases.

The tragedy of the anti-American Left is that, having achieved an unprecedented victory in helping stop an appalling war, it proceeded to commit suicide. It helped force the United States out of Vietnam, where the country had no constructive work to do—either for Vietnam or for itself—but did so at the cost of disconnecting itself from the nation. To a considerable degree, it substituted the pleasures of condemnation for tactics designed to pursue further improvement. The orthodoxy was that "the system" precluded reform—never mind that the antiwar movement had already demonstrated that reform *was* possible. Human rights, feminism, environmentalism—these worldwide initiatives, American in their inception, flowing not from the American establishment but from our own American movements, were not in the picture. The only America in the picture was the America of wealth and weaponry—the corporations, the Pentagon, the CIA. According to the anti-imperialist dogma, the wholesale, indiscriminate anti-Communism that led to imperial overthrows in Iran, Guatemala, Chile, Nicaragua, El Salvador, and elsewhere was the essential America, the inevitable consequence of a history poisoned at the root. When, in the '90s, too haltingly, the Clinton administration mobilized armed

force on behalf of Bosnia and then Kosovo against Milosevic's genocidal Serbia, the hard Left could only smell imperial motives. In
their eyes, the democratic, antigenocidal motive for intervention was
a paper-thin mask. Milosevic's Serbs were cast as deserving victims.

In short, just as America seemed trapped in an essence, so did its
opposition. By the '70s, the outsider stance had become second nature.
Even those who had entered the '60s in diapers came to maturity
thinking patriotism a threat or a bad joke. It did nothing for them. To
be on the Left meant to negate it. But anti-Americanism was, and
remains, a metaphysics more than a politics. Indeed, the demonology
substituted for politics, because politics was delusional, entangled with
a fatally flawed system. Viewing ongoing politics as contemptibly
shallow and compromised, the demonological attitude naturally ruled
out patriotism. There was no reason for deep engagement in the political life of the country, and every reason to avoid it. This Left prided
itself on *dis*connection from a history ruined from the start by original
sin. Marooned (often self-marooned) on university campuses, in left-
wing media and other cultural outposts—all told, an archipelago of
bitterness—what sealed itself off in the post-'60s decades was what
Richard Rorty calls "a spectatorial, disgusted, mocking Left rather
than a Left which dreams of achieving our country."

From this outlying point of view, the attacks of September 11,
2001, revealed a symmetry that the hard-bitten Left had long
expected. America was condemned by its history. The furies were
avenging, chickens were flying home, American detonations were
blowing back. No one could see the truth but the saved. They had
little time, little interest, little hardheaded curiosity to comprehend a
fanatical Islamist sect that set no limits to what and whom it would
destroy. Whoever was killed in America, Americans must still end
up the greatest of Satans. Thus did Noam Chomsky belittle the September 11 attacks—so incredibly far as to claim, in a Belgrade radio

interview, as the ash still rained on lower Manhattan, that the United States was responsible for vastly more deaths in Sudan after the bombing of a chemical plant in 1998—as many as a million deaths!— all this on the strength of the thinnest of evidence and the thickest of rageful passions. Intent on blaming America first, these anti-Americans bent and selected the reports and rumors that suited them to find respectable reasons for anti-American sentiment, which they regarded as strictly derivative—not blameless, exactly, not necessarily quite justifiable, but always, "ultimately," traceable to American malfeasance. From the legitimate fear that misguided American policy had the effect of recruiting more terrorists, the hard anti-Americans leaped to the unwarranted assumption that terrorists were not terrorists. Soft anti-Americans did not go so far but were quick to change the subject.

Their moral balance was badly askew, but they shared with the rest of America the revelation that there is more than enough destructive power to go around. There are connoisseurs of apocalypse in the world, forces like al-Qaeda that are more than willing to slaughter Americans (not to mention inconvenient others) in the name of their own version of empire. Indisputably, there are forces in the world that, if victorious, would leave the world far worse off than American power. For examples, you don't have to look any further than the Nazi and Japanese empires, or the Islamist totalitarianism that al-Qaeda evidently longs for (insofar as it troubles to offer what Jefferson would have called a "decent respect to the opinions of mankind" and "declare the causes which impel[led] them" to their massacres).

A patriotic Left disputes American policies. But it criticizes, however vociferously, in an insider's voice, without discarding the hope, if not of redemption, at least of improvement. It deplores the deplorable in a tone that displays the critic's shared membership with the criticized. It acknowledges—and wrestles with—the strange dualities of America: the liberty and arrogance twinned, the bullying and tolerance, myopia and energy, standardization and variety, ignorance and inventiveness, the awful dark heart of darkness and the self-reforming zeal. It wants to address the whole of America, but not from the outside looking in. It does not labor under the illusion that the world would be benign but for American power; or that capitalism is uniformly the most damaging economic system ever. It lives inside, with an indignation born of family feeling. Its anger is intimate.

4. Lived Patriotism

TO REPEAT: PATRIOTISM IS conventionally understood as a combination of feelings and ideas. Words are its proofs. We recognize patriotism when it is professed, we bemoan its absence when it is not professed. But patriotism in this sense is claimed too easily. The ease devalues the real thing and disguises its deep weakness. The folklore of patriotism lends itself to symbolic displays wherein we show one another how patriotic we are without exerting ourselves too strenuously. We sing songs, pledge allegiance, wave flags, display lapel pins, mount bumper stickers, attend (or tune in to) memorial rites. We think we become patriotic by declaring that we are patriotic. This is activity, but of a limited, I would say desiccated, sort. It is striking how many of these touchstones we have now—how rituals of devotion are folded into ball games and concerts, how flags adorn the most commonplace of private activities. Their prevalence permits foreign observers to comment on how patriotic the simpleminded Americans are. But such displays are not so straightforwardly proofs of patriotism at all. They are at least equally substitutes. John H. Schaar's stricture is apt here: Patriotism "is more than a frame of mind. It is also activity guided by and directed toward the mission established in the founding covenant." Patriotic activity starts with a sense of responsibility but does not discharge it with tributary rites of celebration and memory. Patriotism in this sense, genuine patriotism, is not enacted strictly by being expressed in symbolic fashion. It is with effort and sacrifice, not pride or praise, that citizens honor the democratic covenant.

To put it this way is to erect an exalted standard. Yet to speak of the burdens of patriotism points to something not so flattering about the patriotism Americans so strenuously claim. Perhaps we celebrate our patriotism so energetically because, when we get past the breast-beating, our actual patriotic experience is thin on the ground. Perhaps Americans feel the need to tout Americanism and rout un-Americans precisely for this reason—not because we are such good patriots but because our substantial patriotic activity is weak. Ferreting out violations is the lazy person's substitute for a democratic life. If civic patriotism requires activity, not just symbolic display, Americans are not so patriotic after all.

What do I mean by substantial patriotic activity? The work of civic engagement—the living out of the democratic commitment to govern ourselves. Actual patriotic experience in a democracy is more demanding—far more so—than the profession of sentiments; it is more easily advertised than lived up to. Whatever Woody Allen thinks of life, 90 percent of patriotism is not just showing up. Democratic patriotism is also far more demanding than signifying loyalty to the regime. In a kingdom, the patriot swears loyalty to the monarch. In a totalitarian society, the patriot is obedient in a thousand ways—participating in mass rituals, informing on enemies, joining designated organizations, doing whatever the anointed leader requires. But democratic loyalty is something else, stringent in its own way. If the nation to which we adhere is a community of mutual aid, a mesh of social connections, then it takes work, engagement, time. It is likely to take money. It may take life. It is a matter, to borrow a magnificent phrase of 1776, of pledging "our lives, our fortunes, and our sacred honor." Most disturbing of all to the prime commitments of our private lives, it may well require that we curb our individual freedoms—the indulgences that normally we count as the highest of values.

In other words, lived patriotism entails sacrifice. The citizen puts aside private affairs in order to build up relationships with other citizens, with whom we come to share unanticipated events, risks, and outcomes. These citizenly relationships are not ones we choose. To the contrary. When we serve on a jury or in Teach for America, or ride in the subway, we do not choose our company. The community we partake of—like the whole of society—is a community of people whom we did not choose. (Thus the embarrassment to the liberal ideal of self-creation, already discussed.) The crucial difference here is between a community, consisting of people crucially *un*like ourselves, and a network, or "lifestyle enclave," made up of people *like* ourselves.* Many "communities" in the sense commonly overused today—"the business community," "the academic community"—are actually networks, a fact that the overused term disguises. Cosmopolitanism is also usually lived out as a network extension: It invites connections with people like ourselves (writers, academics, liberals, members of the same profession, what have you) who happen to live in other countries.

Undemocratic societies require sacrifice, too, but unequally. There, what passes as patriotism is obeisance to the ruling elite.

---

*Robert N. Bellah in *Habits of the Heart: Individualism and Commitment in American Life* uses the term "lifestyle enclave." The commonplace use of "network" came later.

Democracy, on the other hand, demands (for one thing) a particular sort of sacrifice: citizenly participation in self-government. This is not the place to explore the difficult questions of where participation must stop and professional management must start; but the important principle is that the domain of popular involvement should be as large "as possible," the question of possibility itself deserving to be a vexatious one. At the very least, at the local level, the citizens should approve the agenda for governmental action. The result is twofold: not only policy that takes distinct points of view into account, but a citizenry that takes pride in its identity as such. When the citizen enters the town meeting, the local assembly, or for that matter, the jury, disparate qualifications hardly disappear, but they are tempered, counterbalanced by a common commitment to leave no voice unattended.

Decision making aside, democratic life also requires spheres of experience where citizens encounter each other with equal dignity. Put it another way: A democratic culture is one in which no one is exempted from common duties. Commonality and sacrifice are combined. This is the strong side of what has become known as communitarianism, which has also been called civic liberalism. As Mickey Kaus argued in *The End of Equality,* social equality requires bolstering three spheres: the armed forces and national service; public schools; and adult public domains (transportation, health, day care, public financing of elections). The operative word, of course, is "public." It is in these sectors that the republic's commonality lives, on the ground, in time and space. In the armed forces, life is risked in common. In national service, time is jointly invested in benefits that do not accrue to self-interest. When loopholes are closed, class mixing becomes integral to life. Privilege, however extravagant in the rest of life, can't buy you everything. In public schools, privilege doesn't buy superior opportunities. In amenities like public transportation, governments provide what private interests would not, and individuals experience themselves as sharing a common condition. As these public spheres dwindle, sheer wealth and income grow in importance, and vice versa. (For purposes of this argument, it doesn't matter which comes first.)*

We also need some common sacrifice of our self-indulgences— not to test our Puritan mettle but to prevent ecological breakdown. Americans having proven averse to eco-efficiency in production, consumption, and transportation, despite our robust achievements in global warming and air and water pollution, we have a particular responsibility to lean less heavily on the earth. Since oil dependency is a considerable factor behind some of America's most egregious foreign policies, true patriotism is fully compatible with, indeed intertwined with, ecological sanity that lowers fossil fuel guzzling and promotes sustainable sources like solar and wind power. Yet Detroit automakers steadfastly resist hybrid gas-electric cars and increased fuel efficiency, and Washington permits them to get away with their profligacy. Patriots ought to endorse the environmentalist Bill McKibben's suggestion that "gas-sucking SUVs . . . should by all rights come with their own little Saudi flags to fly from the hood."

Overall, egalitarian culture is patriotism's armature. No matter how many commemorations Americans organize, no matter how many pledges we recite and anthems we rise for, the gestures are

*Kaus argued in his 1992 book that liberals are mistaken to overemphasize economic inequality, and I do not follow him all the way to his bitter end. Surely the appalling inequalities in the ratio between CEO and worker salaries, for example, of the order of five hundred to one, do not serve the entrepreneurial purposes that laissez-faire advocates rejoice in. The fact that it would take confiscatory tax rates to eliminate this discrepancy does not mean that lesser reductions are pointless. Reducing the high-low income gap would work toward the principle of social equality.

inessential. At times they build morale—most usefully when the suffering is fresh—but they do not repair or defend the country. For that, the quality of social relations is decisive. And the contrary follows, too: The more hierarchical and less equal the nation becomes, the less patriotic is its life. Not that the culture as a whole should be in the business of enforcing egalitarian norms—the ideal that populism defended and Stalinism made murderous. But there must be zones of social life, important ones, where the same social goods are at stake for everyone and individual distinction does not buy exemption. The most demanding, of course, is the military—and it is here, where the stakes are highest and the precedents most grievous, that universality is most important. It must not be possible to buy substitutes, as the Union's wealthy did in the Civil War. Many are the inequalities that are either morally legitimate or politically unbudgeable, but there must be equalities of sacrifice and encounter—not in order to strip the high and mighty of their individuality, but purely and simply to treat everyone equally. Financial sacrifice on the part of the privileged is a proof that money cannot buy anything—it may not even be able to buy the most important thing, namely, personal safety. As long as equality prevails in one central phase of life—the most dangerous phase—the inequality of rewards in other phases does not become the be-all and the end-all of existence.

Many liberals will be inclined to demur. For whatever its merits, conscription surely grates upon the ideal of self-control—that is precisely one of its purposes. Let's face it: Most of us don't like to be told what to do. Moral preachments not only grate, they offend our sense that the only authority worth taking seriously is the authority of our own souls (or senses). Moral preachments about our duty sound to many Americans, left, right, and center, like claxons of a police state. To live our patriotism we would have to pick and choose, to overcome—selectively—some of the automatic revulsion we feel to laying aside some of our freedoms in the name of a higher duty. It isn't clear how many of us are willing to overcome our inner frolickers. I think of myself as rather civic-minded but much of the time it isn't clear to me how much of my own initiative *I* will gladly surrender for the common good.

Which raises this related question: Where does a onetime antiwar activist and would-be conscientious objector get off defending conscription now that he is several decades away from vulnerability? (At the very least, I am not the only man of my generation to have rethought the principle of the draft. I wonder, though, whether any of the so-called chickenhawks, who defended the Vietnam War but not for themselves—to name only a few recent Republican office holders: Dan Quayle, George W. Bush, Dick Cheney, Trent Lott, Tom DeLay, Paul Wolfowitz, Richard Perle—has rethought his own. "I had other priorities in the '60s than military service," Vice President Cheney has said.) This is no mere debater's point. The principle of universal conscription is not only an abstract tribute to equality—worthy as that would be—but it undermines arbitrary warfare. If the citizens asked to support a war are the ones (or their relatives) who will have to fight it, the chickenhawk factor weakens—the fervent endorsement of war in Iraq, for example, by Republican leaders who thought the Vietnam War a "noble crusade" (Ronald Reagan's term) that they in their own persons somehow never found time for. The principle that wars must be popular with their soldiers is a good democratic requirement. Let it not be forgotten that Richard Nixon terminated the draft not to end the war—in fact, he continued the war from the air, killing at a pace that exceeded Lyndon Johnson's, often in secret (as in Cambodia)—but to insulate it from public exposure and dissent.

Equal sacrifice of liberty in favor of conscription ought to dovetail with equal civic opportunity of other sorts. We talk a lot about equality of opportunity, but as a nation we are ill-prepared to amplify the principle—to enlarge it to the right to be healthy, to be cared for, to participate in government. As the election of 2000 demonstrated, we are not even terribly serious about guaranteeing the right to vote—and have one's vote counted. In a formula: Lived patriotism requires social equality. It is in the actual relations of citizens, not symbolic displays, that civic patriotism lives. In these palpable relations, no one is elevated. Status does not count, nor wealth, nor poverty. One person, one vote. Absent these ideals in action, patriotism lapses into gestures—Pledges of Allegiance, not the allegiance itself. Considering the shallowness of patriotic experience, there is a particular pathos in expecting the current president, so little of whose life has been concerned with public service, to ignite civic virtue.

A unifying logic links many of George W. Bush's public statements on and after September 11, 2001. There is the inadvertently comic spectacle of this man, who spent much of *his* September 11 flying aimlessly around the country as his staff fabricated security threats, soon thereafter appearing on a television commercial urging people to get back on planes and visit Disney World. In July 2002, pooh-poohing the significance of corporate corruption, and therefore the need for political remedies, he resorted to these words: "I believe people have taken a step back and asked, 'What's important in life?' You know, the bottom line and this corporate America stuff, is that important? Or is serving your neighbor, loving your neighbor like you'd like to be loved yourself?" No contradiction here: The mediocre oilman with the triumphal career expresses the logic of a business civilization—consumption *as* citizenship; political withdrawal as a noble act. His not-so-comic equivalent was urging Congress to stick with tax-cut legislation almost all of whose benefits would flow to the rich. How striking the contrast to World War II's dollar-a-year men, who attested by financial sacrifice—and noblesse oblige—to the cause's transcendent virtue (though romantics should not forget that war profiteering remained common)! Even trivially, children during that war collected scrap metal to link their fate to the country they loved. Air-raid wardens did their part. So, of course, did soldiers, sailors, and war workers. So did those who accepted their rations without resorting to the black market. Yet in a drastic break from precedent, Bush proposed to cut taxes (especially for the better-off) in wartime, promoting "bombs and caviar," in the words of the *Los Angeles Times*'s Ronald Brownstein, and guaranteeing "bigger federal deficits and a larger national debt, which amounts to shifting to defending the nation onto our children. . . . With this push to slash taxes during wartime, Bush broke from 140 years of history under presidents of both parties."

Forget Afghanistan: After September 11, 2001, millions of Americans wanted to enlist in nation building *at home*. They wanted to fight the horror, to take their fate in their hands, to make community palpable. They wanted to rescue, save, rebuild, restore, recover, rise up, go on. From their governments, nothing much materialized by way of work for them, for the principal version of patriotism on offer today demands little by way of duty or deliberation, much by way of bravado. What duty might ignite if it were mobilized now, we do not know. How Americans might have responded if their political leadership had invited them to join in a Marshall Plan that would, among other things, contain anti-Americanism and weaken the prospects of terror, we do not know. How they would have responded if told that it was now a matter of urgent self-defense as well as environmental sanity to free America from oil dependency, we do not know. These invitations were not issued. After the week of mutual aid, patriotism dwindled into symbolism. It was inert, unmobilized—at most, potential. In the current state of desiccated patriotism, Election Day is all the politics most citizens can manage, and for most of them that single day is not the culmination of their political activity, it is the sum of their political activity.

Take it as symbolic, then, that September 11, 2001, was, among other things, New York City's primary day for Democratic mayoral candidates. The primary was the least missed loss of that day. Terrorists smashed up our political life, as well as our economic and personal lives. Our professionals, our public institutions, and our volunteers roared into action. Our police, our firefighters, our ironworkers, our emergency workers threw themselves into action in a style that deserves to be called noble. A mayor previously unmarked by eloquence responded eloquently. Take it as symbolic that our official politics, and our loss of them, didn't seem to matter much. Politics didn't live. America's survivors did.

5. Patriotism Unembarrassed?

A FEW WEEKS AFTER SEPTEMBER 11, my wife and I took down our flag. The lived patriotism of mutual aid had fallen off and the symbolic substitute felt stale. Leaving the flag up was too easy, too easily misunderstood as a triumphalist cliché. It didn't express my patriotic sentiment, which was turning toward political opposition of various sorts (though not in the key of the antiwar left). The unexceptionable part of the war on al-Qaeda and the Taliban was in place, and while the United States proceeded to commit several terrible wrongs in Afghanistan, and many vexatious questions remained about how to proceed there, these were not questions that could have been asked, let alone answered, without the intervention.

But with the passage of weeks, the hardening of American foreign policy and the Democratic cave-in produced a good deal more triumphalism than I could stomach. The patriotism of the activist passengers of Flight 93 slipped into the background; the spectacle that replaced them in my imagination was of unnamed, unrepresented detainees turned deportees. Deep patriotism, patriotic activity, was not bouncing back. Americans were watching more news, even more foreign news, but the political debates about means and ends that needed to happen were not happening. Democrats were fearful of looking unpatriotic—in other words, patriotism was functioning in the most poisonous way, chauvinistically, as a silencer. We needed defense, absolutely—lurking in the background was the most interesting question as to why we had not had it on September 11, 2001—but what *was* a "war on terror" that was, in effect and in principle, interminable, unlike the righteous war against imperial Japan and Nazi Germany, for it would be declared won (as Secretary of Defense Rumsfeld declared soon after the attacks) when and only when Americans *felt* safe? What kind of war was that, and what did missile defense and the reckless demolition of such treaties as Kyoto and antiballistic-missile defense have to do with it, and was there not the disconcerting fact that five or six individuals without a legitimate claim to democratic rule were calling all the important shots? By the time George W. Bush declared war without end against an "axis of evil" that no other nation on earth was willing to recognize as such—indeed, against whomever the president might determine we were at war against, just when he said so—and declared further the unproblematic virtue of preemptive attacks, and made it clear that the United States regarded itself a one-nation tribunal of "regime change," I felt again the old estrangement, the old shame and anger at being attached to a nation—*my* nation—ruled by runaway bullies, indifferent to principle, their lives manifesting supreme loyalty to private (though government-slathered) interests, quick to lecture dissenters about the merits of patriotism.

So once again patriotic sentiment bangs up against a wall of small-mindedness. Not since the last big bank loan to Argentina has credit been squandered as rapidly as when the administration of George W. Bush drained away the moral capital that came America's way after the massacres of that bright, scorched day of September.

For good and bad reasons, people love to hate, love, and otherwise be transfixed by America, so it was not altogether predictable that instantly in September 2001, as the acrid stench still hung over lower Manhattan, millions of people on every continent would stand up to declare that they identified with America and Americans. Mirabile dictu! In candlelight vigils and front-page headlines, they declared a common humanity (*Libération:* WE ARE ALL NEW YORKERS. *Le Monde:* AMERICA STRUCK, THE WORLD SEIZED WITH DREAD, with a photo of the Statue of Liberty over the smoke and void). To feel this solidarity, people had to move their grievances—and everyone has grievances against the imperial center—to the back burner, and many millions of people did that, did it spontaneously and, I think, sincerely. It was as if the awfulness of mass murder drove them not only to share in the losses but to remember who they were and to draw a sharp existential line. On *this* side, the best of the American idea. On *that* side, the abyss of apocalyptic violence. Even as anti-Americans came forward to insinuate that time spent grieving for the American lost was time stolen from the more deserving victims of American power, anti-Americanism had never looked so ugly, petty, and frozen.

The outpouring of plain human solidarity was all the more impressive because to that date the Bush administration had already piled up a considerable due bill from the moment of its anointing by the Republican majority of the Supreme Court, delighting in go-it-alone crusades, its blustering imperiousness so unremitting in its unilateralism, so contemptuous of "a decent respect to the opinions of mankind," that it seemed to have lasted twenty-one years, not a mere twenty-one months, at the moment when the fuel-laden jet missiles exploded us into a new epoch. Osama bin Laden had, at a stroke, given anti-Americanism a bad name. When I spoke to Greek students at an American studies conference in Athens in April 2002, arguing that theirs, too, was the cause of the West against absolutism, that it was possible to dissent, as I do, from much of American foreign policy without changing sides, I was happily struck by their openness to my case. Greeks have a propensity to look for "dark forces" at work, frequently American, frequently Zionist, but by comparison with the suspicions circulating in recent years, I was pleasantly surprised at the straightforward sympathy, the absence of rancor.

Much of this goodwill is gone. Monumental arrogance is the hallmark of Bush's foreign policy—it *is* his foreign policy. Not surprisingly, anti-Americans are back in gloat mode. Hi-Yo Silver, the Lone Bully rides again. So I find myself thrown back on the familiar old brew of emotions—pain at the losses, love of Americans, suspicion of power, fury at the enemies of humanity who hijacked the jets and would cheerfully commit more mass murders, fury at their apologists who had not a moment to spare to mourn—and a vigorous dissent from Bush's recklessness. Patriotism must make room for a robust no, too.

If mobilized—it hasn't yet been—liberal patriotism would find many friends among troubled Americans. Perhaps surprisingly, the American public cares about acting abroad through alliances and with the sanction of the United Nations. It rejects—though not actively, by and large—Bush's go-it-alone adventures. On the domestic front, little love is now lost for the corporate chiefs, those of gargantuan appetite for whom this administration so loyally fronted until they were shocked, shocked to discover there was gambling going on in the casino. With the bursting of the stock-market bubble, deregulation no longer looks like an economic cure-all. Whom do Americans admire now, whom do we trust? Americans did not take much reminding that when skyscrapers were on fire, they needed firefighters and police officers, not Enron hustlers or Arthur Andersen accountants. Yet we confront an administration that passes out capital gains and inheritance tax cuts to the plutocracy, whose idea of sacrifice is that somebody in a blue collar should perform it for low wages.

Surely many Americans are primed for a patriotism of action, not pledges or SUVs festooned with American flags. The era beginning on September 11, 2001, would be a superb time to crack the jingoists' claim to a monopoly of patriotic virtue. Instead of letting minions of corporate power run away with the flag (while dashing offshore, gobbling oil, and banking their tax credits), we need to remake the tools of our public life—our schools, social services, transport, and not least, security. We need to remember that the exemplary patriots are the members of the emergency community of mutual aid who brought down Flight 93, not the born-again war devotees who cherish martial virtues but somehow succeeded in getting themselves deferred from the armed forces.

Post-Vietnam liberals have an opening now, freed of our '60s flag anxiety and our automatic rejection of the use of force. How to feel—and live—pride in the nation when the nation's power is hijacked? Only by working to ripen our institutions. To live out a democratic pride, not a slavish surrogate, we badly need liberal patriotism, robust, unapologetic, and uncowed. For patriotic sentiment, that mysterious (and therefore both necessary and dangerous) attachment to the nation, moves only in one of two directions: backward, toward chauvinistic bluster and popular silence, or forward, to popular energy and democratic renewal. Said the French essayist Charles Péguy: "Everything begins in mysticism and ends in politics." Patriotism, as always, remains to be lived.

It's time for the patriotism of mutual aid, not just symbolic displays, not catechisms or self-congratulation. It's time to diminish the gap between the nation we love and the justice we also love. It's time for the real America to stand up.

KANAN MAKIYA

Arab Demons, Arab Dreams: 1967–2003

A WEEK OR SO AFTER THE COLLAPSE of the World Trade Center towers and the attack on the Pentagon, I had this conversation with a friend who shall remain unnamed.

"They could not have been Arabs," he said.

"Of course they were. Read the list of names. Look at the pictures."

"No Arab is capable of planning an operation like this."

My friend is an Arab himself. He was, a long time ago as a young man, an activist in the al-Da'wa Party, an Iraqi Islamist organization that waged an underground war in the 1980s against the Baathist regime of Saddam Hussein after all secular, nationalist, military, and liberal forms of opposition had collapsed. The intolerable oppressiveness of his own regime drove him to Islamic politics at a time when Iraq had launched a war against the Islamic Republic of Iran, a war that was being supported, from the mid-1980s onward, by the United States. For him, in those days, these two things were connected—the brutality of Saddam Hussein's regime and American support for it. Hounded out of Iraq, he has spent fifteen years as a refugee hopscotching from one country to the next. Had he been born in Saudi Arabia or fallen into a fringe radical

Islamic circle in Egypt, he could very well have ended up as one of the hijackers.

I make this observation not by way of passing any kind of judgment on my friend. For a variety of reasons, he does not identify with the perpetrators of September 11. Nor am I able to condemn his actions against the Iraqi regime two decades ago—he will not be too specific about what he did in those days, but I surmise he was part of an Islamist plot to assassinate Saddam Hussein and was one of the lucky few who succeeded in hightailing it out of the country after the conspiracy was uncovered. Today he is a happily married man with too many kids, and if his English were up to it, and he could read my saying he might have, in some earlier incarnation, been one of the September 11 terrorists, he would get very upset.

And yet his anger, like that of the September 11 hijackers and much of the Arab-Muslim world today, was, until the fall of 2002, directed at the United States. My friend justified his anger by the belief, shared with an overwhelming majority of Iraqis inside and outside Iraq (until the fall of 2002), that the United States deliberately left the Iraqi tyrant in place after the Gulf War, and then went ahead and imposed a regime of sanctions that made ordinary people, like my friend's family living in Iraq, pay the price for Saddam's actions in 1990. Like most Iraqis, he used to get angry when I said that he was wrong, that the United States wanted nothing more than for Saddam to be replaced through some sort of palace coup. Before September 11, America was simply unwilling to shoulder the responsibility of doing the job itself; moreover, it feared, or did not have any confidence in, radical structural change in Iraq.

I MADE THE HYPOTHETICAL STATEMENT about my friend's potential for being one of the hijackers because normal, ordinary people perpetrated September 11, however horrific and bestial their behavior, and we need to understand the reasons they turn to terrorism, or away from it: They were not born terrorists, nor are they inclined toward violent solutions of their problems by the tenets of their religion. I say this not wanting for a second to excuse or justify what was done on September 11, but because of the urgency of understanding what it is we are dealing with—if for no other reason than to be able to fight it more effectively.

I brought up my friend's denial because he was not alone. A very large number of Arabs and Muslims refused to accept that their coreligionists or fellow Arabs took part in September 11. This refusal came effortlessly, almost naturally, like the deeply distressing but widely accepted story in Egypt and the Gulf Arab countries that Jews or Israelis, not Muslims, were behind what happened in New York, Pennsylvania, and Washington, D.C. On the face of it, the statement that the hijackers could not have been Arabs because no Arab is capable of planning such an operation sounds simple, almost as if it were a naive comment on the facts. But it is nothing of the sort. If we only knew how to unpack all that produced it—by no means an easy task—it would encapsulate tendencies in Arab politics that have been decades in the making.

Notice, for instance, the element of self-deprecation and inner defeat implied by the idea that Arabs are not capable of pulling off such a remarkable feat of planning and organization; it had to be someone like the Israelis, who have an interest in making "us" look bad, and who are, everyone knows, very smart. What is going on here? Is it only that my friend is so horrified by the event his first instinct is to distance himself from it? This would be a reasonably positive political impulse, however wrongly founded. Does my friend's denial arise out of a sense of shame or deep anxiety that the perpetrators might in fact turn out to be Arabs or Muslims? On the first day, I, too, hoped—hoped against all hope—that the hijackers would turn out to be some homegrown group of Timothy McVeighs. Or is there, in my friend's denial, perhaps layered onto his shame, overtones of admiration for the feat of the hijackers?

Whatever my friend's reasons, the fact is that most Arabs, and some Muslims, have not yet come to terms with what happened on September 11. You will note I said most Arabs and some Muslims. That is because we should not let the initial Afghani focus of the "war against terrorism" obscure the fact that September 11, whatever else it may be, is an outgrowth of the problems of the modern Middle East, not the whole Islamic world as bin Laden would like us to like to believe. Not one of the hijackers or their al-Qaeda bosses is an Afghan. They are all Arabs who have exported their problems to that unfortunate country.

Facing a civilizational challenge such as they have not had to face since the fall of the Ottoman Empire, the Arab world is hunkered down and battening the hatches, unaware that in the years to come the greatest price to be paid for the terror unleashed upon the United States on September 11, 2001, will be borne by individuals of Arab or Muslim origin, wherever they might live.

That price goes much deeper than bombing campaigns in various Muslim countries, or efforts to hunt down Arab terrorists from the suburbs of Boston and Hamburg to downtown Cairo and Karachi, or enduring humiliating slurs and racist attacks everywhere in the West. It is the much greater price brought about when large numbers of people sink ever deeper into denial and a sense of their own victimhood, whether at the hands of the United States, or Israel, or the world economic system, or what nowadays is called globalization. It almost no longer matters which label is held responsible.

The "anti-Americanism" of the Arab and Muslim worlds that we see manipulated by Osama bin Laden is built on this sense of victimhood and abdication of responsibility that I have been talking about; it is not a new phenomenon for the Middle East but rather the latest and most virulent variant of an idea nurtured originally by secular, nationalist Arab intellectuals like myself in the immediate aftermath of the 1967 Arab-Israeli war. In those days it went under a variety of different labels: anti-imperialism, anti-Zionism, Arab socialism, pan-Arabism. Whatever else you might care to say about this older class of labels, at least they took as their point of departure genuine grievances, some of which, of course, were more legitimate than others. Among the legitimate grievances, priority of place must be given to the profound injustice caused by the real dispossession of millions of Palestinians that accompanied the birth and consolidation of the state of Israel in 1948. In the hands of Arab nationalists and leftist "anti-imperialists" of my generation (of whom I was one), this sense of grievance failed to get channeled into building civil societies based on hard-won expansions of civil liberties wrested from tyrannical regimes such as happened in Latin America in the 1980s. Democratization began, and even took off in some parts of that continent in the 1980s, but not in the Middle East. Why? Could it be, perhaps, because unlike Latin Americans we remained stuck with a "national question," namely a situation where the collective rights of a whole people to self-determination were still, until Oslo at least, being denied in theory and in practice? Certainly that is part of the answer. But it is also the kind of answer that can all too quickly be turned into an excuse. The fact remains that my generation failed to even pursue issues of individual and civil liberties in the 1960s right through the 1980s. Our failure left a vacuum that was increasingly filled by a conspiratorial view of history, one reinforced by those consolidating tyrannical regimes like Saddam Hussein's or Hafez al-Assad's, a view of history that ascribed all of the ills of one's own world to either the Great Satan, America, or the Little Satan, Israel.

The terribly dangerous, unstated corollary of this view was the notion that "we Arabs" had no, or hardly any, agency to change the terribly unjust way that the world works. Arabs in particular increasingly began to see themselves as the great "eternal" victims of the second half of the twentieth century, consigned to a Sisyphean "struggle" against absolute or satanic injustice. Lost was a sense of ourselves as authentic political agents aiming toward concrete and gradual political gains in the political arena. It is important to remember that Arabs are not the only ones to wrap themselves up in the comforting mantle of victimhood; the modern Israeli sense of identity was, after all, forged on the foundations of the Holocaust just as surely as Palestinian national identity was forged into shape by Israel's harsh treatment of Palestinians under occupation. Such symmetries (and there are many others) have created a powerful complex of victimhood that not only undermines reconciliation efforts like Oslo but is applicable to one degree or another to all peoples of the Middle East (Palestinians, Israelis, Kurds, Armenians, Chaldean Christians, Turkomans, Shias, and Sunnis). It is very difficult to find a real peace between peoples when at some deep and primal level, all these collectivities are still stuck in competition with one another over who has suffered the most and whose cause is more just.

Among Arabs in particular, especially after Israel's stunning and totally unexpected victory in the Six-Day War of 1967, this complex began turning itself into the driving force of politics and culture; it grew into the foundation upon which such murderous regimes as Saddam Hussein's Iraq and Hafez al-Assad's Syria were built. From the hands of secular Arab nationalists, the murderous anti-American brew was passed on to previously marginalized religious zealots. In 1979 it fused with anti-Shah sentiments to become one of the animating forces of the Iranian revolution. In the wake of that seminal event, it overwhelmed major sections of the Islamic movement from Algeria to Pakistan.

Any "politics of victimhood" is inherently unreasonable. But in the Arab part of the Middle East that inherent unreasonableness (as typical of Israelis as of Kurds, for instance) is fueled by failure. The Arab world today comprises a veritable basket case of collapsing economies and mass unemployment overseen by ever more repressive regimes. This is a world that has been defeated in one war after another with Israel. It is a world that has been torn apart by coup d'états, occupations, intifadas, wars, and civil wars that in tiny Lebanon alone killed 140,000 people, wounded 400,000, and made refugees of one in every three Lebanese. The eight-year-long Iran-Iraq War, to take another defining event of our times, has killed more people than all the Arab-Israeli wars rolled into one; its effect, on the countries that waged it, was no less than World War I on, say, France or Germany.

The extraordinary depths of human suffering in Iraq today, after the Iran-Iraq War, the Gulf War, and twelve years of sanctions, is simply a special case in a whole ocean of misery. The problem is that on all the indices—economic, political, and social—the problems have become worse in the decade that came on the heels of the Gulf War. When you think of the emergence of bin Laden during the 1990s in the Middle East from this point of view, remember the emergence of Hitler out of the rubble of Germany after World War I. The economic lot of the average Palestinian today is orders of magnitude worse than it was when the Oslo peace process started. Nothing better symbolizes how much worse these problems have become since the hope-filled days of Oslo than the continuation until very recently of the regime of Saddam Hussein in power, a regime that was no longer capable of projecting its power outside its own borders, perhaps, but was for all practical purposes given free license to do what it wanted with its own citizenry. And it was given this license under the hypocritical gaze of a world that passively sat by and watched even as it was doing so. Is it any wonder that my Iraqi friend, like so many other Iraqis during the Clinton years, grew so bitter?

When you factor all of these post-1967 wars, revolutions, occupations, acts of ethnic cleansing, intifadas, and civil wars into the condition or perception of being a victim, a murderously explosive brew is the likeliest outcome. We saw that brew ignite once before, in 1990, with the Iraqi occupation of Kuwait. On September 11, 2001, it did so again. I have been speaking of a failure of systems and institutions of government, such as armies and states. But in many ways the greatest failure of all has been intellectual, specifically a failure of the intelligentsia—people like myself, writers, professors, artists, journalists, and so forth—who, with few exceptions, failed to meet the challenges of their strife-ridden times; in particular they failed to challenge the region's and their respective regimes' wildest and most paranoid fantasies. If anything, they sometimes buttressed them by becoming propagandists for political parties and armed-struggle organizations and by in general refusing to break out of nationalist paradigms, for instance, by not extending the hand of solidarity to their counterparts in Israel.

Instead, many of us who were formed politically by the 1967 war, acted as "rejectionist" critics who largely excoriated their own regimes for being insufficiently anti-Zionist or anti-imperialist. Lost in all of this was the hard work of creating a modern, rights-based political order out of or from within those very regimes, one that could eventually form the basis for a wider-based, more general prosperity.

In the absence of that kind of alternative focus, in the thick of all that endlessly self-pitying victimizing rhetoric, is it any wonder that despairing young middle-class individuals like Mohamed Atta and Ziad Jarrah, two of the men that flew the planes into the World Trade Center, men who are a generation younger than someone like me, gravitated toward ever more radical and presently terroristic activities aimed at smiting the demonized Other? Atta and Jarrah lived through on the ground—not in exile, or in the West—the practical consequences of the failure of what had been my generation's well-intentioned dreams and hopes. We by and large either sold out to our homegrown autocracies and tyrannies or packed our bags and left for one reason or another. We went on to do things like turn a city like London into a new cultural capital of the Middle East—five daily Arabic newspapers, Arab businesses, and Arab commerce operate today out of cities like London, Paris, and Hamburg. But the generation that followed ours for the most part stayed behind; they had to fight the wars and dodge the bullets; therefore, in an important sense, they had to pay the price for our failure, a price that we were either unwilling or fortunate enough not to have to pay.

Consider the case of Mohamed Atta, the ringleader of the hijackers, and quite probably the author of the five-page manual that is the only available document into his mindset at the time of the attack. Atta was born in 1968, the year the Baath came to power in Iraq, which was the year I left Baghdad to study abroad. He came of age in an Egypt that was waging an unofficial and undiscriminating underground war on the Islamism that had in its most extreme offshoot led to the assassination of President Anwar Sadat. Thousands of people were killed, civil liberties were trampled upon, and the easygoing secularism that had been the Egyptian way for the greater part of the twentieth century was giving way in the 1980s to what Fouad Ajami, a shrewd observer of the Arab scene, called a new "anxious, belligerent piety." As Gamal Abdel Nasser's drab national socialist Egypt of the 1950s and '60s was suddenly plunged into Sadat's more competitive and glamorous world of the 1970s and '80s, corruption grew, wealth was conspicuously flaunted, and society reacted by turning to Islam as a way of protecting itself from the onslaught of Western mores and ways. Young women took to the veil, and young men began to grow their beards and make their way into Islamist politics. These were the symbols of what Ajami called "a cultural war" whose main arena was the extremely overcrowded campuses of Egypt where the young Mohamed Atta was being educated. This was a war that Atta's nationalist parents, products of the Nasserite experience of the 1950s and '60s, could not understand. Atta's autocratic and reasonably well-off father took to berating the swarms of foreign reporters who came to him after September 11. He was outraged, it seems, as much by the claim that his son was a hijacker—which he denied—as by the reports that his son may have been drinking vodka and playing video games days before he boarded American Airlines Flight 11.

The elder Atta ended up sending his son to study in Germany. Mohamed Atta left in 1993 without, it seems, a single political thought having yet implanted itself in his head. Religion did not come to him in Egypt in spite of the fact that it was all around him. It came in Germany, in Hamburg of all places, where he had gone for a degree in urban planning. So how did a young man like Atta metamorphose from a studious child of a pampering mother and an ambitious and pompous father to a cold-blooded mass killer? It is hard to to answer that question with any kind of precision at the moment because much of the evidence about the Hamburg cell of terrorists has been sequestered or is very hard to obtain. I surmise Atta was an extremely complex and intelligent individual—a would-be urban planner who, even after he had made his fateful decision to go on a suicide mission for the sake of the uncompromising brand of Islam that he had come to believe in, insisted on finishing his thesis at Hamburg Technical University. This work had been on hold for a few years while Atta seems to have traveled all over the world, including, investigators think, spending a long stint in bin Laden's training camps in Afghanistan. Atta successfully defended his thesis and graduated with high honors in 1999, and then came to the United States to carry out a plan he seems to have been entrusted with directly by bin Laden, as implied by the December 13, 2001 videotape found in a house in Kandahar.

The subject of Atta's thesis was the problem of preserving the traditional forms and structures of Arab cities faced with rampant Western-style development. I can to an extent identify with this, having been a practicing architect in the 1970s working in Muscat and Bahrain with a brief to conserve and rebuild traditional forms and structures in those rapidly developing cities. But why a young man who had already hitched his destiny to an apocalyptic project to kill himself and change the world should also worry about such things remains a puzzle for me.

Consider next the case of Ziad Jarrah. He was born in 1975, the year the Lebanese civil war began. I am twenty-six years older than Ziad and had already spent years cutting my teeth in Palestinian politics by the time of his birth. His family, after September 11, claims he was sheltered from the ravages of the civil war, although that is hard to believe of anyone who was growing up during the 1980s in Lebanon. What his good parents probably meant to say is that he was spared a direct experience of its horrors. After all, they had sent him to the relatively more sheltered environment of a Christian school in Beirut, like so many of his upper-class Muslim counterparts. I went to an American Jesuit high school in Baghdad, some 75 percent of whose students were Muslim. In Lebanon, these are originally European (mostly French and Catholic) missionary schools that train the Lebanese elite and have become part of the Lebanese social landscape. Individual experiences in such schools vary considerably; however, it is fair to state that attending missionary schools does not present any significant religious or cultural problems for Muslim students, culture being largely a function of social class in Lebanon, not community of origin.

You could expect Ziad, thus, to have lived a social life virtually indistinguishable from that of his peers in the West—partying, dating, seeking fun as well as success—in spite of the precarious environment of war-torn Beirut. Behind the scenes, one could speculate about two areas of difference between this son of Beirut and any Westerner: religion—he happened to be a Muslim—and, more important, politics.

But what did religion mean to Ziad in those years? Probably not much. Perhaps on religious occasions like the Muslim Eid al-Fitr, Ziad practiced his faith, understanding it, as did his family, community, and most Muslims across the world, as being about truth, justice, and tolerance. Certainly politics was something set apart from religion while Ziad was still living in Beirut. His political views, prior to joining the terrorist cell in Hamburg, would have been those of his community at large, marked by frustration and anger at the injustice he certainly would have believed was being suffered by fellow Arabs in Lebanon, Palestine, and Iraq. That is also how I grew up in Baghdad in the 1950s and '60s.

A key difference between Ziad and a person like myself, however, was that the "isms" that my generation had believed in had all hit the dust during the years when Ziad was growing up—Arabism, nationalism, socialism, Marxism, Third Worldism. He grew up knowing our failure in his bones, so to speak. He may not have been able to theorize about them, and he may not have even accepted fully that they were failures. But growing up and seeing the streets of Beirut taken over by gangs of young men toting Kalashnikovs and extorting "protection" money from ordinary folk in the name of these high-minded "isms" teaches a young, well-intentioned, and probably highly moralistic young man things no book or theoretical treatise can teach. People imbibe these lessons, without even knowing that they are doing so, and, in the case of specially dedicated and conscientious people, they soon begin to seek alternatives.

Ziad Jarrah almost certainly did not himself join in the butchery of the Lebanese civil war that was euphemistically called the "armed struggle" during the years of his adolescence. And that is what his shocked family tried to say to the news reporters banging on their doors. Nonetheless, Ziad surely grew up suffering from its corrosive effects. For him, I suspect, there was nothing left to believe in, nothing that had not been tried out in some form or another in the streets of Cairo, Beirut, Ramallah, and Baghdad. Nothing, that is, except faith in a holy cause, which so often in politics is a substitute for lost faith in ourselves.

One "ism" had not yet been fully tested out and proven bankrupt by what men—and they were largely men—had done with it on the ground: political Islam. When did Ziad become attracted to this new and rising ideology fueled by the success of the 1979 Iranian revolution? We don't really know. We know that Ziad went to, Hamburg sometime after Atta in the mid to late 1990s, probably sent by his family to continue his studies. We know that something happened to him there. What exactly, we don't know. We can speculate, however. Once in Hamburg, acquainted for the first time with the phantasmagoric vision of an Islamic utopia that would redress all wrongs, Ziad, in need of answers and a degree of certainty in his life, found the Islamism of the Hamburg cell, which recruited him and provided all that certainty. He probably went through a long process of acculturation and adjustment into the cultlike environment of his new reality. Some of the statements made by his German girlfriend and his family do indicate a change in his approach and behavior—the kind of thing that happens to young people when they are recruited into cults. Can the idea of a utopia, any utopia, wreak such havoc upon the mind of a conscientious young man?

Dostoyevsky's novel *The Demons* tells the story of a secret society of nineteenth-century Russian revolutionaries. A group of men conspire to bring havoc to a small provincial town. They end up burning down one section of the town and murdering three people. Characters in *The Demons* seem to be possessed—an earlier translation was entitled *The Possessed;* they are somehow driven to evil forms of behavior by an external force that operates on their bodies, changing their entire mode of behavior. These external forces are the "demons" of the novel's title. But what are they?

The whole point of the novel is that they are ideas, in particular, ideas foreign to Russia, at least as Dostoyevsky came to see things. The demons of the title are that legion of "isms" that came to Russia from the West: idealism, rationalism, empiricism, materialism, utlitarianism, positivism, socialism, anarchism, nihilism, and, underlying them all in its demonic power by the end of the novel, atheism. While a person is being "eaten up" by such ideas—this metaphor is used frequently in the novel—his character and very personhood gets more and more deformed, to the point of self-destruction in one character's case or madness in another's.

Another artistic device employed in *The Demons* is that every so-called demonic idea ends up an inverted version of its original self: The would-be freedom sought by the nihilists ends in despotism; the ringleader's adoration of his guru—the closest thing to a bin Laden in the group—turns to hatred. The extreme lucidity of another character increases his blindness, and finally the first real act of the terrorist leader who would liberate all mankind is arson and the murder of his former comrade. In other words, in our passion to find and bring about the greatest good, human beings often tend to do the greatest evil. Or, as Lenin was to put it half a century after Dostoyevsky, "The road to hell is paved with good intentions." Notice that the content of what the fanatic thinks—be it the Russian terrorist's nihilistic atheism or Mohamed Atta's brand of Islam—is not the point at issue here. Dostoyevsky does not let his politics, which were reactionary, get in the way of his insights into the human condition. In this novel in particular, that happened to be investigations into his own wayward conduct as a young man, because in his youth the great Russian author had flirted with secret societies and revolutionary politics. Only after spending ten years in Siberia did he turn against them. This novel is his way of settling accounts with his past.

The irony is that in the realm of ideas, our September 11 story is an inverted version of Dostoyevsky's tale. Our terrorists were religious fanatics, and their victims—at least the occupants of those two symbols of high capitalist finance, the World Trade Center towers—were ideologically at least their polar opposites. And so it would seem from this comparison that what is finally "demonic" about the kind of terrorism that we saw on September 11 is not the ideological reference system—atheism or Islam—but an insidious political temptation that is in some ways more fundamental: the temptation, as the political theorist Judith Shklar put it, to so hate the hypocrisy and injustice of the world, as to be willing to do virtually anything to get rid of it. What student of the twentieth century can deny the political consequences of such misanthropy?

IT IS STRIKING TO NOTICE that while what I have been saying applies to Lebanese who experienced, on top of their own terrible civil war, an Israeli war and occupation of their country that only ended a short while ago, and it applies to Palestinians living in Gaza and the West Bank, and it applies to Iraqis who suffered under an intolerable regime that they blamed the United States for not doing away with during the Gulf War, precious little of what I have been saying applies to someone like Osama bin Laden, or even to some of his key lieutenants like Ayman al-Zawahiri. Saudis have, after all, not been colonized or occupied by anybody; they have one of the highest per capita income levels outside the Western world; and bin Laden returned to Saudi Arabia from Afghanistan in 1989 neither defeated nor a victim. In fact, he returned as a kind of hero, flushed with the mujahideens' victory over the Soviet Union.

Unlike the wrath of the earlier post-1967 generation of Arabs, which was formed over the Arab-Israeli conflict, bin Laden's is directed not at Israel in the first place, but at the whole post-Ottoman Arab order. Bin Laden, even more than Saddam Hussein during the 1990–91 Gulf crisis, is an unconvincing convert to the Palestinian cause; he featured it at the bottom of his list of grievances against the United States in his October 2001 al-Jazeera videotape.

What explains the 1990s emergence of a terrorist "grand alliance" led by such a man onto the center stage of Arab politics? I would suggest that we are looking at something new in Arab politics, something perhaps analogous to what Russia went through in the second half of the nineteenth century, with the rise of revolutionary nihilist movements described by Dostoyevsky in *The Demons*. The revolt of bin Laden and his cohorts, like that of Dostoyevsky's characters, is a nihilistic all-out revolt of the sons against the fathers who had to make all the compromises and broker all the dirty little deals that created the constellation of ultimately failed states that we see today in the Middle East. The great-uncle of bin Laden's right-hand man, Ayman al-Zawahiri, for instance, was the first secretary-general of the Arab League set up in the wake of the fall of the Ottoman Empire; bin Laden himself is a son of the mega-rich generation of Saudis who, quite literally, in the case of bin Laden's father, built modern Saudi Arabia. Such would-be leaders are a very far cry from the men who dominated the Arab political scene since 1967, men like Yasser Arafat or thugs like Saddam Hussein, Muammar al-Gadhafi, and Hafez al-Assad, all of whom rose to power from lowly beginnings in nondescript towns and villages through political parties or state institutions like the army and the secret police.

And, if not the Arab-Israeli conflict, what is the driving force of this movement's bid for leadership of the Arab world? Bin Laden, in a statement issued in 1998, after President Clinton's pointless missile attack on al-Qaeda's training camps in Afghanistan—the statement in which he calls on Muslims to kill Americans wherever they may be in the world—puts at the top of his list of grievances the fact that the Saudi regime allowed non-Muslims, namely American troops during the Gulf War, to pollute "the land of Muhammad," the phrase he used in his 2001 al-Jazeera video clip. The psychopolitical makeup of a man who cares more about the polluting effect of an American presence in Arabia than anything else that has been going on around him for the last thirty years is very different from that of a desperate, would-be suicide bomber in Gaza or the West Bank who lashes out wildly because he has, quite literally, nothing left to lose. I can't think of anything coming out of the Middle East in recent years that compares with it. Needless to say, bin Laden's scapegoating of the United States is not new. Here he is intersecting with the mainstream discourse of victimhood and victimization that has been in the making since the 1967 war. But his style of reasoning, the motivating impulse behind his actions, the application of notions of purity to parts or perhaps even the whole of the Arabian peninsula in modern times, is strange and in need of explanation.

Obsession with questions of purity is a characteristic feature of Wahhabism, the eighteenth-century creed founded by the fanatical reformer Muhammad ibn 'Abd al-Wahhab (1703–1787), who went on to ally himself with the tribal warlords that eventually became the Saudi dynasty. The creed was unknown in Pakistan or Afghanistan or anywhere outside the Arabian peninsula before Saudi oil wealth spread it around. So extreme is the original form of this puritanical image-hating Muslim sect that it views all non-Muslims—as well as non-Wahhabi Muslims like myself, by the way—as a form of "pollution." Osama bin Laden not only grew up with this ideology, which is taught today in all Saudi schools, but he turned it against his own regime when it violated its own principles during the Gulf War.

Through the oil wealth and power of the Saudi dynasty, and because it could always count on its alliance with the United States, Wahhabism has been able to spread its regressive, archconservative vision of Islam around the world, both within the Islamic world and to the West. Billions of Saudi dollars a year are pumped into madrasas and mosques along with the very particular type of Wahhabi Islam that parades itself as the real thing from one end of the world to the next. It is those billions, not bin Laden's allegedly great personal fortune, that directly and indirectly financed al-Qaeda camps in war-torn Afghanistan.

But there is still a problem of transition, of understanding how bin Laden got to his radical jihadi worldview from the Wahhabism of his education and his experiences fighting the Soviet Union in Afghanistan in the 1980s. The seminal moment here, where so many of the roots of September 11 intersect, is the Gulf crisis of 1990–91. There is no easy explanation—no one wrong or great act of historical injustice—that lies behind what happened on September 11, and yet many of the threads lead back to that 1990–91 crisis, to how the war against Saddam was waged, and above all, to the irresponsible way in which it was left unfinished with the whole population of Iraq left to fester. The Palestinian question, foundational though it is for the peace of the whole region, is just one of those threads. Moreover, we know from the bits and pieces of bin Laden's personal information that have begun to surface that the experience of 1990–91 was a turning point for him.

Shortly after bin Laden returned as a hero from Afghanistan, Saddam Hussein invaded Kuwait. Bin Laden reacted in a very interesting way: He called upon the Saudi ruling elite into which he had been born to let him deploy his "Arab Afghan" fighters, battle-hardened by their experiences against the Soviet army, to expel Saddam Hussein from Kuwait. Iraqi troops, who did not want to be in Kuwait in the first place, would be a pushover, he must have argued. Bin Laden was turned down, of course. The Saudis preferred to go the route of paying the United States to fight the Gulf War on their behalf. And the United States, having become accustomed to tailoring its policies in the Middle East to autocratic, authoritarian regimes of this nature, was happy to go this route. In retrospect, it is worth examining bin Laden's position back in 1990 more carefully. To begin with, it was very unusual. I say unusual because there were very few Arabs who held the position that Arab should fight Arab, and if necessary, die in the thousands, to expel the Iraqi invader from Kuwait in 1990. In fact I only know of two: bin Laden and myself. One of the biggest shocks I have had to contend with in the aftermath of September 11 is the realization that on this existential question of Arab politics back in 1990, bin Laden and I, coming as we do from entirely opposite sides of the political spectrum, shared what amounted to the same extremely unpopular position at the time concerning the seriousness of the Iraqi occupation of Kuwait and what ought to be done about it.

My position came straight out of the experience of writing about the Baathist regime in *Republic of Fear,* my first book, which was published in 1989. My Palestinian, Lebanese, or Jordanian counterparts, on the other hand, were understandably preoccupied with Israel and its policies in the region; they did not feel threatened by the Iraqi annexation of Kuwait in the same way Kuwaitis or Iraqis suffering under Saddam did. A homegrown tyrant was not the absolute center of their universe. Perhaps, large numbers of Arab intellectuals allowed themselves to think, Iraq's much touted military strength would act as a counterweight to Israeli arrogance, forcing Israel to make concessions it would not otherwise make. There were those who argued that Kuwait, being an artificial creation of the oil companies, was hardly worth fighting for. More technocratic types convinced themselves that Saddam could be prevailed upon by the Arab League to leave of his own accord. They tended to think that negotiations over Iraqi withdrawal before the outbreak of hostilities broke down only because of America's perfidy and its desire to pursue a war strategy at all costs. In the United States, Noam Chomsky, among others, made the same argument.

Saddam, however, was counting on such sentiments; he was

counting on the state of a world that he knew to be psychologically defeated. He was not about to leave Kuwait because he did not believe anyone would force him out. Who could have predicted the coalition that President George H. W. Bush put together in 1990? The America that Saddam knew had been defeated in Vietnam; it had been humiliated in Iran, and when it tried under Reagan to intervene in Lebanon, one deadly car bomb was all it took to send the U.S. Marines scuttling back to their ships. This America looked weak and irresolute in the eyes of Saddam. And so he gambled everything on its inaction over the issue of Kuwait. Saddam was wrong about the United States in 1990, but he was right about the state of the Arab world. Once the fighting had started in January of 1991, and it became clear that Arab armies were there as window dressing and were not going to be at the head of the drive to evict Saddam from Kuwait, I changed my position and called upon the Allied coalition to finish the war by taking out the tyrant and opening up the possibility of democratic change in the Middle East.

Bin Laden also changed his position, but in the opposite direction. He turned his wrath against the U.S. puppet master who was manipulating the Saudi puppet, as he now saw the relationship between the Saudi regime and the United States. How bin Laden today rationalizes his apocalyptic vision of the clash between the force of "true" Islam, which he claims to represent, and Western civilization must be distinguished from how he arrived at it. I have talked only about how he arrived at his positions. His rationalizations and use, or rather abuse, of the Qur'an to justify what he certainly thinks of as a war of civilizations have to be the subject of another essay (see my article entitled "Manual for a 'Raid'" in the January 16, 2002 issue of *The New York Review of Books*). Suffice it to say for now that his use of the Qur'an to justify terrorism is in the end about as Islamic as a reading of the story of Sodom and Gomorrah that justifies nuclear holocaust on the new Babylon that is New York, is Jewish.

There can be no rational exchange with such a perverted reading of texts; the very attempt to do so bolsters the project of the perpetrators of the heinous act of September 11, which is to blur the lines that separate a terrorist sect like al-Qaeda from the millions of ordinary Muslims and Arabs in the world. One needs to distinguish between this doomed exchange and engaging with the "culture" of anti-Americanism in the Middle East that bin Laden is exploiting to broaden his appeal. The former is a cultlike distortion of reality that it is impossible to reason with; the latter is an amorphous but nonetheless real sentiment grounded in desperate and extreme conditions of hopelessness, defeat, occupation, and, in a case like Iraq, gradual societal meltdown. Bin Laden's apocalyptic vision, like that of the Russian nihilists of the nineteenth century, is not going to materialize. His defeat was never really in doubt. The important question is, What will his demise mean for a world whose own failures are responsible for creating bin Laden in the first place?

IN THE WINTER OF 2001, "regime change" in Iraq became the official policy of the United States. Months later, senior American officials began talking about a long term American role in post-Saddam Iraq, that included democracy and reconstruction—in short, the very "nation building" that this particular administration had shied away from before it came to office. Condoleeza Rice was quoted in *The Financial Times* as saying that the United States was "completely devoted" to the reconstruction of Iraq as a unified, democratic state in the event of a military strike that toppled Saddam Hussein. She suggested that the United States was willing to spend time and money rebuilding Iraq and that the values of freedom, democracy, and free enterprise did not "stop at the edge of Islam." She underlined U.S. interest in the "democratisation or the march of freedom in the Muslim world."

Iraqis everywhere, including my friend cited at the outset of this essay, took a number of months to even begin to consider the idea that the United States had actually undergone a sea change in its policy toward Iraq. But in those moments when he lowered his guard enough to let hope triumph over experience, to the great horror of all his non-Iraqi Arab friends he welcomed the war, and has even begun to get excited about the possibilities it opens up for him (returning to family and friends he has been cut off from for nearly twenty years).

These kinds of sentiments have opened up a division in Arab politics that first made its appearance during the 1990–91 Gulf crisis. The fact is, Iraqis, as individuals and as oppositional political groups, have broken the mold of Arab politics as it was set by the 1967 Arab-Israeli war. For them, the debate over regime change that has taken place in the West and in the Arab world has by and large been a selfish one, centred on the threats to the West and its friends on the one hand, and on the moral issues arising from American hegemony on the other. It has been all about Western fears and Arab nationalist illusions, not about those who have had to live inside the grip of one of the most brutal dictatorships of modern times. Among non-Iraqi Arabs, it is hard to speak of any kind of real debate over the possibility that this war may actually end up being a force for good in the Middle East as opposed to the unmitigated disaster that almost all non-Iraqi Arabs seem to think it will be. The spectrum of what it is politically possible to talk about in non-Iraqi Arab politics still runs from Palestine at one end to Palestine at the other, with no room for the plight of the people of Iraq, the overwhelming majority of whom believe that military action was a price that they were willing to pay to be rid of a regime that they themselves helped bring into the world.

What might become of this divide in the months and years to come depends entirely on how willing the United States is to follow through with regime change coupled with nation building and the building of democratic institutions in Iraq; mere regime change is not enough. There is a great deal more at stake in Iraq than the elimination of weapons of mass destruction, and the removal of Saddam Hussein, as important and real as these are as considerations. At stake is the triumph of a new, self-critical, nonnationalist political paradigm.

Nothing illustrates the new paradigm emerging inside the Iraqi opposition better than a signature-collecting campaign around a document called Charter 1991 to which I added my name along with those of hundreds of other Iraqis of every ethnic and religious denomination and from all walks of life. The relevant passages read as follows:

> *The notion that strength resides in large standing armies and up-to-date weapons of destruction has proved bankrupt.*
>
> *Real strength is always internal—in the creative, cultural and wealth-producing capabilities of a people. It is found in civil society, not in the army or in the state. Armies often threaten democracy; the larger they grow the more they weaken civil society. This is what happened in Iraq. Therefore, conditional upon international and regional guarantees which secure the territorial integrity of Iraq, preferably within the framework of an overall reduction in the levels of militarization of the whole Middle East, a new Iraqi constitution should:*
>
> *Abolish conscription and reorganize the army into a professional, small and purely defensive force which will never be used for internal repression. Set an absolute upper limit on*

expenditure on this new force equal to 2 percent of Iraqi National Income.

Have as its first article the following: "Aspiring sincerely to an international peace based on justice and order, the Iraqi people forever renounce war as a sovereign right of the nation and the threat or use of force as a means of settling international disputes. The right of belligerency of the Iraqi state will not be recognized."

I am convinced that if the territorial integrity of a post-Saddam Iraq were to be guaranteed by an outside power like the United States, the overwhelming majority of Iraqis, certainly its Kurdish and Shiite populations, will vote for such a far-reaching transformation of priorities. Like post-war Germany, the country will need powerful internal law and order institutions. But Iraq's future, like that of Japan and Germany after World War II, lies in unshackling itself in no uncertain way from the burden of its past and focusing all the creative energies of the country on reconstruction and cultural renewal. Work on a road map for such a transition, of which demilitarization is only one plank, is already well under way among Iraqi intellectuals. From this point of view, whatever other legitimate problems of regime change in Iraq might have, I am convinced that it also provides a historic opportunity that is as large as anything that has happened in the Middle East since the fall of the Ottoman Empire. The question that I cannot answer, however, is this: Will the new resolve that America has discovered in itself after September 11 rise imaginatively to the level of the opportunity it may be about to create in the Middle East?

Susie Linfield

The Treason of the Intellectuals (Again)

"I always start anything by saying, 'A and B are not the same.'"
—Hannah Arendt,

DESCRIBING HER ANALYTIC METHOD

Introduction

S EPTEMBER 11 MADE ME THINK about many things, and one of
them was judgment. Actually, I had been thinking about
judgment for several years because I teach criticism, and I teach it
to students who often don't like to make judgments, though they
want to be critics. Even worse, they think—though certainly
they've only imbibed this from their elders—that not making judgments might be somehow connected to being a "fair" person or a
"good" person, whereas I think it's connected to being a person who
has renounced her own autonomy and is therefore unlikely to be
either fair or good.

But after September 11, I began thinking about the long-term
failure, especially by some liberal and leftist intellectuals (who con-
stitute the "we" of this piece, and in whose indictment I must too
often include myself), to make certain kinds of judgments in the political realm—particularly in regard to the so-called Third World or
underdeveloped world or, one might bluntly say, the chronically
poor, dangerous, and unlucky world. Terrified of being called racist
or elitist, we had stopped holding the Third World to standards

once proclaimed universal, and we thereby condoned politics both brutal and mad. September 11 made me think about the ways in which this too was connected, at least in our minds, to being fair people or good people or liberal, tolerant people. I began to wonder if a uniform way of thinking, or not-thinking, had seeped into two seemingly distinct spheres (the one of arts and culture, the other of politics). And then the connection between the two, and the similarity of our epistemological approach to them, emerged with a clarity I could not ignore because the urgent, fierce ugliness of September 11 would not let me ignore it.

In both the political realm and that of the arts, the refusal to make judgments advertises itself as a defense of the powerless, as an egalitarian practice, and as an easing of oppressive hierarchies. This self-promotion is at best a delusion and at worst a lie. The refusal to make judgments does not make the world a fairer place, a better place, or a more beautiful place. In fact if not in theory, the refusal to make judgments means nothing less than the refusal to make choices and, even more, the refusal to create value. Without value there are no ethical possibilities—the very lifeblood of freedom and equality, or at least of freedom and equality in a meaningful rather than rhetorical sense. The refusal to make judgments is fundamentally antidemocratic and fundamentally antipolitical. It shrivels the moral universe; it closes down the world. It is, I now believe, the modern-day version of the treason of the intellectuals: a betrayal of rationalism and human solidarity.

I. Politics: The Age of Leveling

"THE MURDEROUS FANATICS WHO DESTROYED the World Trade Center . . . took the issue of multiculturalism out of the fetid atmosphere of the graduate seminar and into the streets," the conservative critic Roger Kimball wrote in a post–September 11 essay in *The New Criterion*. He is right (though most classrooms are reasonably well ventilated). Still, it shouldn't be forgotten that multiculturalism—which, contrary to current assumptions, emerged after World War II (exemplified by organizations like UNESCO) and not as a result of 1960s activism—had salutary, indeed noble origins. Westerners in the developed world could no longer ignore the barbarism to which assumptions of racial or cultural superiority had led (the Belgians' savage rule in the Congo being just one of far too many examples). Nor, of course, could any sentient person be unaware of the key part played by notions of Aryan superiority in Nazi ideology and practice. Multiculturalism—a respect for the plurality of ways in which people throughout the world organize their societies and their lives—originated in an entirely fitting sense of horror and shame.

But like virtually every emotion, shame can either clarify or blind. In this case the shame spread too far, mutating into guilt and then ossifying into cowardice. As the political movements of the 1960s morphed into the identity politics of the 1970s and '80s; as the plump satisfaction of the developed world contrasted ever more starkly with the immiseration of the rest; as real political change became harder to make and bravado took its place—as all these unhappy things occurred, it became too easy to stop thinking about the actual, rather than wished-for, trajectory of the formerly colonized world. In a dialectic that combined tragedy and farce, the sense of shame, originally a fit corrective to the arrogance of imperialism, itself became a blank check for cruelty. Thus, for instance, the Marxist historian Raymond Williams could explain Pol Pot's evacuation of Cambodia's cities—not just a disastrous policy but a murderous one—as an effort "to feed the population without American grain" and thereby avoid "colonial subservience."

This is a kind of reverse Eucharist (or, one might say, a kind of voodoo) in which the blood of agony is mysteriously transformed into the wine of justice. It exemplifies what I would call the age of leveling: the denial, indeed erasure, of crucial distinctions under the rubric of purported fairness and supposed equality.

Leveling is a cheat, for in the real world things are rarely fair and never equal. It is a shortcut that uses neat words to bypass messy realities and to create instant, consoling similarities out of sharp dissonances. It makes judgment both impossible and unnecessary. Though it is often used to excuse harshness, it is mostly soft and fuzzy, which is why it dissipates in the cold light of day. Leveling is a form of wishful thinking, which means it retreats from the world instead of changing it. Leveling is based on abstraction, and a big problem with abstraction is its tendency to turn away from immediate injustice and immediate suffering in the service of an always greater, almost-there good and an always higher, almost-realized ideal.

So whether the realm was "native rituals," such as female genital mutilation, or overtly political: Virtually any practice, no matter how grotesque, could be rationalized or fudged or, at the very least, "contextualized." A recent article by the British journalist Richard Gott, for instance, explained that the rebels in Sierra Leone have been deprived by the West of sophisticated weapons and, therefore, are "forced to rely on the axe and the machete" to hack off the limbs of their countrymen. (Just *think* what they'd accomplish with AK-47s!) But there was something odd about this relativism, for though it professed to be radical and subversive, it directly negated the long and priceless lineage of radical, subversive thinkers who understood that without judgment, not only morality but actual politics wither away. Take for instance the anarchist militant Cornelius Castoriadis, founder of the group Socialism or Barbarism, who wrote simply that "How can we judge and choose?" is "the political question *par excellence*." The point is not that Castoriadis had all the right answers but that he had the right question. And the Western origins of that question, it must be noted, bothered Castoriadis not a whit; bluntly, he observed, "This activity of judging and choosing . . . is a Greco-Western activity and idea—it has been created within this world and nowhere else."

Yet as the postwar decades progressed, the question par excellence was successfully ignored, par excellence, in both the arts (where "quality" became a dirty word) and politics (where tyrants were transformed into liberators). Nonetheless, some differences developed between the two realms. As judgment declined in the artistic arena, a fetishization of novelty emerged; due partially to the demands of publishing, and certainly to the demands of the marketplace, critics almost hysterically sought out the next big thing. (This is, of course, different from being open to the next big thing and different, too, from being able to discern when the next big thing is a wonderful thing and when it is not.) In contrast, in the political realm, a suspicion of newness and an unthinking adoration—at least in regard to the underdeveloped world—of cultural customs, of nativity and authenticity and "keeping it real," became commonplace.

This reverence for the ancestral was something new, for liberals and the Left, starting with the philosophes of the Enlightenment, had always defined themselves as *critics* of tradition, of inheritance, of passive adherence to the past—which they viewed as dangerous and cruel rather than peaceful and benign. Either the Left was modern, skeptical, and universalist or it was nothing. Yet in adopting what the French philosopher Alain Finkielkraut calls "the cult of time-honored beliefs," the postwar Left and its liberal friends replicated the nostalgia-drenched values of the French counterrevolution and of German Romantics—their historic, deadly enemies—while perversely renouncing their own forward-looking, optimistic worldview. "The idea of the rights of man came into existence precisely to challenge the authority of traditions," Finkielkraut writes. "It was *at the expense of their culture* that European individuals gained, one by one, all their rights. . . . It is the critique of tradition that constitutes the spiritual foundation of Europe."

Let us put aside, for the moment, the question of how traditional most traditions are, or how "authentic." And let us allow, for the moment, that traditions can be indisputably good: sources of stability, collective nourishment, and historic memory. Yet how quickly that moment passes, for it is equally, simultaneously true that traditions can be indisputably bad: sources of violence, repression, and ignorance. On the very day that I write this, for instance, I cannot help noting a *New York Times* article on a Nigerian Islamic court's affirmation of a death sentence—by stoning—for Amina Lawal, a poor thirty-one-year-old divorced mother deemed "guilty" of adultery. On the same day, by chance, a Johannesburg *Mail & Guardian* piece catches my eye; it reports the murder of three children in Swaziland "believed to have been killed as part of traditional rituals to bring luck to election candidates." Datelined Mbabane, it continues with noticeable understatement, "Traditional leaders are generally detested by common people because of their unlimited authority. . . . Although the police have promised to apprehend the murderers, the chances that they will ever be found are slim."

Still, the obsession with native origins has stubbornly persisted. It has meant, quite simply, that wretched art and savage actions are too often approved, or at least "respected," so long as they are creations of the Third World. This is populism at its crudest, infused with a shameful obsequiousness. And though parading under the rubric of antiracism and anticolonialism, this adulation of origins has, ironically, reproduced the assumptions of racism and colonialism. What has yet to be grasped, or grasped firmly enough, is that neither glory nor guilt can be found in origins; the only things we can take pride in, and responsiblity for, are those we create through thought and action, never those we inherit at birth.

The fixation on origins has led not just to the sometimes-passive defense of the indefensible but, furthermore, to an outright rejection of great civilizational achievements such as liberal democracy's rule of law, separation of church and state, and protection of minorities. Indeed—in some odd leap of logic that I've always found puzzling—liberal democracy itself, because it emerged in the West, is accused of (and condemned as) being foundationally, and forever, "Western." By this reasoning—which posits that ideas and things are eternally "owned" by their creators—pencillin should work only for the English, $E = mc^2$ and dialectical materialism are Jewish concepts, only Greeks can write tragedies, paper and umbrellas are "essentially" Chinese, and the modern numeric system is the exclusive property of Indian Hindus.

Such provincialism—which seems absurd, and is—represents another bizarre reversal. It refutes in particular the universalist credo of those twentieth-century black intellectuals (social conservatives, liberals, socialists, and militant Marxists alike) who saw, rightly, that emancipation meant entry into, rather than exclusion from, the richness of world culture. Thus did C. L. R. James, the West Indian Marxist writer and organizer, declare, "I denounce European colonialist scholarship. But I respect the learning and the profound discoveries of Western civilisation"—under whose tutelage, he added, "my eyes and ears have been opened and I can today see and hear what we were, what we are, and what we can be."

Thus did W. E. B. DuBois insist that every ex-slave had not just the ability but the right to read Aristotle, Shakespeare, and Balzac. (It was precisely through the assertion of this right that freedom would expand from a narrowly defined legal concept into a capacious existential one.) Thus did Ralph Ellison and Albert Murray declare the entirety of American culture—indeed, the entirety of world culture—to be the organic province of African Americans. Marx and Engels, too, had hailed the creation of a transnational "world literature" and "spiritual . . . common property." But it was Goethe who expressed this idea most beautifully when he wrote that "the value of anything with true merit lies in its belonging to all humanity."

All these thinkers conceived of the world as a shared project; "all men are created equal" means nothing if it doesn't at least mean this. To believe that the world's wealth and physical resources belong to all but that its achievements—artistic, intellectual, or moral—can or should be compartmentalized would be merely silly were its repercussions not so severe.

2. The Arts: Critics Without Criticism

IN THE CULTURAL REALM, the prejudice against judgment is not new. But it is a not-new problem that has been vastly exacerbated in the past several decades.

"Value-judgments require discrimination, an ugly word in liberal-democratic America," Dwight Macdonald observed in *Partisan Review* in 1960. What was considered ugly in 1960 is now viewed as a sin. Criticism today, especially among multiculturalists and postmodernists, is derided as authoritarian, patriarchal, sexist, unegalitarian—the cultural equivalent of tyranny. Of course, in the world of artistic creation, diversity *is* quite nice—what could be lovelier than a hundred flowers blooming?—but the inability to distinguish the rose from the weed is, perversely, mistaken for an act of liberation rather than recognized as an evasion of intellectual maturity. An art critics' roundtable in a recent issue of the postmodern journal *October* (titled, perhaps fittingly, "Obsolescence") is a sad and excellent illustration of this tendency. The critics in question are a strikingly crabby lot, but they are in general happy agreement that, as one says, they have successfully worked "against this identification of criticism with judgment." They seem to not know, or not care, that their project furthers a corroding nihilism rather than an enhancing freedom. Yet others, more aesthetically traditional but politically radical than they, have seen this clearly; as the Marxist art critic John Berger wrote a quarter century ago, "The refusal of comparative judgements about art ultimately derives from a lack of belief in the purpose of art. One can only qualify X as better than Y if one believes that X achieves more, and this achievement has to be measured in relation to a goal."

In an aristocratic culture—or, alternately, a totalitarian one—the antipathy to judgment doesn't matter. In the former, the definition of beauty, and of art, is dictated by the wealthy; in the latter, it's decreed by the state or the party. But in a democratic society—and most especially in the United States, where the membrane between high and low art is so porous—judgment is the linchpin upon which the health of the culture depends. In this environment the making, and forthright assertion, of critical judgments is the *only* way to nurture a culture of high achievement and quality—which, in a democracy, is a gift to (and responsiblity of) all.

Frequently though, the critic, and especially the critic who does not mirror the public's tastes, is viewed as democracy's executioner rather than its midwife. "For some reason, objections to the giving-to-the-public-what-it-wants line are often attacked as undemocratic and snobbish," Macdonald wrote of what we now call mass culture but which Macdonald viewed as anticulture. "Yet it is precisely because I do believe in the potentialities of ordinary people that I criticize Masscult." A century before Macdonald, writers steeped in the exuberance of transcendentalist democracy echoed his hopes if not his fears, fervently desiring a new literary culture that would be modern, egalitarian, widely disseminated—and highly accomplished; in fact, they believed that American democracy would fail in the absence of such a cultural formation.

Walt Whitman, for instance, insisted that new modes of being, feeling, and thinking, not political institutions, would determine the shape of the demos and its ability to survive. Thus he advocated the creation of a literature—and of an authoritative, indeed "sacerdotal," class of authors—that could permeate "the whole mass of American mentality, taste, belief, breathing into it a new breath of life, giving it decision, affecting politics far more than the popular superficial suffrage . . . For know you not, . . . that the people of our land may all read and write, and may all possess the right to vote— and yet the main things may be entirely lacking?" And Whitman's contemporary, the journalist Margaret Fuller, clearly understood that criticism is not an expression of elitism but an offering of mutuality, an I-thou relation in practice: "We will go to the critic who trusts genius and trusts us. . . . He will be free and make us free from the mechanical and distorting influences we hear complained of on every side. He will teach us to love wisely what we before loved well, for he knows the difference between censoriousness and discernment, infatuation and reverence." Yet who among our current critics is willing to boldly "give decision" to popular taste and political ideas, or to speak of freedom, love, wisdom, or reverence without an ironic smirk?

The antijudgment school of criticism is a rejection not only of forebears like Whitman and Fuller but also of the energetic, joyous tradition of American modernist criticism. Its major exemplars were Gilbert Seldes, a cultural critic of the 1920s; James Agee, who worked as a film critic throughout the 1940s; and Pauline Kael, best known for her film criticism at *The New Yorker* in the 1960s, '70s, and '80s. Each reveled in the fluidity of American culture, in the fertile dialectic between high and low; each dug the spunky, demotic aspect of American life and American art. (As did the modernist masters like Balanchine; he wasn't slumming when he called Fred Astaire the greatest male dancer of his time, nor when he choreographed to Gershwin.) Agee, for instance, praised the "unobstreperous, poor, metropolitan" moviegoers in a Times Square theater as "the finest movie audience in the country," far superior in taste and judgment to "the 'art-theater' devotees."

But these modernist critics never mistook trash for art; never thought it elitist (or unimportant) to distinguish the two; never put forth that there was any connection, organic or otherwise, between the widely accepted and the good. Writing in 1924, Seldes celebrated the wonderful American talent for burlesque, vaudeville, ragtime, and he considered the Krazy Kat comic strip—a "despised medium," he admitted—to be "the most amusing and fantastic and satisfactory work of art produced in America to-day." Yet he had not the slightest doubt, when a friend brought him to Picasso's studio to view a recent painting, that "we found ourselves, with no more warning than our great admiration, in the presence of a masterpiece" of an entirely different order.

And unlike today's mandarins at magazines like *The New Criterion*—whose dearest wish is to stifle the uncouth vox of the populi—these earlier moderns weren't threatened by the vivacity of

American culture, and they resisted the temptation to turn high and low into Abel and Cain. "There is no conflict," Seldes flatly insisted. "The battle is only against solemnity which is not high, against ill-rendered profundity, against the shoddy and the dull." Kael, too, rejected all forms of purism: "Movie art is not the opposite of what we have always enjoyed in movies, it is not to be found in a return to that official high culture, it is what we have always found good in movies only more so." The point, for Kael, was not to suspend judgment but to let pleasure guide us toward it: "In the darkness at the movies where nothing is asked of us and we are left alone, the liberation from duty and constraint allows us to develop our own aesthetic responses. . . . Trash," Kael concluded, "has given us an appetite for art." All the more reason, then, not to confuse them: "If an older generation was persuaded to dismiss trash, now a younger generation . . . has begun to talk about trash as if it were really very serious art. . . . It's a peculiar form of movie madness crossed with academicism, this lowbrowism masquerading as highbrowism."

Equally important, these critics knew there was "no conflict" between reason and feeling; between, that is, assessing art and enjoying it. Thinking needn't dampen joy, but can enhance it; emotion needn't obliterate judgments, but might initiate them. (To understand this is to be an intellectual without apology—or tears.) "The life of the mind is supposed to be a terrible burden, ruining all the pleasures of the senses," Seldes wrote. "This idea is carefully supported by 'mental workers' (as they call themselves) and by the brainless. The truth is, of course, that when the mind isn't afflicted by a desire to be superior, it does nothing but multiply all the pleasures, and the intelligent spectator . . . feels and experiences more than the dull one." Even Kael, the most passionately emotive of critics, believed that the viewer who approaches a film saturated with his feelings but devoid of thought "does not respond more freely but less freely and less fully than the person who is aware of what is well done and what badly done in a movie, who can accept some things in it and reject others, who uses all his senses in reacting, not just his emotional vulnerabilities."

The suspension of judgment is an intimate friend of the cult of unexamined feelings; both purport to brim with democratic virtue (in the realm of the senses we are all created equal, or so they say). But a closer look reveals the utter vacuousness of this duo. In what way could the refusal—or inability—to make judgments foster democracy or promote equality? For the democratic system depends, if it is to exist in anything but name only, precisely on each citizen's ability to develop rational criteria as to what constitutes the good, the just, the wise, the worthy, and then to act accordingly. Is it possible that we could lose our power of discrimination—which represents nothing less than our intellectual and moral autonomy—in the arts and culture, but maintain it in the political realm?

Hannah Arendt answered no. Arendt reminds us that the ancient Athenians regarded those with the ability to judge beauty (and the spectacle of the games) as "the most noble group of the freeborn men," for "to look for the sake of seeing only was the freest . . . of all pursuits." (In contrast, she writes, the failure to "know how to choose . . . was deemed to be barbarian.") To weigh, to analyze, to distinguish: These were matters of aesthetics and politics, which indeed could not be disentangled. Both culture and (democratic) politics depend on our ability to form, debate, and act upon subjective values—to be, in short, intellectually and morally *alert:* "Culture and politics, then, belong together because it is not knowledge or truth which is at stake, but rather judgment and decision." In Arendt's view (following Kant), the development and expression of an aesthetic is not a frivolous or even private matter but a profoundly social activity, "an anticipated communication with others."

Judging, then, becomes "one, if not the most, important activity in which this sharing-the-world-with-others comes to pass."

Far from nurturing freedom, our inability to make critical judgments has strangled public conversation. Far from connecting critics to their audience, it has severed the two. (Obsolescence, anyone?) Far from leading to a more democratic culture—one that is created by and open to all, but that maintains and debates critical values—it has impoverished us in a flattened desert of meaningless equivalences. In short, the demagogic populism we mistakenly substituted for democratic practices has borne a high cost. Leveling is not inclusion.

Though the dream of a democratic culture—the dream of Seldes, Agee, and Kael, and of earlier forebears like Fuller and Whitman—has failed, I do not believe we can abandon it. Yet the problem that Macdonald saw so clearly—how to push for greater equality in political life without blurring all distinctions in the cultural—remains, and the solutions to it are less clear than ever. The conservative response offers little; Roger Kimball, for instance, prescribes the restoration of the cultural hierarchy and "sacred order" that reigned in Matthew Arnold's day, which suggests that the new criterion is a clone of the old. (Osama bin Laden, from what I understand, is also an ardent fan of the past's hierarchies and its sacred orders, though his preferred century is different.) But all such "solutions" will of course fail, for change is our human condition and, regardless of our desires, the only possible direction is forward. The conservative attitude refuses the challenge of constructing a future and, ironically, thereby negates its aims: Rather than preserving the past, it fosters disintegration.

To begin again—and yet again—is our curse and our gift; the question is not whether we do so, but how.

3. September 11: Something Happened

BUT IF CHANGE IS OUR FATE, what of the mantra—repeated cease-lessly by the press after September 11—that "Everything's changed"? This suggests not so much a facing up to certain realities, which is long overdue, as the absolutist worldview of a child (usu-ally accompanied by wistful scenarios of "if-onlys" and pining for lost Edens). There is no single event that changes everything—nor one that has no effect at all. Since September 11, many things have been altered yet much remains the same. It behooves us to have the humility to admit that we do not always know which is which, and to reject both the hysteria of catastrophism and the lullaby of denial. "Knowledge," the Polish poet Adam Zagajewski once wrote, "grows slowly like a wisdom tooth."

Some things, big things, have of course changed, and others will continue to. In the political world, for instance, there is Russia's move toward NATO, the United States' invasion of Iraq, and the Bush administration's bold assertion of preemptive warfare as a po-litical and moral prerogative, all results of September 11. In the intellectual and cultural world that is the focus of this essay, the changes are perhaps less obvious but, I suspect, equally grave. It is no exaggeration to say that September 11, 2001, may be for my gen-eration (and perhaps for yours) what 1956 was for that of my par-ents, when the faith of many Western intellectuals in Soviet Communism was destroyed.

The analogy is not perfect. Many intellectuals of my parents' generation, and in my own family, came of age in the fight against fascism and were ardent believers in Soviet Communism; Khrush-chev's 1956 speech, which revealed some of Stalin's crimes, was a hand grenade hurled at the very foundation of their convictions.

(Other hand grenades, such as the show trials of the 1930s, had of course been lobbed, as subsequent ones would be, like the crushing of Prague Spring.) Intellectuals of my generation have not, obviously, been adherents of Islamic fundamentalism. But some of us have believed that the forces of superstition and fanaticism were in retreat; that people in the underdeveloped nations might be slowly gravitating toward democratic humanist values; and that, despite or because of the twentieth century's incalculable violence, the rich and poor sectors of the world were moving toward more unity. I can defend this as a kind of necessary optimism; I can argue that it is not utterly stupid; but I cannot deny it is a worldview ever harder to sustain. Hope and history are not rhyming well.

So now my generation, like that of my parents, is forced to confront our delusions and, more painfully, their epistemological foundations. (And forced, also, to drop the glib superiority we too often felt toward our woefully misguided elders.) We are forced, that is, to investigate why we refused to see the strength and the ugliness of the fundamentalist movements. We are forced to confront our loss of perception, of our ability to make crucial distinctions, of our intellectual courage. We are forced to see that, by severing ourselves from our own proud tradition of judgment-as-freedom, we allowed conservatives to "own" the realm of judgment (just as some black students, in a perverse paroxysm of self-defeat, have relegated intellectual achievement to whites). We are forced to realize that critical thinking and relativism are not uneasy partners but irreconcilable ones, and that we must choose between them. It is not that we failed to predict the events of September 11, an obvious impossibility, nor even that we were "wrong" on any particular question. It is, rather, that we neglected the *discipline* of clear thought.

And yet the source of the failure is deeper still, and strikes at the very heart of the thinking process. What we took to be the activity of thinking was actually the reproduction of old thoughts; it is thinking-as-creation, rather than as replication, that we must now teach ourselves. This means the learning not of new words but of a new syntax—one that, in particular, does not rely on slippery and misleading analogies. It means discarding the Xerox machine that exists in each of our heads, and that seduces us into mistaking tired, generic formulas for fresh, distinct analyses.

"A crisis," Arendt wrote, "becomes a disaster only when we respond to it with preformed judgments." How capable are we of forming new judgments—of living through an upheaval rather than creating a catastrophe? I am not sure, but I have observed, broadly speaking, three main responses to the massacres of September 11. None inspires confidence.

The conservative response is best represented by the book *Why We Fight* by William Bennett, former secretary of education for Ronald Reagan and "drug czar" for the first President Bush. Bennett seems genuinely grieved by the September 11 attacks. But there is a creepy triumphalism to his descriptions of their putative effects on America and Americans. "Across the nation, patriotic ardor burned bright," he writes with undisguised relish. "Suddenly flags were flying everywhere, and everywhere we were singing the national anthem. . . . In the wake of September 11, the doubts and questions that had only recently plagued Americans about their nation seemed to fade into insignificance. . . . It was, in short, a moment of moral clarity." Bennett praises the "open, curious, free spirit" of Enlightenment rationalism, but the moral clarity that he hails is directly endangered by that spirit—and there is no doubt which he will choose. By the book's end, it's evident that rather than seeking Arendt's new ways of thinking, Bennett actually despises them; for him, critical thinking is not the handmaiden of moral clarity but its gravedigger. "What I fear," he writes, "is the erosion of moral clarity, and the spread of indifference and confusion, as a thousand voices discourse with energy and zeal on the questionable nature, if not the outright illegitimacy, of our methods and our cause." He condemns the "turmoil" that those terrible thousand voices "introduce into our public discourse" and cites, as a pernicious example of the coming anarchy, "the frenzied debate over civil liberties." Democracy and freedom are fine things, apparently, so long as they remain unsullied by the messiness of conflict, contestation, and competing ideas.

Among liberals and Leftists, the response has been different but also highly problematic. First, there are those who suggest that because the event was horrible, it is divorced from human history. The title of a new September 11 book by the staff of the *New York Times* epitomizes this view; it is called *Out of the Blue*. But while the planes may have come from there, al-Qaeda—not to mention the far deeper, broader movements of Islamic fundamentalism, anti-Semitism, and antimodernism that it represents—certainly didn't. The title, then—which represents the work of some of the most influential journalists in the country and therefore the world—is a silly mystification. Why would, and how could, the hideousness of an event propel it outside of time—which, after all, has no normative aspect at all? Here again is the viewpoint of a child who can only watch, passively, as bad things mysteriously happen to good people, and who lives in a kind of black-magic world conjured by nasty gods, evil spirits or, perhaps, terrible parents. And though it is possible to envision the United States playing many roles in the world, a passive child is surely not among them.

Alternately, there is the perspective that September 11 is a kind of payback—or "blowback," in the more sophisticated, indeed gleeful, parlance—for specific acts of the evil (American) empire. In this view, which appears hyperrational but is also a kind of magical thinking, everything that happens in the world is not just embedded in history but embedded in predictable and ultimately "fair" ways. What goes around comes around; the chickens have come home to roost; every nation creates its own karma: The clichés, each one a bit stupider than its predecessor, are familiar by now. This perspective replaces sheer bewilderment with irresolute certainty; and whereas the first view fetishizes the sense of shock, the second denies that anything that happens can *ever* be a surprise. On the one hand, then: absolute wonder, disconnection, and impotence; on the other: absolute knowledge, causality, and power.

Neither of these latter approaches can take us anywhere worth going. The first attempts to maintain American dissociation from the world—always a false and self-serving stance, especially for the world's only superpower and especially unsustainable since September 11. The second, put forth most forcefully by Noam Chomsky and his many followers here and abroad, assumes that the United States is the world's sole source of evil, the master of the universe who controls all peoples, movements, and events. It suggests that some kind of cosmic justice is at work in the world—an invisible hand of righteousness, so to speak. (This is what the Greeks called hubris and my grandparents called chutzpah.) It conflates victims and perpetrators. It confuses just war and terror, politics and mass murder, states and civilians. It insists that a crime is a punishment. It mistakes the ecstasy of Thanatos for the politics of justice.

And, on a philosophic level, it refuses newness. To say that an event has introduced something unprecedented into the world does not suggest its rupture from history—just as to understand a crime does not imply forgiveness toward its perpetrators. (Comprehension doesn't exclude judgment but, rather, establishes a rational basis for it.) The American, French, and Russian revolutions, for instance, each introduced newness into the world. So did the Holocaust, and the dropping of the atom bomb on Hiroshima.

These were political events, which means they were made by human beings, and they were the result of conscious decisions. They were acts of creation. They changed the world irrevocably and—of course—in ways their makers could never have anticipated. They were not simply variations, even magnified ones, on an already-existing theme. The Russian Revolution was not just a longer, fiercer version of the 1848 Revolutions or the Paris Commune; the Holocaust was not just a very big, very bad pogrom; the dropping of the atomic bomb was not just a continuation of previous modes of warfare. These events were *qualitatively* different from their predecessors; to focus on their terrifying quantitive aspects is to evade their essential meanings. Similarly, the horror of September 11 lies not just, or even primarily, in the number of victims but rather in the new kind of politics the attacks made real. Our primary job is to grasp that. As the cultural critic Greil Marcus wrote post–September 11, "Real intellectuals admit that it is in the nature of the human condition that it will inevitably, at unpredictable times, in unpredictable ways, produce events that leave every conceptual apparatus in ruins, and that real intellectuals value nothing so much as the chance . . . to do their work there."

Can we do that work? Do we have a choice not to? Can we participate as active citizens in the shaping, and reshaping, of our country's political future rather than sullenly standing by? Can we learn from the past without lazily assuming that the present is a replication of it? (The past is not always prologue—and certainly not in the ways we had hypothesized.) Can we tell the difference between principles and dogmas? Can we think instead of feel? Can we look at our own culture, and those of others, with discrimination, taste, and judgment—and regard doing so as a right and responsibility rather than a source of guilty embarrassment?

I make no predictions. But I do remember something one of my graduate students told me in response to September 11. She was a Hindu of South Asian descent, though she was raised in Hong Kong, educated at one of the most exclusive women's colleges in the United States, and now works as an editor in New York City: a true child of globalization. She defined herself, for obvious and good reasons, as an anti-imperialist and she was, for obvious and good reasons, vastly suspicious of U.S. military and economic power. But she also thought of herself as a feminist and a humanist, and she adored Salman Rushdie. On September 12, she realized that her previous politics—her instinctive alliance with the Third World, her belief that globalization's losers would always choose justice—no longer worked.

She and I subsequently had many debates—sometimes uncomfortably heated, sometimes in deep sorrow—about modernity, power, inequality, and ethics. "I feel as if the ground is shifting under my feet," she exclaimed one day in November. "I no longer have a steady place to stand."

To which I could only reply, "That's terrific!"

Conclusion

THE MASSACRE OF SEPTEMBER 11 was many things, including a surprise and an atrocity. It is also an opportunity, for it challenges us to regain a sense of realism. By this I do not mean pessimism or hopelessness—nor, certainly, a mimetic style in literature or the arts.

Realism is, rather, a way of understanding one's existence as intimately enmeshed with what John Berger called "the production of the world." This is the realism of George Orwell, who believed that all lies, even the most well-intentioned, are counterrevolutionary; of Martin Buber, who understood love not as a private emotion that you feel but as a mutual relation that you live; of Primo Levi, who discovered beauty, and an ethic, in the periodic table; of Hannah Arendt, who trusted limited, man-made rights over infinite, "natural" ones. Realism is based in respect for the actual things, including the actual histories, that we make. It is an embrace of the world as it is and as it could be; it can encompass hopes but not illusions, tragedy (which reveals us to ourselves) but not sentimentality (whose aim, always, is to obfuscate). It is creative. It is an exploration and an invitation. It is not heroic, but it requires us to stay awake. It values reason, though it does not dishonor mystery. It seeks truth not because the truth is happy but because it is the only path to knowledge. It enables us to distinguish between skepticism and cynicism, flexibility and moral relativism, conviction and ideology, humility and despair. Realism is the basis, I would argue, of principled politics and good art. The opposite of realism is not optimism or imagination but evasion and bad faith.

And realism requires us to understand a simple fact that is also a complex paradox: Though we do not create the world, we are responsible for it. All of us, as Arendt noted, enter the world as strangers, more or less bewildered; to become an adult means transforming an alien universe into a home, albeit not quite the one we had envisioned. That the conditions under which we do this are always and unforgivably unfair is irrelevant; that the resulting home is always and unforgivably imperfect makes it none the less ours.

It is a world we must—indeed can only—make with others. This is not a sweet and comforting fact but a harsh and terrifying one. And it is, or so I hope, a fact we will no longer seek to deny, for it holds the key to transforming brotherhood from an altruistic sentiment into necessary action.

William Finnegan

Globalization Meets Pachamama

WHY DO THESE MATCHES COME FROM SWEDEN?" Luis Bredow lit a cigarette and shook a red matchbox. "Why can't we make our own matches here in Bolivia? We have trees, we have people who need work." Bredow and I were sitting in the courtyard of the Hotel Cochabamba, high in the Bolivian Andes—a long way from Sweden. He is a newspaper editor, tall and wry. He rattled the Swedish matches again. "And, you know, every one of these matches is perfect, and a box costs twenty centavos. If we made matches, half of them wouldn't light and a box would cost fifty centavos. Something is strange here, something is wrong. Is this globalization?"

In a word, it is. But this exhausted word conceals, by now, more than it reveals. Defined narrowly, it means simply international trade as a swiftly rising percentage of world economic activity. Less narrowly, it means world economic integration and all the exploitation, opportunity, cultural and political domination, and cross-pollination that this entails. But to answer Bredow's question—to unpack the bafflement of underdevelopment and begin to see why advantage, both between nations and within nations, seems to flow, in much of the world, ever more heavily to the already advantaged—

it helps to stick to cases. So let us stay for a moment with Bolivian matches—or their nonexistence.

Bredow's matches were made by the Swedish Match Company, which is the largest match producer in the world. It sells its products in 140 countries. According to the company, it has, in Sweden, the world's most technically advanced match production line. Bredow's matches were probably made, however, in Brazil, where the company has a production plant and is also the market leader. All the company's plants use high-speed Swedish peeling lathes, splint choppers, and other state-of-the-art machines. This is why every match seems perfect. Although the company has annual sales in the billions of dollars, it employed, because of its advanced automation, fewer than six-thousand workers in 2001. This is why its matches are so cheap.

Which is not to say that Swedish Match enjoys a global monopoly. The match business is competitive. The Swedes got a head start, since both the safety match and the first automated match machine were invented in Sweden—in 1844 and 1864, respectively. But competitors soon emerged: There were more than a hundred match factories in Poland in the late nineteenth century. To keep its modern market share, Swedish Match does, among other things, a frantic amount of branding—entering a yacht in the Whitbread Round-the-World race, sponsoring the Swedish Open tennis tournament, staging its own sailboat-racing series. In countries where its market dominance might be resented, on the other hand, Swedish Match has quietly taken over national brands with strong local identities, such as Redheads, the most popular matches in Australia.

Could an aspiring Bolivian match producer hope to compete with this global corporate juggernaut? Certainly trees and cheap labor would not by themselves be enough to gain comparative advantage—the necessary grail of market economics. And yet historical context and the policies of governments determine the course of trade and industry as surely as the raw facts of economics. Consider the Swedish Match Company's experience in India. In the last great round of trade globalization, which took place in the decades before World War I, Swedish matches began to be sold in bulk in India. The war abruptly ended that era, and in India temporarily ended Swedish match imports. Locally owned factories sprang up around Calcutta, using Japanese technology. After the war, Swedish Match returned, and in 1924 introduced mechanized match production to India. The Calcutta factories could not compete, and shut down. But entrepreneurs from South India had by then learned the trade. They started a cottage match industry in faraway Tamil Nadu, Kerala, and neighboring states. And the Indian government chose to encourage, particularly after national independence in 1948, small-scale, handmade match production, which employed large numbers of people. The government used tariffs and differential excise taxes to protect the Indian match industry, and it limited the Swedish Match subsidiary's market share. Eventually, Swedish Match, which was the only large-scale automated producer in the country, was limited to 18 percent of the Indian market. Still, its operations were profitable, and it continues to coexist today with its many Indian competitors.

A serious answer, then, to Bredow's question about the absence of Bolivian matches must include local history and government policies, which in Bolivia's case means consideration, also, of its relations with its primary overseer in the developed world, the United States.

FIRST, THOUGH, WHY BOLIVIA? It's a decidedly minor player on the world stage, and that, actually, is why. If every underdeveloped country is underdeveloped in its own way—and it is—none can stand in any comprehensive sense for the scores of others. Bolivia, which is landlocked and thinly populated (8.5 million people, spread over a territory larger than France and Spain), contains abundant natural resources and an unusual variety of terrain, including vast rain forests and a high, cold, mineral-rich plain known as the altiplano. It is, however, both mired in ancestral poverty and, in 2003, sufficiently "in play," politically and economically, to reflect, at least in part, the situations of many poor countries. For all the experience it shares with the rest of Latin America, it is the poorest country in South America, with living standards and development prospects more precisely comparable to much of sub-Saharan Africa. And development—meaning the host of economic and moral questions surrounding desperate poverty—remains, even while terrorism, Middle East conflict, or American military campaigns fill the headlines, the single most urgent political issue in most of the world's countries.

Bolivia's peculiar relationship with the North American hyperpower makes it, moreover, an informative spot from which to look at this sprawling galaxy of things we call globalization—to look at it from the other end of the telescope, as it were.

In Bolivia, before the United States, there was, of course, Spain. The conquistadores of the sixteenth century stormed through the New World in search of rumored El Dorados, and in the mountains of what is today western Bolivia they found one. "They say that even the horses were shod with silver in the great days of the city of Potosí," writes Eduardo Galeano, in his classic study, *Open Veins of Latin America*. "In the mid-seventeenth century silver constituted more than 99 percent of mineral exports from Spanish America. Latin America was a huge mine, with Potosí as its chief center." In 1573, the now-forgotten city had 120,000 inhabitants, "the same population as London and more than Seville, Madrid, Rome, or

Paris. . . . By the beginning of the seventeenth century it had thirty-six magnificently decorated churches, thirty-six gambling houses, and fourteen dance academies." Most of Potosí's wealth, "this jugular vein of the viceroyalty," nonetheless went for export. "Silver shipped to Spain in little more than a century and a half exceeded three times the total European reserves," Galeano writes. "The metals taken from the new colonial dominions not only stimulated Europe's economic development; one may say that they made it possible."

And yet the historic transfer of wealth from Bolivia and other outposts of the Spanish Empire was more than just a textbook case of colonial extraction, for the truth was that by the seventeenth century Spain was broke, and most of the money simply flowed through Seville directly to the Crown's bankers and creditors elsewhere in Europe. For citizens of the dozens of countries desperately in debt today, this arrangement may sound familiar. Of course, for the Andean Indians forced to work in the mines and haciendas of the invaders (as many as eight million slaves are believed to have died in the silver mines), the details of European financial relationships made little difference—just as independence from Spain, achieved in Bolivia in 1825, only slightly eased their peonage. Local politics were conducted exclusively by and for a small, white-skinned elite. Tin eventually replaced silver as the country's leading export. Shipped to Britain for smelting on railroads built largely with British capital, tin created vast new fortunes for investors and entrepreneurs while leaving most Bolivians as destitute as ever.

The emergence of the United States as a world power first registered strongly in Bolivia in the early twentieth century, when American bank loans allowed the country to complete crucial railroad lines. By the 1920s, the terms of the government's debt effectively gave the United States direct control over Bolivian tax policies. Oil had been discovered in the country's eastern lowlands, and the Standard Oil Company of New Jersey gained special concessions to operate there. These bald extensions of U.S. power into national life were politically controversial, and when Bolivia lost the bloody and pointless Chaco War (1932–35) to Paraguay—and lost, in the process, a large swath of territory—popular anger was directed at Standard Oil, which was accused, unfairly, of causing the war, and had its operations confiscated.

Something remarkable, although not widely remarked, happened in Bolivia in 1952: a full-scale popular revolution. The old feudal haciendas were seized by peasants, their lands redistributed; owners and managers who resisted were killed. Major industries, including the tin mines and railroads, were nationalized. The army was effectively disbanded, replaced by peasant militias. Universal suffrage was introduced, the Indian majority was freed from legal bondage, and a new class of communal peasant landowners was created, as it were, overnight.

Just as remarkable, in its way, was the U.S. response. This was early in the Cold War, at a time when the CIA was violently destabilizing left-wing governments in Guatemala, Guyana, and around the world. The Bolivian revolutionaries pleaded with Washington not to intervene. Yes, there might be Communists in the movement, particularly in the labor unions, but the leadership itself was not Communist. A 1953 visit to Bolivia by Milton Eisenhower, the president's brother, who gave the revolution his blessing, led to a decision in Washington to try something different in Bolivia. Rather than oppose the revolution, the United States would co-opt it. After demanding, and receiving, a new investment code that allowed American companies back into the eastern oil fields, the Eisenhower administration sent large amounts of food aid to help Bolivia avoid starvation. It was agreed that something called "state capitalism" would be the new official economic model.

U.S. aid became a mainstay of the Bolivian economy. The army was slowly reestablished and, in 1964, a group of officers, trained in "counterinsurgency" in the United States, overthrew an elected civilian government, plunging the country into a long night—nearly two decades—of military rule. Many of the revolution's gains were reversed, as regime cronies amassed land and resources. The repression of the unions and other sectors of the left was fierce, although not, on the whole, as bloody as the "dirty wars" waged on civilians by the neighboring dictatorships in Chile, Paraguay, Argentina, Brazil, and Uruguay. Still, U.S. support of the "anti-Communist" regional security alliance known as Operation Condor has left a well of bitterness in Bolivia (and in neighboring countries) whose depths, though often hidden, remain profound.

When Bolivia emerged from military rule in the early 1980s (it did so partly because of Carter administration pressure on the government to improve its human-rights record), there was widespread hope for a new, nonaligned, democratic dispensation. And yet the country was in an impossible position. It had been looted by the generals. Its foreign debt was overwhelming. And then world tin prices collapsed and inflation exploded, in 1985, to a surreal annual rate of 25,000 percent.

Politically and financially prostrate, Bolivia had no choice but to consent to radical treatment. Enter "the Boys," also known as "the Chicago Boys," after a group of Chilean economists, trained at the University of Chicago, who implemented free-market policies under General Pinochet. The reformers in Bolivia were led by the minister of planning (later president), Gonzalo Sánchez de Lozada (another Chicago graduate), who was closely advised by Jeffrey Sachs, the American economist who later became famous for the "shock therapy" he designed for post-Communist Poland.

Bolivia's shock treatment was ferocious. The currency was devalued, price and wage controls were abolished, government spending was slashed, and the state-owned tin mines were closed. The economy plunged into recession; unemployment soared. Miners, teachers, nurses, and factory workers were especially hard hit. But the inflationary death spiral was broken. Bolivia's relations with its foreign creditors—and, most important, with their de facto enforcement arm, the International Monetary Fund—were restored. Loans and foreign investment began to flow again.

But the IMF and the World Bank (the Bank's development loans helped keep the country afloat) took effective control of large areas of public policy. Like many poor countries, Bolivia was subjected to what is blandly known as structural adjustment—a set of standardized, far-reaching austerity and "openness" measures, which typically include the removal of restrictions on foreign investment, the abolition of many public subsidies and labor rights, reduced state spending, deregulation, lower tariffs, tighter credit, the encouragement of export-oriented industries, lower marginal tax rates, currency devaluation, and the sale of major public enterprises. In Bolivia's case, the latter included the national railways, the national airlines, the telephone system, the tin mines, and a long list of municipal utilities. Many indebted countries have had to be forced to accept structural adjustment, but Bolivia's small, wealthy political class seemed to have come to a quiet understanding with the international bankers. The power of the workers and peasants was clearly broken; all of the major parties were now business-aligned. And so the parties began to trade the presidency around peaceably every election cycle, and their leaders found that they could collaborate profitably with the international corporations that came in to run the phone company or pump the oil and gas. The World Bank warmly dubbed Bolivia an "early adjuster." It is still being adjusted today. As Luis Bredow, the newspaper editor in Cochabamba, explained it, "The World Bank *is* the government of Bolivia."

Since both the World Bank and the IMF are based in Washington, D.C., and the "market-friendly" policies that they urge on countries throughout the world are known as the Washington Consensus, it should not be surprising that some Bolivians discerned a certain continuity between structural adjustment, Standard Oil, and Operation Condor—there were elements, after all, of that old-time Yankee imperialism in this new globalization regime. It wasn't, to be sure, gunboat diplomacy (except when it came to the war on drugs, an entirely different sore subject in Bolivia), and it wasn't a purely North American operation. The cheap foreign products that flooded the country after 1985 came from all directions, as did the foreign investors. The matches in the shops were *Swedish,* for god's sake.

But the hundreds of local factories that went bankrupt, unable to compete—including one that made an inferior brand of matches called Condor—were, for the most part, Bolivian. And, contemplating what the anthropologist Lesley Gill calls the "imposed disorder" of postshock Bolivia—the havoc and deep social pain caused by structural adjustment—contemplating, especially, the mysterious power of these faceless institutions, the World Bank and the IMF—both ostensibly public agencies dedicated to the reduction of Third World poverty—many Bolivians must have asked one another, echoing those suave gringo outlaws, Butch Cassidy and the Sundance Kid (who died, it may be remembered, after robbing a mining company in Bolivia), "Who *are* those guys?"

THEY WERE CONCEIVED during the latter part of World War II at a conference of American, British, and European economists and civil servants held in Bretton Woods, New Hampshire, and dominated intellectually by John Maynard Keynes. The World Bank was originally intended to help finance the reconstruction of postwar

Europe. After the Marshall Plan made that purpose redundant, the Bank had to look farther afield for a raison d'être, and it shifted its focus to Asia, Africa, and Latin America, where it loaned money to poor governments, usually for specific projects. Eventually it wandered into areas far beyond its original mandate, such as conflict resolution—demobilizing troops in Uganda, clearing land mines in Bosnia. Today, the Bank has around 10,000 employees, 184 member states, and lends nearly $20 billion a year. The IMF, whose founding purpose was to make short-term loans to stabilize currencies and the balance of payments, promote international economic cooperation, and prevent another Depression, has similarly had to shape-shift with the times. It now makes long-term loans as well, functions almost entirely in the developing world, and, by interpreting its mandate to maintain international financial stability as broadly as possible, seeks to actively manage the economies of many poor countries. Because nearly all significant aid and loans to poor countries hinge on the IMF's assessment of a nation's financial soundness, the Fund has the leverage to dictate public policy in large areas of the globe. The Bank and the IMF work together closely. They are the two most powerful financial institutions in the world. And that's just the beginning of who those guys are.

Power within the institutions was originally apportioned among governments according to their relative financial strength and contributions, which meant that the United States had the leading role from the start. Although the managing director of the IMF is traditionally a European, the United States is the only country with an effective veto over IMF actions. The president of the World Bank has always been an American.

During the Cold War, loans were often granted on a crudely political basis. Indeed, the World Bank's first loan—$250 million to France, in 1947—was withheld until the French government purged its cabinet of Communists. In the Third World, friendly dictators were propped up by loans. Robert McNamara, after presiding over the Vietnam War, became president of the World Bank in 1968, and he expanded its operations aggressively, pushing poor countries to transform their economies by promoting industrialized agriculture and export production. There were fundamental problems with this development model. By the time McNamara retired, in 1981, his legacy consisted largely of failed megaprojects, populations no longer able to feed themselves, devastated forests and watersheds, and a sea of hopeless debt.

Both the World Bank and the IMF passed through an ideological looking-glass in the 1980s. They had been established and run on Keynesian principles—on assumptions that markets need state guidance, whether to stabilize currencies and prevent panics (IMF) or to build infrastructure necessary for economic development (the Bank). But with the ascendance of Reaganite (and Thatcherite) free-market economics in the West—among their rich-country masters, that is—both institutions changed their operating philosophies. They began pushing privatization, deregulation, fiscal austerity, the lifting of tariffs, liberalization of capital markets, and other policies laissez-faire.

Unfortunately, they have had even less success with the new philosophy. Financial panics and crises continue to roil the IMF's clients, from East Asia to Argentina. (A recent study found that IMF programs have had, overall, a *negative* effect on economic growth in participating countries.) The idea that open markets and increased trade lead invariably to economic growth may be sound in theory, but it has repeatedly failed the reality test. Rapid import liberalization, for instance, has often caused mass unemployment and deindustrialization, as it did in Bolivia, with no significant local upside, and certainly none for the poor. Increased exports have frequently been just as disappointing. In Latin America as a whole, according to Oxfam's Kevin Watkins, "rapid growth in exports has been associated with rising unemployment and stagnating incomes. Real minimum wages in the region were lower at the end of the 1990s than at the start."

The World Bank's declared mission of reducing poverty has been a bust so far. More than a billion people are now living on less than one dollar a day—the figure in 1972 was 800 million—while nearly half the world's population is living on less than two dollars a day. When Catherine Caufield started the reporting for her book, *Masters of Illusion: The World Bank and the Poverty of Nations* (1996), she asked the Bank to direct her toward some of its most successful projects. The Bank's press officers made repeated promises, but produced no list. Finally, as Caufield was leaving for India, which happened to be the Bank's largest client, the Bank came up with the name of one project, the South Bassein Offshore Gas Development Project. Caufield could find no one in India who had heard of it. Later, she discovered that the project was a gas field in the Arabian Sea, and was known in India by a different name. The Bank had loaned $772 million to the project and, because no villagers had needed to be resettled from the open sea, had managed to avoid controversy—this was apparently the successful part. The project had taken twice as long as expected to complete and, according to Bank records, more than a third of the loan had ultimately been written off "due to misprocurement."

Bank officials have consistently vowed to improve this sorry record, to start funding projects that benefit not only big business and Third World elites but also the world's poor. Accordingly, projects with nongovernmental organizations (NGOs) and other "civil society" groups, along with efforts to promote access to health care and education, have increased. But Bank contracts are typically worth millions, and multinational corporations have remained major beneficiaries. In 1995 Lawrence Summers, then of the U.S. Treasury Department (now president of Harvard), told Congress that for each dollar the American government contributed to the World Bank, American corporations received $1.35 in procurement contracts. This was an unusually candid admission by a leading Bank supporter that one of its main activities is, in fact, corporate welfare. Those donated American dollars come, after all, from ordinary American taxpayers—few of whom know anything about what the World Bank does.

The Bank does many things, of course, and employs many people who are undoubtedly devoted to the idea of reducing poverty. (So does the IMF.) It provides technical assistance to poor countries, some of it clearly useful, and even tolerates a degree of internal debate. William Easterly, a senior Bank economist, tested the limits of that tolerance in 2001 when he published *The Elusive Quest for Growth,* a book that chronicled the failed development panaceas the Bank has promoted over the years. In a prologue, Easterly applauded the fact that his employer "encourages gadflies like me to exercise intellectual freedom." In the preface to a paperback edition, published in 2002, however, Easterly was obliged to revise this assessment. In truth, the Bank, he had learned, "encourages gadflies like me to find another job."

The more serious consequences of World Bank policy rigidity tend to occur in the poorest corners of the globe. In the Indian state of Rajasthan, peasant villagers are starving as I write. India achieved self-sufficiency in grain production decades ago, and huge surpluses of wheat are in fact rotting in fields and warehouses in neighboring Punjab, just a few hundred miles from the starving. This atrocity is the unintended result of many factors, notably the influence of a powerful farm lobby on the Indian government. But World Bank pressure to reduce food subsidies has been a main contributor to recent hunger in India. It will be a new day indeed, though, when we hear the Bank take any responsibility for the starvation in Rajasthan.

Both the Bank and the IMF are locked in unhealthy relationships with their client governments. Easterly provides a stunningly long list of "adjustment loans" that accomplished nothing, and dryly concludes, "The operation was a success for everyone except the patient." Governments recognize, obviously, that their poverty is a precondition for the flow of aid, and for the less scrupulous among them, this can turn the poor themselves into a valuable commodity, their pitifulness a resource not to be squandered through amelioration. On the donors' side, lending is essential to the continued health of aid bureaucracies and the advancement of careers—not the best environment in which to make wise decisions. Then there is the merry-go-round of fiscal crises and bailouts, aboard which the Bank and the IMF and rich-country bilateral lenders regularly make new loans to deeply indebted countries in order to avoid the embarrassment of nonperforming loans. Because it helps condemn the world's poor to a fate of permanent debt, the Bank's self-description as a "pro-poor" development agency is at best self-deluding. (Bolivia, like many other countries, spends more on debt servicing than it spends on health.) The Bank's core constituencies remain the corporations and the poor-country bureaucrats and politicians whom it enriches.

Conspicuous among those corporations has been Enron. Between 1992 and its collapse in 2001, Enron received *more than $7 billion*—in public financing for projects in twenty-nine countries.

Many of these projects involved privatizations pushed by the World Bank and IMF. In Bolivia, Enron dined well at the banquet of post-shock privatizations. Bolivia's state-owned oil and gas company was privatized in 1996, after which the Bank approved a $310 million loan to support construction of a $2 billion natural gas pipeline to Brazil. Enron was among the major investors in the pipeline, which runs across more than a thousand miles of fragile dry tropical forest, wetland, and rain forest. Perhaps because the project has been strongly criticized by environmental and indigenous groups for its destruction of habitat and livelihoods, the World Bank's political risk-insurance arm provided a $14.6 million guarantee directly to Enron. This was after Gonzalo Sánchez de Lozada, who was Bolivia's president at the time, had awarded Enron a suspiciously disproportionate share of the profits from the Bolivian side of the pipeline. Enron, it is worth noting, did not include its Bolivian operations in its bankruptcy filing of December 2001. Company officials say the Bolivian pipeline is a key feature of its reorganization plan.

DOES A PROMISING DEVELOPMENT PATH exist for a country such as Bolivia?

Angel Villagomez, a retired state road inspector, wanted to know the same thing when I visited him. Villagomez lived with his family in one of the dozens of dusty *barrios marginales* that have sprung up in recent years around the city of Cochabamba, which has a population of 800,000. The Villagomezes, like most of their neighbors, were economic refugees from the mining districts around Potosí, districts that have been hemorrhaging people under structural adjustment. We were sitting outside their house, a simple adobe structure on a steep hillside. Behind Mr. Villagomez, glistening in the afternoon sun, I could see Mount Tunari, a snow-covered, seventeen-thousand-foot peak that towers over the Cochabamba Valley. Villagomez, a vigorous, engaging man in his sixties, was wearing a Nike cap and complaining that local politicians all campaigned with their left hands raised but, once they attained office, always turned out to have hearts that beat on the right. He struck the right side of his chest for emphasis. "It's very sad," he said. "Here in Bolivia we are sitting on a chair of gold—oil, gas, minerals—and yet all the wealth goes to foreigners."

This is a common view and the image recalled, almost exactly, the description in an influential 1951 UN report. Bolivia, the United Nation said, was "a beggar sitting on a throne of gold." The national revolution of 1952 was meant, of course, to overturn this state of affairs, and yet the economic development theories of the revolutionary movement, known as the Movimiento Nacional Revolucionario, or MNR, soon converged to a large extent with the theories followed by the United States and other international aid and development agencies that became increasingly active in Bolivia during the 1950s. While the MNR broke up haciendas and distributed land to former peons, all of the directors of development projects, national and foreign, saw the "primitivism" of the indigenous Aymara- and Quechua-speaking Indians as a major obstacle to progress. All favored some form of "imported development."

Indeed, the main study that the U.S. embassy and its various rural aid programs used for decades did not even mention the native camelids (llamas, alpacas, vicuñas) that Andean farmers have been relying on for five thousand years—animals superbly adapted to the cold, dry, high-altitude environment of the Bolivian altiplano. Cattle and sheep better suited to the American Midwest were introduced, leading to severe overgrazing. (Cattle and sheep have been in Bolivia since the Spanish arrived in the sixteenth century, but U.S.

aid in the postwar period has greatly intensified their impact.) The same mistake was made with modern seed hybrids, which were brought in and proved inferior to native grasses, grains, and, especially, potatoes. Even the cultivation of quinoa—a fantastically nutritious grain that Andean Indians have grown and, indeed, worshiped for millennia—began to decline. Thousands of tractors and mechanized plows were imported. Most of these were soon lying disused for lack of spare parts. DDT and other pesticides were widely distributed, until peasant farmers, who in Bolivia still call the earth Pachamama, after an Andean earth deity, began to speak of *Puchamama drogado*—drugged Mother Earth.

The futility of applying Western farming methods to the smallholdings of the altiplano eventually became clear, as did the hopelessness of trying to turn Indian peasants into modern farmworkers overnight—something the MNR attempted by systematically replacing traditional village elders with zealous young cadres. Increasingly, both the government and the foreign-aid agencies shifted their attention and resources toward the sparsely populated eastern lowlands, where agribusiness had better prospects and vast forests lay waiting only for timber-industry roads. Those lowlands, served by the quickly growing (now million-plus) city of Santa Cruz, have been the scene of nearly all of Bolivia's economic growth in recent decades. Large cattle ranches, timber companies, and monocropping for export (rice, sugar, cotton, and, later, soybeans) have flourished—although the profits from these industries have tended to accrue to an elite no less tiny than the layer of *latifundistas* who ruled Bolivia in hacienda days.

The MNR's main economic strategy was what is known as import substitution. This strategy seeks to replace imports with domestic production—it's the common-sense philosophy behind Luis Bredow's vexed question about Swedish matches. Import substitution was popular among Latin American governments in the 1950s, and it later drove, in various forms, the development policies of many newly decolonized states in Africa. The idea is to reduce a poor country's dependence on richer countries, while diversifying the national economy. Its drawbacks tend to include lack of consumer choice and, over time, large budget deficits. In Bolivia, behind a wall of protective tariffs, the MNR successfully reduced the country's dependence on foreign oil, achieved self-sufficiency for a number of basic foodstuffs, and nurtured a small, vibrant, unionized manufacturing sector. But the country's exports remained almost exclusively raw materials. Bolivia's industries and agriculture were still relatively inefficient—unable to compete with other countries'—and its lack of a seaport, together with an acute shortage of paved roads, made transportation costs prohibitive.

This is not to say that the "throne of gold" does not exist. The minerals, the vast reserves of oil and gas, are there. It's just that having rich natural resources is not enough—is never enough—to make a country rich. Everything depends on who exploits the resources and how.

From broad indicators such as literacy and life expectancy, it is clear that some economic and social progress were made under state capitalism. But the gulf between the poverty of Bolivia (and of many other countries practicing import substitution) and the wealth of the industrialized West continued to grow. Then the army seized power and the already bloated, corrupt state sector began to swell—to lose whatever transparency and accountability it had under the MNR—and ultimately to distort all development hopes with its greed and violence, particularly after the emergence of a vast world market for cocaine in the 1970s.

It was the MNR, ironically, that finally came back and killed state capitalism in 1985. The party had been pro-fascist during World War II—before becoming the spearhead of left-wing revolution. Now it was neoliberal (as Latin Americans call pro-corporate politics). It implemented structural adjustment, and it has been regularly in and out of power since. Gonzalo Sánchez de Lozada, still the party's leader, was elected president once again in 2002.

After seventeen years, it seems fair to ask whether neoliberalism is proving itself a viable development model in Bolivia. The country has certainly put on and dutifully worn what Thomas Friedman, the great sloganeer of globalization, calls "the Golden Straitjacket" of liberalized economic policies—no matter how socially and politically uncomfortable that garment has been. And the promised foreign investment has materialized, largely in the form of multinational corporations taking control of privatized entities. But has prosperity followed? Agribusiness has prospered in the eastern lowlands, particularly among large soybean farmers, whose exports help brighten the macroeconomic picture. Public health, as measured by infant mortality and life expectancy, has continued to improve slowly. Nearly one child in ten still dies before the age of five, however, and Bolivia remains the poorest country in South America. Two-thirds of the people live on less than $400 a year. Inflation is under control, and there has been modest economic growth, but its benefits have been concentrated among the wealthy, exacerbating a centuries-old problem of extreme inequality.

The once-powerful labor unions have been smashed, and hundreds of thousands of workers have been thrown into what economists call "the informal sector," which in Bolivia means sweatshops producing knockoffs of brand-name clothing, street peddling in the towns and cities, and coca farming. A recent study of a "home-based enterprise" (small sweatshop) in Cochabamba ended with the owner's wife taunting an employee who dared to ask for time off on May First, "What, you suppose you're a worker?" (*¿Acaso eres trabajador?*) She and he both knew that the era of workers' rights—

indeed, the very idea of the modern worker—was over in Bolivia.

Peasant farmers, too, have found it increasingly difficult to make ends meet, as prices for their cash crops have fallen under the pressure of foreign competition. They abandon their lands and move to the cities in droves. Many Bolivians of all classes leave the country entirely. They can earn better pay in the sulfur mines of Chile or the sweatshops of Buenos Aires than they can at home. Every year thousands go on, many of them illegally, to Spain or the United States.

The outlook is bleak, as even Jeffrey Sachs, who continues to advise the Bolivian government, concedes. "Belt-tightening is not a development strategy," he recently told the *New York Times,* criticizing the IMF. As for Bolivia: "I told the Bolivians that, from the very beginning, that what you have here is a miserable, poor economy with hyperinflation; if you are brave, if you are gutsy, if you do everything right, you will end up with a miserable, poor economy with stable prices."

It is also possible to march backward, of course. Some privatizations, for instance, succeed in improving service, while those that go badly can be catastrophic. Bolivia's national railways were awarded, in a forty-year concession, to a consortium led by a Chilean multinational called Cruz Blanca. The terms of purchase allowed Cruz Blanca to discontinue service on lines it found unprofitable. Accordingly, it soon closed a number of freight and passenger lines, including the rail line connecting Cochabamba, Bolivia's third-largest city, to La Paz, the capital. (It was the only rail line connecting Cochabamba to anywhere.) Given Bolivia's rugged terrain, and its awful roads, this was a serious blow to the national infrastructure. The closure, moreover, seemed to be indefinite. The Cochabamba train station was turned, willy-nilly, into a vast marketplace, shanties were built over the track bed, and photos began to appear in local papers showing collapsed stretches of track in the mountains. Bolivia's railroads were built a century ago, when labor economics made such monumental construction possible. Such railroads will not be built again. Cruz Blanca may abandon as many lines as it chooses, and nonmaintenance for even a few Andean winters will render them irrecoverable. The Sánchez de Lozada government elected in mid-2002 seemed to realize that a historic fiasco was in progress. Within weeks of taking power, the government announced that it planned to reopen the main line from La Paz to Cochabamba. The announcement contained no details, however, and it did not mention Cruz Blanca, and no one seemed to believe a word of it.

ARE ANY SMALL POOR COUNTRIES finding a viable development path? A few are making slow progress, but there are no recent success stories. The handful of countries that have managed to escape mass poverty since the 1950s are concentrated in East Asia—South Korea, Taiwan, Singapore, and, to a lesser extent, Thailand and Malaysia. The industrializing strategies of South Korea and Taiwan used aspects of import substitution. High protective tariffs were raised, for instance, around certain fledgling industries. (This is sometimes known as the "infant industry" strategy.) But these industries were selected for their export potential, and when they were ready to compete internationally, they quickly found markets. Before long, the local standard of living began to rise. This development strategy is similar to what all the Western powers once did to encourage their own industries, but it is anathema under the free-trade dogma of the Washington Consensus, and it could not be implemented by any underdeveloped, indebted country today. It relies heavily on tariffs and state planning, and is thus noxious not only to the IMF and World Bank but, equally as important, to the

World Trade Organization, which is the third Bretton Woods institution. The WTO is dedicated, even more unequivocally than the others, to eliminating "barriers to trade."

South Korea, Taiwan, and Singapore also managed, each in its own way, to turn some of the early waves of the current flood of corporate globalization to their advantage. When manufacturing started fleeing the high-wage nations of the West, opening assembly plants in Latin America and Asia, the countries that came to be known as the Asian Tigers successfully imposed local-content laws (requiring that investors buy locally produced components when possible) and consistently cut better deals for the transfer of technical skills to their own workers than, say, Mexico did. Thus, when the multinationals moved on to Indonesia and Vietnam in search of cheaper labor, Taiwan and South Korea were ready to let the sweatshops go, and assume a higher position in the global production chain.

None of this wise planning meant that the Tigers were immune to pressures from the multilateral financial institutions. The IMF, in particular, was determined that the newly prosperous East Asian countries liberalize their capital markets, and its success in prying open those markets contributed to the devastating regional economic crisis of 1997–98. In the crisis, only Malaysia seriously defied the stern—and, in retrospect, disastrous—advice of the U.S. Treasury Department not to impose capital controls. (These are laws that impede international investors—or speculators, or currency traders—what Thomas Friedman calls "the Electronic Herd"—as they try to move money in or out of a country.) By no coincidence, Malaysia emerged from the wreckage more quickly and less scathed than any of its neighbors. (Chile, which has made more progress against poverty under neoliberalism than any other Latin American country, also uses capital controls.)

China and India, although poor, have the populational heft to ignore many applications of Western pressure, which has helped each of them ride the globalization wave at least in the right general direction. China offers foreign corporations some of the world's cheapest labor, particularly in what are called export-processing zones, or free-trade zones. EPZs are tax-free manufacturing zones, where local labor and environmental laws (if any) are often relaxed or suspended in order to attract foreign capital. Tens of millions of people in more than seventy countries work in EPZs today. They are where the American (and Canadian and Western European) manufacturing jobs go when they go South. Or, rather, parts of the jobs go there, temporarily, because multinational firms have found that it is often most profitable to distribute the different aspects of production and assembly to different contractors and subcontractors, often in different countries, with the lowest-skilled, most tedious, unhealthy, labor-intensive work typically going to the least developed country. Mobility is essential to this arrangement—the ability to quickly transfer operations from country to country in search of the cheapest production costs and least hassle from local authorities. Thus, the facilities in EPZs, the vast prefab sheds and plants, are rarely owned by the contractors who use them, let alone by the multinationals who place the orders. They are leased.

EPZs are not a viable development model. Wages are extremely low, and workers are typically drawn not from local communities but from distant villages and rural areas. With the constant threat that firms will pick up and leave if they are taxed or regulated, local governments rarely profit in any significant way. Local-content laws and knowledge transfer are seldom, if ever, part of the package. A few corrupt officials, along with managers drawn from local elites, profit, certainly, but the great influx of foreign technology and capital that EPZs are supposed to bring rarely materializes.

And this seemingly minor, disappointing fact undermines a crucial assumption, widespread in the West, about the new global division of labor. The assumption is that the developed world is turning into one big postindustrial service economy while the rest of the world industrializes, and that, yes, sweatshops, child labor, egregious pollution, health and safety nightmares, and subsistence-level wages come with industrialization, but that any country that wants to develop must go through all that. *We went through it. So did Western Europe.* This assumption, though not usually stated so crudely, underpins every serious argument for corporate-led globalization. The problem is that the industrialization that Indonesia, Honduras, the Philippines, and dozens of other countries are now experiencing is not the same industrialization that we in the West experienced. It's true that people are moving from farms to factories, and that urbanization is proceeding at a rampant rate. But exploitation and immiseration are not development. And unregulated, untaxed foreign ownership, with profits being remitted to faraway investors, will never build good infrastructure. It is simply not clear how, under the current model, the poor majority in most poor countries will ever benefit from globalization.

China has achieved and maintained impressive growth, even in the present world recession. And yet China, while increasingly integrated into the world economy, and recently admitted to the WTO, is following a development path very much its own. It has strict capital controls. It forbids foreigners from owning many forms of stock. It has gone slowly with privatization. (Russia already demonstrated how to do it fast and badly.) The state retains control of the banking system. Still, everybody wants to do business with China, if only because of the size and docility of its labor force and the size of its consumer market, which is expanding swiftly, along with its urban middle class. Politically, China remains, of course, a one-party state—a police state, in fact—nominally Communist, with little interest in human rights, the rule of law, or other democratic niceties that theoretically come with a market economy.

India, the world's largest democracy, has achieved less growth, and it has been racked by battles over some of the main salients of corporate globalization, such as seed patenting and the construction of giant World Bank–backed dams that have displaced millions of villagers. But the Indian middle class (also growing) has enjoyed the fruits of a technology-led boom, thanks to a thick slice of the world's software programming and back-office work being outsourced to a few Indian firms. The government, meanwhile, has continued to protect many domestic industries—and to use capital controls—basically thumbing its nose at the imprecations of the Bretton Woods institutions to stop. Swedish Match is still the only foreign match producer allowed to operate in India.

While such policies preserve many jobs—an achievement whose value can hardly be overstated—they also preserve, it must be said, many corrupt practices and much exploitation. The rules governing the handmade match industry, for instance, specify that, to qualify for lower excise taxes, an enterprise must not exceed a certain size. Through "disarticulation"—by breaking up production, that is, into many units, each under the specified size—and by playing ownership shell games, eighteen families, known as the Match Kings of South India, have come to dominate the industry, controlling two-thirds of all national match production. Their supposedly small-scale factories are, moreover, unregulated, which means they are dangerous, nonunion, rely on child labor, and pay very poorly. Based solely on the benefits they receive from legislation, it seems safe to say that the Match Kings enjoy close relationships with major Indian political parties.

Another type of disarticulation has been occurring at another level of the business world. It can be seen most easily in two figures: First, the total assets of the one hundred largest multinational corporations increased, between 1980 and 1995, by 697 percent; second, the total direct employment of those same corporations during that same period *decreased* by 8 percent. This was more than mere downsizing. It demonstrates, again, that a great many of the jobs that left the United States (and Canada and Western Europe) over the past twenty-five years did not, in fact, rematerialize elsewhere, in the Global South, where labor is cheaper. Because the question turned out to be, in many cases, again, not *where* to produce goods but *how* to produce them, and the answer turned out to be not by owning factories and having employees, but by ordering products from contractors and subcontractors and sub-subcontractors in poor countries. This arrangement has allowed the multinationals to take vast profits, while cutting their workforces and devoting more of their budgets to marketing. EPZs have been instrumental to the success of this strategy.

Bolivia, by the way, has EPZs. Nobody wants to use them, though. Transportation costs alone—in a landlocked country with bad roads and disappearing railroads, far from major markets—deter potential investors. Then there is the country's tradition of labor militancy, which frightens foreign investment and is not a problem in, say, Thailand (and certainly not in China, where independent labor unions are illegal). Bolivian trade ministers end up in the same position as many trade ministers from sub-Saharan Africa. They would be delighted to have foreign corporations come and exploit their people. But the corporations see better opportunities elsewhere.

I WAS WALKING DOWN A PATH in a village outside Cochabamba, talking with a local student. Another American, a filmmaker, was videotaping our conversation for a TV documentary. A middle-aged man from the village stumbled past. He was drunk, glassy-eyed in the heat of the afternoon, and he did a double take when he saw us. He stopped, and began to regale me loudly and sadly with the troubles of his village. They lacked all services—water, sewage, garbage collection. They had thought they had a friend in the mayor's office in Cochabamba, but he had forgotten them, forgotten them completely. My companion, the student, was embarrassed. He gently interrupted the man, telling him that the filmmaker and I were not, in fact, *las autoridades.* We were just foreigners, looking around. The man regarded us forlornly, uncomprehendingly. We were *white,* he said finally. Why the hell couldn't we at least put in a word with the whites who ran the world?

The Bolivian people have enjoyed, if that's not too strong a word, twenty years of unbroken democracy. No politican has gone and "knocked on the barracks door," and people are proud of that fact. This isn't to say that the structures of authority and influence are transparent, or that the country's traditional pigmentocracy is not still in place—the drunk villager's assumptions about us were eloquent in that regard. And corruption is reportedly epidemic at every level of officialdom. Indeed, local political practice is enough to drive conscientious foreign analysts to blame the country's under-development, as a recent World Bank paper did, on "public sector dysfunction" and the "'informality' of public administration" and "the patrimonial dynamics of party politics." (That means who you know in the mayor's office.)

Many Bolivians distrust party politics so deeply that they regu-larly march across the country, shut down cities with barricades, stage mass hunger strikes, even crucify themselves to make their grievances known—or to demand, as they have done lately, the cre-ation of an extra-parliamentary "constituents' assembly." This would mean a restart, so to speak, for representative democracy, with more peasant and proletarian input than the business-friendly mainstream parties have.

But not all the parties in parliament are mainstream. I was surprised to learn, for instance, that the *cocaleros,* Bolivia's coca farmers, have a parliamentary brigade. I went to see its leader, Evo Morales, at his office in La Paz. His office turned out to be a dimly lit room in a high-rise government warren. People clumped in the shadows, and it felt a bit like a meeting back home of the National Organization for the Reform of Marijuana Laws, particularly after I told Morales and his aides that I had recently chewed coca leaves to combat altitude sickness on a drive through the high mountains, and they all cackled happily.

Morales was short, dark, handsome, round-faced, with a long pageboy haircut. His father had been a peasant potato farmer, he said, and he himself still farmed a coca plot in the Chaparé, a jungle district east of Cochabamba. Most of the coca farmers were ex-miners, he said, "on the run from neoliberalism." They had been fighting for years with the Bolivian army, which was being heavily supported by the United States in an ambitious coca-eradication effort known as "zero coca." Although the government (and the U.S. Drug Enforcement Agency) was claiming victory in the campaign, most independent analysts believe the effort is futile, since poor farmers in other parts of South America have always proved willing to raise coca when there is a market for it. Squeezing coca farmers in one area is often likened to squeezing a balloon. Morales was concerned with his little corner of the balloon, though, and there had recently been, he said, a great deal of hunger and army violence in the Chaparé.

In Bolivia, I should explain, and in other Andean countries, there is coca and there is coca. One type of leaf is for chewing, brewing tea, and traditional use—religious, recreational, occupational (it eases hunger as well as altitude sickness). It is sold in markets and shops. The other type of leaf is illegal. It's for processing into cocaine. The latter is the type of leaf they grow in the lowlands of the Chaparé, although most of the processing labs today are in Colombia. Morales didn't want to discuss the drug business, except to say that in Bolivia it was certainly not a military problem. He preferred to frame the U.S.–Bolivian war on drugs as a war on his people, the Quechua and Aymara, who have been growing coca for thousands of years, and have been suffering attacks from white colonizers for centuries. "Zero coca means zero Quechua and Aymara," he said. "They see us as animals. They enslaved us. When we learned to read, they cut out our eyes."

Evo Morales was a significant Indian politician, but a rival of his named Felipe Quispe was getting more press at the time I visited, and seemed to have a larger popular following. Quispe's group had recently shut down all the highways into La Paz, and he was giving thunderous interviews to reporters, denouncing not just party politics but laws themselves as part of the white oppression of Bolivia's indigenous people. The whites should simply leave the country, he said.

Making the rounds of government offices, I asked the president's press secretary if Quispe and Morales might, if they combined forces, threaten the Bolivian state. A pale, high-strung young man with a constantly ringing cell phone, the press secretary considered the matter. He shrugged. "They will never combine forces," he said. "Quispe wants a conventional political career."

A conventional political career for a man opposed to the concept of laws?

The press secretary shrugged again. That was revolutionary rhetoric, he suggested. That was for now. Quispe would later move toward the mainstream. But he would never succeed there if he were allied with Morales. "Because Evo is not accepted by the embassy."

The embassy?

"The U.S. embassy," he said, as if I were thick. "The Americans hate Evo. They will never give him a visa. Not only does he grow coca, but he took a million dollars from Gadhafi. So Quispe can never be allies with him."

I had heard about Gadhafi and the million dollars. It seems the Libyan dictator gives an annual prize and a million dollars to the person he thinks has done the most to annoy the Americans that year, and Morales had won it for opposing coca eradication.

The U.S. embassy in La Paz confirmed the story, but assured me that the political career of Evo Morales had peaked years earlier, and that he would soon be found in the dustbin of Bolivian history.

That was in early 2001. In 2002 Morales ran for president on a socialist ticket. He vowed, if elected, to end Bolivia's participation in the U.S. war on drugs, and to end, moreover, Bolivia's participation in the failed neoliberal experiment. All the industries and utilities that had been privatized? They would be renationalized. To the horror of the local authorities, not to mention the Americans, Morales began to rise in the polls. His radical ideas clearly appealed to a fair number of people. As election day neared, the embassy seemed to panic. Ambassador Manuel Rocha announced that, if Morales won the election, the United States would have to consider cutting off aid to Bolivia. This threat was taken ill, apparently, by Bolivian voters. Support for Morales surged, and on election day he finished second, behind Gonzalo Sánchez de Lozada. Since no candidate had received a majority of votes, there was a runoff between the top two finishers. Fortunately for Goni, as Sánchez de Lozada is known, the voters in the runoff were not the Indian majority of Bolivians, in which case Morales would probably have won. They were, instead, the Bolivian parliament, whose members over-whelmingly favored the wealthy, well-educated white man, Goni.

THE AMERICAN PRESENCE IN BOLIVIA is less brainlessly imperial than Ambassador Rocha made it seem. The embassy understands, for instance, that the relative success of the coca-eradication pro-gram has been a major blow to Bolivia's economy. Jorge Quiroga, Goni's predecessor as president, told me that, when the Chaparé still supplied a third of the world's coca leaf, the income from coca had accounted for more than 8 percent of Bolivia's gross domestic prod-uct, and 18 percent of exports. "Imagine wiping that out," he said. "All the unemployment and suffering, all the multiplier effects. In the United States, it would be like wiping out the mining and agri-cultural sectors combined." The embassy did not dispute these numbers or the analogy (and Quiroga is a *supporter* of eradication). Partly because the war on drugs causes hardship, the United States remains by far the largest source of bilateral aid to Bolivia, as well as the prime mover behind the World Bank's local largesse.

And it should be noted that some of the smaller units within the Bank—and also within other mammoth aid bureaucracies, such as the U.S. Agency for International Development—have long aban-doned the crass and destructive approaches to aid work that saw indigenous culture as an obstacle to progress and Westernization as a development goal. It is now generally accepted that dumping surplus American wheat into poor rural communities to prevent the spread of Communism did far more harm than good, and an effort to actually understand and help revitalize local cultures, technologies, incomes, diets, and biodiversity through small, carefully targeted, sustainable programs (microcredit, self-management, popular education) has replaced, particularly among smaller foreign and local NGOs, the old blunderbuss approach to development. For many rural Bolivians, llamas and quinoa are the future as well as the past.

The World Bank also recognizes the impossible burden that international debt places on nearly all poor countries, and it has lobbied for partial debt relief for certain poor countries that it considers fiscally responsible, including Bolivia. The Bank has seen, furthermore, enough social and financial fallout from hasty privatizations to realize, belatedly, that in many sectors, such as utilities, a strong regulatory framework to protect the public interest is essential to successful privatization. In most poor countries, the modern regulatory body is a novel concept. The Bank has therefore started sponsoring courses to train would-be regulators from countries undergoing structural adjustment. The courses are said to be first-rate, although problems can arise with the students sent to them by client governments. "They always send the minister's nephew," a regulation advocate in Bolivia told me. "Somebody who thinks of regulation the same way he thinks of a job in government, as a way to make money from bribes." The patrimonial dynamics of party politics strike again.

"Structural adjustment," incidentally, has caused so many riots in so many countries, caused so much suffering and received so much bad publicity, that it is currently being rebranded, by both the Bank and the IMF, as "development policy support lending," which has a much less Procrustean sound, I think.

The U.S. embassy is not, of course, a charitable organization. It exists to represent U.S. interests, which in Latin America has traditionally meant the interests of U.S. business. This is as true today as ever. Even at the World Bank, and at each of its regional develop-

ment banks, the United States has, under order of Congress, an offi-
cer of the U.S. Commercial Service assigned to look out for U.S.
business interests. And the economic big stick is at times still crudely
wielded. In late 2002, for instance, the Colombian defense ministry
expressed interest in buying forty light attack planes from the leading Brazilian aircraft manufacturer. Colombia, which is racked by
civil war, is a major recipient of U.S. military aid. General James T.
Hill, head of the U.S. Southern Command, learning of the Colom-
bians' interest in purchasing Brazilian planes, fired off a letter to the
Colombian government warning that future U.S. military aid could
be jeopardized by the purchase. The Colombian air force should be
buying American-made C-130s, the general wrote, mincing no
words. When this letter unexpectedly became public, a Southern
Command spokesman claimed it was merely a technical evaluation
of Colombia's military needs.

The top priority of the Bush administration's policy toward
Latin America is the creation of a hemisphere-wide free-trade zone
known as the Free Trade Area of the Americas (FTAA). If and
when it goes into effect, the FTAA, which was first seriously pursued during the first term of the Clinton administration, will be a
sort of super–North American Free Trade Agreement (NAFTA),
including in its embrace thirty-four of the Western Hemisphere's
thirty-five countries—all but Cuba. Like NAFTA, the FTAA is a
brainchild of big business, whose interests it would serve from start
to finish. It would virtually eliminate barriers to foreign investment,
strengthen investor rights with a new hemispheric legal framework,
eliminate tariffs, ban capital controls, and establish secret trade
courts in which multinational corporations could sue governments
over health, labor, or environmental laws that could be shown to
impede profits. The FTAA would actually go beyond NAFTA,
with mandatory requirements that national markets be opened to

foreign corporations not only for basic services such as banking and insurance but also for public services such as health, education, and water. Within Latin America, there is broad popular and political opposition to the FTAA, which is widely seen as an economic onslaught on sovereignty. North American firms, it is believed, simply want more access to Latin American markets, on grossly unfair terms. U.S. embassies in the region thus spend a great deal of time parrying such arguments—presenting the FTAA as a win-win deal, trying to woo local businessmen, politicians, and opinion makers onto the bandwagon.

Their job would be easier if the United States did not flout the principles it espouses. In the spring of 2002, for instance, President Bush, responding to domestic political pressure, imposed steep new tariffs on steel imports. Loud protests came from Europe, East Asia, and Brazil, and complaints were soon being filed with the WTO. The hypocrisy was stark: The United States shoves free-trade doctrine down the throat of every country it meets while practicing, when it pleases, protectionism. Even more hypocritical, and economically painful, to dozens of countries in Africa and Latin America has been the latest round of U.S. farm subsidies, which may total as much as $180 billion over the next decade. Most of that windfall goes directly to big agricultural corporations (all of them big political contributors). These subsidies effectively close American markets to many poor-country food producers (we also have tariff barriers in place, just in case), while allowing U.S. exporters to flood foreign markets with cheap food, often putting poor-country farmers out of business. Global trade rules, as codified in the WTO's Agreement on Agriculture, do allow countries to make direct payments to their farmers. But only rich countries, for obvious reasons, have that option. This is one of the many ways that the "level playing field" extolled by free traders does not look level from the Global South.

Our NAFTA partners (Canada and Mexico) are exempt from the new steel tariffs, a fact sometimes pointed out by U.S. diplomats campaigning for the FTAA. The implication is that members of a free-trade pact may actually practice free trade with one another. But since the advent of NAFTA in 1994, the fate of Mexican workers and farmers—especially small corn farmers, the country's rural backbone—has not been confidence-inspiring. Wages have fallen and a half million families have been driven off their land by a collapse of prices as local markets have been swamped with subsidized corn produced by U.S. agribusiness.

Bolivia's experience with free trade is even less encouraging. The Economic Freedom of the World Report, a sententious compendium produced annually by a group that carries the imprimatur of the conservative economist Milton Friedman (mentor of the Chicago Boys), in 2001 ranked Bolivia first in South America in its Trade Openness Index. Worldwide, Bolivia was found to be eleventh in overall economic freedom—ahead of Canada, Japan, and Germany. The report's sponsors are full-volume free-trade advocates, contending that "more freedom translates into less poverty, faster economic growth, and higher scores on the United Nations Human Development Index." Perenially impoverished Bolivia's oddly high ranking (and low scores on the UN's Human Development Index) went unremarked in the group's most recent press release.

That would not surprise Jorge Quiroga, Bolivia's ex-president. Educated in the United States, neoliberal to his boots, and firmly pro-American, Quiroga nonetheless denounced U.S. trade hypocrisy when we spoke. "We are competitive in textiles," he told me. "But they don't give us a chance. They give U.S. factories and farmers arms like Mike Tyson with subsidies, and then make them even longer with tariffs. Then they tie our hands behind our backs, and say, 'Okay, let's see you fight!' "

THE TRUTH IS, no government practices free trade. The European Union subsidizes its farmers even more lavishly than the United States, and Japan does almost as well by its farmers. The WTO is a tariff-trading bourse, where countries dicker and bicker and hash out compromises under arbitration. Its founding document is more than twenty-seven thousand pages long. This is not the yellow brick road to a purified, simplified ("free") global trading system.

But the main problem, from the perspective of poor countries, with the existing system of world finance and trade is simply that the rules drawn up, and decisions handed down, at the WTO, the IMF, and other international tribunals are drawn up and handed down almost entirely by the rich countries. They have the negotiators, the expertise, the financial leverage, and in some cases (such as the IMF and World Bank) the weighted vote to win virtually every dispute. Even when rich countries clearly violate an agreement, their poor-country counterparts may lack the resources (meaning, often, simply the lawyers) to lodge a successful protest.

Lopsided legal contests in trade courts are not tragedies, of course. Those occur, rather, in what international bureaucrats like to call "the field"—when the European Union decides to dump heavily subsidized powdered milk in Jamaica, say, and Jamaican dairy farmers are forced to throw away hundreds of thousands of gallons of fresh milk; or when the United States decides to offload vast quantities of subsidized rice in Haiti, putting thousands of small rice farmers out of business and causing a regional rise in child malnutrition. Haiti, although the poorest country in the Western Hemisphere, does well, incidentally, on the IMF's trade openness rankings.

Beyond the egregious incidents, though, there are the structural obstructions that highlight the inexorability of disadvantage. Consider rich-country tariffs. They are, in the aggregate, four times higher against the products of poor countries than they are against the products of other rich countries. Why? Well, what you got to negotiate *with,* mon? Or consider the twist known as "tariff peaks." These charges, levied at rich-country ports, get higher with the amount of processing that an imported product has undergone. Peanuts? We charge you, assuming that this is an American port, *x*. Peanut butter? We charge you *x* plus *132 percent*. Our peanut butter companies do not appreciate competition. Canada, Japan, and the EU all use tariff peaks to keep out processed foods and other manufactured products. The result is to prevent poor countries from adding any value to their raw commodities—to prevent them, that is, from achieving even the primary stages of industrial development.

Protecting intellectual property rights is a top U.S. priority, spurred by understandable concerns in Hollywood, the software industry, and the pharmaceuticals industry about piracy. The WTO therefore ratified, in 1994–95, under heavy American pressure—but *against* the interests of the great majority of its members—an agreement known as TRIPS, for Trade-Related Aspects of Intellectual Property Rights. Enforcing patents and royalty collections, TRIPS protects, in theory, everyone's "intellectual property." Since all the valuable patents tend to be registered in the rich countries, though, the royalties tend to flow in their direction. Indeed, TRIPS obliges the payment of roughly $40 billion a year to rich countries—$19 billion to the United States alone, according to a recent World Bank study.

To date, there has been one effective antipatent rebellion. Worldwide protests against the high prices of AIDS drugs, along with threats by governments on the front lines of the pandemic to start compulsory licensing, have compelled both the big pharmaceutical companies to cut prices and the WTO to decide, in November 2001, that public health should be a consideration in some intellectual property matters. But this episode is so far the exception that proves a hard rule—that the rich countries, led by the United States (once a great pirate itself, refusing to recognize any other country's copyright laws for most of the nineteenth century), are determined to maintain a rigid system of intellectual property rights that nails yet another barrier across the path to economic development in the Global South.

Some multinational corporations, particularly agrochemical firms, have even found a dubious new use for international patent protections. They have started acquiring patents on plants, seeds, and traditional medicines that have been in common use for centuries, and then trying to charge people in poor countries, including peasant farmers, for their use. It is estimated that between two thousand and three thousand patents on traditional Indian crops and medicines have already been filed in the United States alone. Even Bolivian peasant quinoa farmers, who have lately found an export niche in U.S. gourmet health-food stores, got a scare in 1996 when two American scientists who had worked on the altiplano patented, in the United States, a quinoa variety based on a Bolivian crop grown around Lake Titicaca. A furious protest campaign by Bolivian farmers (conducted primarily over the Internet), along with an ad hoc tribunal on indigenous rights held in New York to consider the ethics of the case, finally convinced the scientists to let their patent lapse. But notice had been served: Corporate biopiracy is coming, and no indigenous community or poor-country government will have the resources to fight each case at the WTO or in faraway patent courts.

It's the perennial mismatch of the powerful center and the weak periphery. In economic policy today, though, it plays out in a particularly perverse way. When a poor country is in recession, for instance, it is usually ordered by its paymasters at the IMF to balance its books. This approach to fiscal management went out in the West with Herbert Hoover. In the rich countries, during a recession we run deficits and apply good countercyclical remedies like lowered interest rates. We don't listen to the IMF's ultraorthodox prescriptions because we don't owe the IMF money. Austerity, like free trade, is for us to prescribe, and for poor countries to practice. Private enterprises in poor countries are expected to compete with rich multinationals, when the interest rates that they must pay to raise capital—pushed dizzyingly high under austerity plans—make fair competition impossible. And all this bitter medicine comes in a bottle labeled "Economic Freedom." As Bolivia's ex-president Quiroga says, "They tie our hands behind our backs, and say, 'Okay, let's see you fight!'"

IT's EASY TO BE CYNICAL about the double binds—the rigged world trade system, to be blunt—faced by poor countries seeking economic development. And the bald contradictions of U.S. policy and preachments suggest, certainly, a degree of official cynicism. But nobody really wants to see economies stultify or implode (nobody except, perhaps, a few financial specialists known as vulture capitalists), and the IMF's great efforts to prevent emerging-economy disasters with emergency bailouts, although frequently unsuccessful, seem basically sincere. The problem lies, rather, with the model. For the set of beliefs that has driven most U.S. foreign policy in recent years has hardened into a dogma, an ideology that George Soros, the financier and philanthropist, calls "market fundamentalism." Like other fundamentalisms, it is largely impervious to argument or inconvenient facts. Big, broad-brush ideas—freedom, democracy, free trade, free markets—get rolled together into a mantra, where they begin to lose all meaning.

Shortly after September 11, 2001, President Bush declared, "The terrorists attacked the World Trade Center, and we will defeat them by expanding and encouraging world trade." Even the resolutely pro-trade *New York Times,* reporting these remarks, felt obliged to signal the president's confusion with a delicate addendum—"seeming to imply that trade was among the concerns of terrorists who brought down the towers." The U.S. Trade Representative, Robert B. Zoellick, who is Washington's lead negotiator on the FTAA, as well as on bilateral trade pacts, was less delicate when he suggested in a speech that critics of corporate free trade might have "intellectual connections with" the terrorists.

Nowhere has this administration's imperious stupefaction on the topic of trade and markets been on more painful display, however, than in a document, "The National Security Strategy of the United States," issued by the Bush White House in September 2002. Presidents are required to submit a security strategy periodically to Congress, but the Bush edition received an unusual amount of attention because of its unprecedented assertion of an American right to strike its enemies preemptively, as well as its vow to maintain American military supremacy over all rivals indefinitely. Just as notable, however, in another way, was the repeated, incongruous insertion of fundamentalist free-trade precepts into this outline of the nation's security strategy. The conflation of pro-business principles and economic goals with military doctrine was both weird and telling.

"We will actively work to bring the hope of democracy, development, free markets, and free trade to every corner of the world," the strategy declares. The possibility that the marines and perhaps high-altitude bombers might need to be involved in this work does not, in context, seem far-fetched. The Bush strategy document claims to have discovered "a single sustainable model for national success: freedom, democracy, and free enterprise." There is, in its authors' view, simply no other way. History has validated this messianic vision, *and* the American role in leading the world to its realization on this earth. "Free trade and free markets have proved their ability to lift whole societies out of poverty—so the United States will work with individual nations, entire regions, and the entire global trading community to build a world that trades in freedom and therefore grows in prosperity." The lockstep logic here, the airbrushed history, suggest a closed intellectual system—the capitalist equivalent to Maoism or Wahhabism. The strategy document also provides a laundry list of the administration's financial and commercial hobbyhorses, including the Free Trade Area of the Americas and "lower marginal tax rates," which it believes every country should adopt.

National-security strategy outlines are written by committee, are full of boilerplate, and cannot be expected to withstand close literary inspection. Still, the Bush strategy's attempt to articulate a worldview, to actually define some of its mantras, is worth quoting in full: "The concept of 'free trade' arose as a moral principle even before it became a pillar of economics. If you can make something that others value, you should be able to sell it to them. If others make something that you value, you should be able to buy it. This is real freedom, the freedom for a person—or a nation—to make a living." The reductiveness of this formulation makes vulgar Marxism look subtle and humane. The only "real freedom" is commercial freedom. Free speech, a free press, religious freedom, political freedom—all these are secondary at most.

The market fundamentalist's version of history and economics is, again, as obtuse as the vulgar Marxist's. The idea, for instance, that greater trade leads to greater general prosperity, which is an unshakable tenet among not only Friedmanite true believers but also among liberal globalizers, including most of the American journalistic establishment and the Democratic Party, is in many cases simply untrue. In Latin America, during the 1960s and '70s—the decades *preceding* the great trade boom of globalization—per capita income rose 73 percent. During the last two decades, with trade expanding rapidly under neoliberalism, per capita income rose less than 5 percent. As with natural resources, everything depends on who is trading what, and on what terms. The same dismal pattern appears in the United States. Between 1947 and 1973, economic growth averaged 4 percent and nonmanagerial wages—that's the pay of more than 80 percent of American workers—rose 63 percent, in real dollars. Since 1973, with international trade soaring, real wages have fallen 4 percent, while economic growth has averaged less than 3 percent. Nobody knows precisely what effect trade has had on American wages and growth, but even conservative economists ascribe a significant amount of the long-term American wage stagnation to the effects of globalization. These effects, when they are acknowledged at all by free traders, are, we are assured, only temporary. But they have lasted more than a generation now and, as the Springsteen song says about good jobs, "They ain't comin' back."

Another core belief, that lower taxes promote economic growth by encouraging people to work harder and invest more, is equally unfounded in reality. Neither U.S. history, which shows no correlation between tax rates and growth, nor studies of other countries, which show randomly mixed results, bear out this article of free-market faith. If a government collects high taxes and then spends the revenue unwisely, economic growth will be impeded, obviously.

If it spends the money wisely, growth may be enhanced. Of course, different groups in society will be affected differently by the progressivity and specifics of any tax regime—this is why wealthy corporations and individuals tend to be especially enthusiastic about lower *marginal* tax rates, which reduce their own tax bills.

But even economic growth, which is regarded nearly universally as an overall social good, is not necessarily so. There is growth so unequal that it heightens social conflict and increases repression. There is growth so environmentally destructive that it detracts, in sum, from a community's quality of life. (Trade itself carries vast, and rarely calculated, environmental consequences, with pollution-spreading ships, trucks, and planes rushing goods around the globe.) Then there is the destruction of communities themselves, when nations frantically reshape their economies around exports and specialization—the mass production of those goods that may afford them comparative advantage in the global marketplace. Finally, there is the peculiar way that growth, or gross domestic product, is calculated, which is as a value-free measure of total economic output, one that does not distinguish between costs and benefits. Thus, resource extraction is a plus, while resource depletion does not register. Strip mining, clear-cutting, overfishing, pumping an aquifer (or an oil reserve) dry—these ravages and permanent losses do not figure in the growth equation. Neither is income distribution a factor, meaning that most people can be getting poorer in a context of economic "growth." Medical bills and legal bills all count as growth, leading to an absurdist universe in which, as two skeptical economists recently put it, "the nation's economic hero is a terminal cancer patient who has just gone through a bitterly contested divorce."

This is not to say that the world's poor are not in need of economic growth, in the sense of greater economic opportunity. They are. And increased international trade certainly *can* be beneficial to the poor. *But it is not automatically so.* The question remains open: What combination of policies and incentives will actually provide greater economic opportunity to the world's poor?

One doesn't look to a U.S. national-security strategy for answers to this question, of course. For all its piety about raising global standards of living—and the Bush administration has in fact pledged to increase its foreign aid budget by half—the U.S. government's job is advancing and protecting American interests (particularly when the subject is national security). Our leaders' passion for "free trade" is not driven by altruism, but by a desire to open new markets for U.S. firms and products.

How will we respond, though, when our overtures are rejected? In Bolivia, Ambassador Rocha's clumsy threat when Evo Morales ran for president on a platform of economic nationalism was retrograde, old-school. So was the State Department's ill-concealed enthusiasm when Hugo Chávez, Venezuela's defiant president, seemed to have been overthrown in a coup in April 2002. Chávez was quickly back in office, and Washington was still wiping the diplomatic egg off its face months later. This incident shook people throughout Latin America, where memories of coups and military regimes are still painful, and where Washington's support for democratic politics is still, unfortunately, crucial.

That support is going to be tested, for there is a major popular backlash building against the Washington Consensus throughout Latin America (and elsewhere). The election, in October 2002, of Luiz Inácio Lula da Silva, a socialist ex-steelworker, as president of Brazil, will likely try the Bush administration's commitment to respecting democratic outcomes. Lula, as he is known, has been a strong critic of neoliberalism and the FTAA, and without Brazil, which has the largest economy in South America, there will be no FTAA (*pace* Trade Representative Zoellick, who, in remarks that infuriated Brazilians across the political spectrum, suggested that if the new government did not join the pact, it would be welcome to trade with Antarctica). While Lula has vowed not to renege on Brazil's international debt, he has ambitious plans to ease his country's terrible inequality, poverty, and hunger, and international bankers and investors have been loudly nervous about the prospect of his presidency. They caused a plunge in the value of Brazil's currency before Lula was even elected, and it is not too much to say that they retain the power to annul the results of the country's election by pulling out investments and calling in loans. The IMF, especially, with its power to extend or withhold loans, and its even greater power, through its influence, to cut off vast lines of credit, holds the keys to Brazil's financial stability—which is another way of saying, since even Jeffrey Sachs calls the IMF "a front for the U.S. government," that the United States holds those keys. In the Bush administration's quasitheological version of political economy, democracy and free markets are two halves of a mystical whole. In reality, they can be deadly opponents, particularly when voters decide to go against the markets.

EVEN MARKET FUNDAMENTALISTS CONCEDE that corporate-led globalization produces both winners and losers. Why should the U.S. government look beyond a strict pro-business definition of the national interest? Because it is *in* our national interest, especially in the longer term, to expand globalization's circle of winners, and to throw lifelines to the billions of people struggling to stay afloat in the world economic maelstrom. The United States currently enjoys a truly rare global preeminence—military, economic, pop-cultural. But power is not, obviously, the same as legitimacy. And every overweening, remorseless projection of American power, every unfair trade rule and economic double standard jammed into the global financial architecture, helps erode the legitimacy of American ascendancy in the eyes of the world's poor. This erosion is occurring throughout Latin America, Africa, Asia. When the Bush administration, under pressure from the big pharmaceuticals, quietly changes its position at the WTO on public health and intellectual property rights, and sends Trade Representative Zoellick to kill an agreement allowing poor countries access to generic medicines, few Americans notice. But in Africa, and Asia, and all the countries directly injured by this decision, millions notice.

President Bush had it all wrong about al-Qaeda and trade, of course. The September 11 attacks were perpetrated by a genocidal death cult, not by unusually determined proponents of economic democracy. Still, there was the long, horrifying groundswell of popular support for Osama bin Laden and the attacks on New York and Washington that surfaced, mainly in the Muslim world. The depths of hatred that the United States has inspired in some of the world's more oppressed corners may be ultimately unfathomable. But the importance of trying to change that, of trying to inspire something less malignant with policies less rapacious, seems undeniable. Even empires need allies. Curbing our blithe rapacity would also be the right thing to do.

Americans always overestimate the amount of foreign aid we give. In recent national polls, people have guessed, on average, that between 15 and 24 percent of the federal budget goes for foreign aid. In reality, it is less than 1 percent. The United Nations has set a foreign-aid goal for the rich countries of 0.7 percent of gross national product. A few countries have attained that modest goal, all of them Scandinavian. The United States has never come close. Indeed, the United States comes in dead last, consistently, in the yearly totals of rich-country foreign aid as a percentage of GNP. In

2000 we gave 0.1 percent. That's 10 cents for every $100 the econ-
omy produces. Even strapped Japan gave more, both relative to its
economy *and* in absolute terms. U.S. aid, moreover, is largely determined by geopolitics. Most of it is not, technically, development
assistance—only a quarter of the total even goes to poor countries.
We give more to Bosnia than to India. Japan, meanwhile, gives
India five times as much development assistance as we do. President
Bush's dramatic proposal, post–September 11, to increase foreign
aid to $15 billion looks rather puny next to the $48 billion increase in
this year's $379 billion military budget.

Along with our delusions about foreign aid, there persists a more
general belief about the rich world trying to help the poor, at least
financially. In fact, the net transfer of moneys each year runs the
other way—from the poor countries to the rich, mainly in the form
of corporate profits and government debt servicing.

But it is simplistic, even misleading, to talk about whole nations
as winners or losers under the current globalization regime, since
there are, in every country, significant groups of both winners and
losers. In China, with its remarkable growth rate and burgeoning
middle class, tens of millions of people have been left unemployed
and destitute in the upheavals caused by the arrival of capitalism,
while millions more find themselves working seven days a week in
dangerous, unhealthy, abysmally paid factory jobs. In dozens of
countries, a dominant ethnic minority is reaping most, if not all, of
the gains of economic integration—this is certainly the case across
Latin America, where small white elites traditionally rule—while
working-class and peasant majorities absorb the shocks and bitter
downsides of trade liberalization. Even in the United States, the
foremost proponent of free trade and presumably its great benefici-
ary, there are those millions of good jobs that disappeared with globalization, leaving their former holders working nonunion at

Wal-Mart. Indeed, there is a strong argument that the United States may be trading itself into oblivion, for it seems that we began, in 1976, running a trade deficit, leading to an international debt that has since ballooned to $2.4 trillion, or roughly 24 percent of gross domestic product. Our major trading partners have yet to call in these enormous debts, but the national balance sheet looks worse every year. With the economy threatening to slip into Japan-style deflation, life as a debtor nation could become quite unpleasant. And in that event globalization, certainly in this corporate-driven form, may start looking like a bad idea to more and more Americans.

The anticorporate globalization movement in the United States was knocked flat by September 11, with the rare student-labor alliance that made its great debut in Seattle in December 1999 soon sundered by differences over the so-called war on terrorism. But grass-roots resistance to structural adjustment, to privatization, to corrupt alliances between multinationals and poor-country governments, and to the whole range of abuses associated with corporate-led globalization is still flourishing in Europe and, particularly, in the Global South. Labor unions, peasant unions, churches, indigenous groups, and popular political movements of many ideological hues are forming alliances across borders and oceans, often relying on the Internet, that quintessential tool of globalization, to organize. And it will surely be this citizen backlash (not individual appeals to the better angels of our leaders!) that ultimately forces any change of course.

As a young man, fresh out of graduate school, I set off for the South Seas with no return ticket and no plan beyond a wish to see the world "before it all looks like Los Angeles," which is my hometown. That worry eventually came to seem quaint, at best. I was also on to something, though. People weren't yet calling it globalization—this was the 1970s—but American pop culture, including TV, was already making its way into remote tropical villages, along with processed foods and Western clothes, while Japanese trucks replaced draft animals. It was the cultural extinction that concerned me more than the depredations of capital, at least at first. Four years later, I came home, worried, by then, about other things.

Outside the cities in Bolivia, the visitor still enters an unfamiliar world. What are those white flags hanging outside the houses? What does that graffito mean, NO A LA FLEXIBILIZACION? You need a local guide. Drive into the high country and you need a Quechua-speaking guide. In a small town at the base of the mountains, I ask around and find a kid who speaks Quechua and hire him. He's a chubby teenager who makes himself comfortable, then tells me that his ambition is to study radio, so that he can make educational programs for campesinos who don't speak Spanish and don't see newspapers or TV but listen faithfully to their radios. What are those white flags? Those are *chicherías,* unlicensed taverns selling *chicha,* a homemade corn beer. The flags mean they're open for business. *Chicha* is the people's brew—cheaper than canned beer, which comes from the German brewery. What is flexibilization? That was the law that took away labor rights, such as the forty-hour week. It was part of structural adjustment, and was bitterly opposed by the unions, to no effect.

Everything feels contested. I ease my rented car through a herd of llamas, and try to remember the story. The sale of llama meat, prohibited for centuries, was only legalized in 1994. What was it, besides the power of the big cattle ranchers, that kept llama meat, which is highly nutritious, off the market? *"Discriminación,"* I am told, against the Indian herders. We pass a group of peasant women in beautiful, beribboned, handmade straw hats. Those hats, which are expensive, take months to make, and now they are disappearing, under an avalanche of cheap baseball caps from El Norte. The Indian women of the altiplano adopted the British bowler hat in the nineteenth century, and made it jauntily their own. Somehow nothing similar seems likely to happen today. We come to a village with a brilliant, multicolored woven flag hanging from a lamppost in the plaza. "That is the *wiphala* of these people." The *wiphala* represents local pride, the organization of local peasants, vehemently distinct from the Bolivian state. It has also become a symbol of resistance to globalization. *Everything feels contested.*

We drive into the high country, far above the tree line. Herds of alpacas drift in the distance, across cold green meadows. The short grass, the occasional whitewashed hut, remind me of the desolate uplands of Ireland. We run low on gas, and find ourselves negotiating with a campesino in his half-tilled potato field. It's all in Quechua, but I gather he has a can of gas somewhere. He's reluctant to part with it, but finally agrees to sell it to us if we'll give him a ride to town. I watch him put away his hoe. His wife comes to the door of their hut and studies me. I've always despised the social-service penchant for classifying hardy peasant self-sufficiency as "poverty." It's such an easy, condescending, incurious, vaguely missionary appropriation of great, unknown worlds of experience and knowledge. This is not a romanticization of peasant life. It's respect. For purposes of analysis and advocacy, of course, the "poverty" classification is useful. I've often been guilty of it myself. The young Quechua woman watches me, unsmiling, as I drive with her husband off down the mountain.

I later find myself at a big commercial *chichería* near a market town, sitting in the garden with a convivial group of local officials. It's a sunny afternoon and a raucous ranchera band plays inside a tile-floored dance hall. Pitchers of cool, earth-tasting *chicha* keep arriving at our table, accompanied by platters of *mote*—huge moist kernels of corn. Drinking *chicha* has its rituals. Four of us share a single drinking bowl, which we pass around, each carefully filling it for the next man. Before each drink, you pour a splash of *chicha* on the ground, and then toast Pachamama aloud. The *chicha* buzz is mild, even after half a dozen pitchers.

A couple of my companions are older men. It turns out that they both fled Bolivia during the days of military dictatorship. One made the mistake of going to Chile, shortly before the military coup that overthrew Salvador Allende. Out of the frying pan, he said, shrugging. He ended up being held for weeks inside the National Stadium in Santiago. Not a nice place to be. We drink a round to civilian rule.

Kissinger, we agree, is a war criminal.

We drink a round to democracy.

Talk turns to the IMF, whose local representative, a U.S.–trained Israeli economist, is in all the papers. It seems he is giving valedictory interviews because his term is up. His parting message to Bolivia? First and foremost, it must solve the corruption problem. That must be done first. Thank you, Señor Kreis.

Seriously, someone asks me, do I think there is any hope for bringing democracy to the World Bank or the IMF? Or, for that matter, to the United Nations and the WTO? Shouldn't the citizens of the world be *electing* representatives to these powerful institutions, so that they might be accountable to someone other than wealthy corporations and their allies in the rich countries? I can't think of any reason why not. We drink a round to this brilliant idea. It is only later, back at my hotel—or maybe it's back in New York— that I remember that it is only people in countries like Bolivia who know or care what the World Bank or the IMF do. In the West, most of us have other things to worry about.

Jeff Madrick

Inequality and Democracy

WHEN I WAS A BOY IN THE 1950s, "equality" was central to the public discourse. The word was seemingly everywhere. Equality before the law was widely thought of as an unquestioned good, charged with positive associations. Equality was an unquestioned component of American greatness, and of its democracy. We experienced it directly. Almost all of us went to public schools, drove on free and quite extraordinary public highways, and got our federally subsidized polio shots. Our GI parents went to college on the government dole and our teachers got federal subsidies for their education after Russia launched Sputnik.

Not all was ideal. Inequality of health care was never adequately or objectively discussed. That millions of African Americans were originally, and for a long time thereafter, excluded from this equality was still the nation's stunning hypocrisy. But in the 1950s, America was at least beginning to address this central tragedy more directly. "Separate but equal," the prevailing idea that justified legalizing school segregation, was disturbing because it clearly meant separate but unequal to a nation committed in its traditions to equality as a principle. Without that tradition, legal racism would have had an even more extended life.

But if equal rights before the law was an accepted principle of democracy, what can we say about economic equality and democracy? In this period, political and economic equality unmistakably went hand in hand. In fact, the association between political and economic equality made the very idea of equality fine and noble for us. In the 1950s, for example, civil rights clearly implied equality of economic opportunity, and equal economic opportunity implied a middle class life. It was a glorious time for the economy. Incomes grew for all levels of workers on average in America in these years, and the income distribution, which narrowed significantly during World War II, remained that way and even improved slightly for the next twenty-five years. The benefits of this most rapid period of growth in American history—at the least, on a par with the more uneven growth of the late 1800s—accrued to a new middle class.

Naïveté still abounded about how widespread prosperity was. In 1962 Michael Harrington's landmark book, *The Other America,* awakened the nation to convincing evidence that a large proportion of the population was still poor. Much of the nation was in truth appalled precisely because equality was a central American value. With the rise of a counterculture and eventual antagonism toward the prosecution of the Vietnam War, America was no longer thought blemish-free, and the fight for equality, or at least rough fairness, became imperative in many spheres. Relatively few disputed that poverty implied unequal opportunity. The majority increasingly favored programs that were outright grants to the poor, which went against the grain of much of American history. In the past, we typically (with a few exceptions) only gave money to those who already worked or sacrificed for their country—Social Security, unemployment insurance, and war veterans. Now, there were new programs, such as expanded welfare and Medicaid, that simply handed out money with relatively few qualifications. The commitment to equality in these years extended to the new feminists, marked by a threshold book, *The Feminine Mystique,* and it was again not confined to matters of civil rights for women. The wide gap in pay for the same work became a key issue in the struggle for equality.

Times are entirely different today, and regrettably so. Political discussion about economic equality has essentially become a taboo. Social Security is no longer the third rail of politics; equality is. Congressmen and senators are cautioned against discussing it because it sounds like class warfare to the public. A wide range of people believe they are put at an unfair disadvantage by affirmative action, welfare, a minimum wage, and other social programs designed to level the playing field. Ironically, the aversion to discussing equality intensified as inequality of incomes and wealth increased over twenty years to levels not seen since the 1920s.

Where does income and wealth inequality start to impinge on civil and political rights, and on America's long commitment to equality of economic opportunity? Where does it both reflect a failure of democracy and contribute to its weakening? There is a good argument to be made that we are already there.

The past few decades are not the first period in which the nation devalued equality. In the second half of the 1800s and in the 1920s, economic inequality rose rapidly. It was accompanied by a contraction of American ideology that limited the nation's focus to the individualistic components and excluded the egalitarian aspects of the national character. Social Darwinism was the simplistic individualistic philosophy of the day in the late 1800s. Survival of the fittest was a natural law with which government should not interfere, its advocates argued. In the 1920s, there was again a momentary return to rough individualism. Rates for the relatively new income tax were slashed, for example.

In the national mythology, if Americans are left to their own devices, to fall and rise according to their talents, the simple values of early America will reassert themselves and all will be well. If there is more inequality as a result, that merely reflects the abilities and tenacity of individuals, not a failure of the nation. The dominant ideological tenet of the time held that, left to their own devices, most Americans would do well.

Was this ever true? There was plenty of poverty in early America, a strong landed plutocracy, and by any modern standards, times were difficult for most. But compared to conditions in the Old World, the romantic notions about opportunity in early America were based in a large measure of fact. Equal rights did mean in the 1700s and early 1800s, to a greater extent than ever before, equal economic opportunity, even if mere self-sufficiency for most. And self-sufficiency meant political independence that was entirely new for most whites. Many people today fail to realize that equality was a reigning principle of the early 1800s and even the colonial years.

America's truest assertions of equality were not made by the Founding Fathers. Romantic ideas about their democratic intentions have never been the same since the historian Charles Beard's effective, if exaggerated, portraits of this propertied class. The quest for equality for whites only rose to its summit in the early 1800s. But by then it was a powerful force. "Most striking to European observers was a newly strident assertion of equality," wrote Charles Sellers in *The Market Revolution, Jacksonian America, 1815 to 1830*. "All whites insisted on being referred to as 'gentlemen' or 'ladies.' Dress was no longer a clue to class." Now everyone could be addressed as "Mr." and "Mrs." Speaking of white society, Gordon S. Wood simply declared in *The Radicalism of the American Revolution* that "by the early nineteenth century, America had already emerged as the most egalitarian, most materialistic, most individualistic—

and most evangelical Christian—society in Western history." It was only in the late 1800s that incomes became disturbingly unequal again.

Consider the vast political changes of the early 1800s. Universal white manhood suffrage (some states were also turning their attention to female suffrage, but none adopted it until after the Civil War, still well before the federal amendment of 1919) was achieved in almost all states by the 1820s. It was not attained in Europe or England for another generation. Primary schooling was made free to all. States changed laws to protect debtors, often the relatively poor, against their rich creditors. Charters to establish corporations were opened to most if not all white comers, rather than held for the elite. The Supreme Court, packed by President Andrew Jackson, struck a permanent blow against elitist monopoly in the Charles River Bridge case, by allowing a competitive bridge to be built nearby. Eventually, almost any white man, not just the privileged, could get a corporate charter. The federal government pursued vigorously the right of Americans to own their own piece of land, even to the extent of supporting squatters' rights.

The simplistic claims of some modern economists that property rights are the central pillar of capitalist development do not survive a serious look at American history. One person's property rights was another person's broken property rights. Such institutions were necessary but they evolved with economic growth and democratic principles; they did not simply exist beforehand. Thus, the yearning for and belief in equality, if critical to the new and exciting consensus about social justice in these early years, was also critical to a dynamic and competitive economy that utilized the abilities of as many citizens as possible.

By contrast, the oppression of the large black minority— the denial of either political or economic rights, including private property—hurt the Southern economy. If it had abandoned slavery sooner, the American South would probably not have remained essentially an undeveloped nation for so long because it would have had a strong internal market to support manufactures and new technologies, and it would have fully utilized the working capacity and talents of its population. Instead, vitality remained in the North and West. The belief that cheap slave labor—the ultimate inequality, we might say—was anything more than a momentary economic boon to America is, I believe, fundamentally wrong. It deprived the nation of a huge amount of domestic buying power, social capital, and talent. The South's poor economy until only recently is a good historical example of how extreme economic inequality and unequal rights, represented by ongoing low wages for whites and blacks well after the Civil War, undermine growth.

The irony is that if equal rights were the simple state of nature, there would be little concern. But someone is always taking away one's rights, and someone must be there to protect them. Through government, early Americans learned to equalize their opportunities. Through government, democracy worked to open up this plentiful economy to the nation's masses. But in the great sentimental national nostalgia, government would remain the enemy. Equality was about destroying aristocracy, and government was always intent, it seemed to early Americans, on preserving aristocracy. Andrew Jackson captured it in a single paragraph. "It is to be regretted that the rich and powerful too often bend the acts of government to their selfish purpose," he said in vetoing the legislation to renew the national bank's charter. "Distinction in society will always exist under every just government. Equality of talents, of education, or of wealth cannot be produced by human institutions. There are no necessary evils in government. Its evils exist only in its abuses. If it would confine itself to equal protection, and, as Heaven does its rains, shower its favors alike on the high and the low, the rich and the poor, it would be an unqualified blessing." In this one man, perhaps more than any other, resided the contradictions of America. Great democrat, landowner and capitalist, slave owner and Indian slayer, he passed equality on to the nation in a serious if narrow way. Protect equality of economic opportunity, he argued, but that included opportunities for the poor. Lincoln at last enlarged the definition of equality to include all Americans.

But the economy changed after those largely agricultural years. Government had a new rival for abuse and power—big business. Many eventually acknowledged that government was necessary to protect workers and other citizens from the power of big oil, big steel, and new giant manufacturers of all kinds. Before the Civil War, the largest mill had some three hundred workers. Henry Ford's largest factories had tens of thousands. Some robber barons were worth hundreds of millions of dollars—and Rockefeller, $1 billion—when workers earned a few hundred dollars a year.

But it took a generation to mobilize government to take action. Exhausted morally by the Civil War, the nation industrialized without any government check. Wages grew in these post–Civil War decades, but the economy fell into deep crevices, which were painful to workers. This was not a world Jackson or Lincoln could have imagined, nor did America fully understand its changes until the 1890s.

America's egalitarian tradition reasserted itself with Republican Theodore Roosevelt and Democrat Woodrow Wilson. Progressive income taxes were passed, women got the vote, new worker protection laws were implemented, monopolies were broken up, and a fairer central bank, the Federal Reserve, finally created.

The progressive tradition enlarged in the New Deal, and was retained even by Republicans after World War II. To the fundamental question—when is the government equalizing rights and

opportunities, and when is it equalizing outcomes?—the nation
gave an intelligent answer. Schools were desegregated, highways
equally free to the rich and poor connected the nation, GIs received
federal support for college, Social Security was repeatedly expanded
and strengthened, voting rights were guaranteed for blacks, a war
on poverty was undertaken, Medicare was passed. All of this was
done in the name of equal opportunity.

When the economy's growth slowed in the 1970s, Americans
began to see expensive social programs as a cause of their own tra-
vails. In the straitened times, equality as an ideal began to lose its
appeal. Instead of meaning growing opportunities to prosper, as it
did in early America, it had come to mean sacrifice and higher taxes
and limited opportunity.

We have now entered another period of ideological contraction
and narrow yearnings similar to the Social Darwinism of the late
nineteenth century and the economic individualism of the 1920s.
Today, we have new but similar ideological rationalizers. The issue
of income inequality is now mostly left to the economists, it seems to
me, many of whom have justified it by arguing that income inequality reflects an increasingly technical and complex economy, in which
the better educated are naturally paid much more. In a globally
competitive age, it is said, American business has little choice but to
compete this way. Not surprisingly, some economists are also the
chief new critics of democracy itself, claiming essentially that attention to social needs by the masses results in unaffordable government spending rather than needed capital investment. A common
claim today is that nations, especially developing nations, need economic development before they need either democracy or a sense of
equality. Surely, the importance of simple measures of democracy,
such as voting itself, has been exaggerated. But as the economist and

philosopher Amartya Sen poignantly points out, freedom is an end in itself.

Economics is not the only social science that is increasingly justifying inequality. *The Bell Curve*, written by Charles Murray and Richard J. Herrnstein and published in 1994, was unusually popular if widely discredited. It claimed a genetic basis for African American sociological differences. But even some more responsible social biologists with less obvious an ax to grind often now argue that unequal economic outcomes reflect our Darwinist selves, and are therefore merely natural. The return of the argument that nature trumps nurture has been vigorous. Let us face the awful truth that people are unequal in ability, we are now frequently told. The way some, though by no means all, practice it, social biology is a new, improved Social Darwinism. Democracy might well be about *protecting inequality* in such a world, goes the argument.

There is also a new fashion in the telling of political history itself that reflects the tendencies already evident in the public discourse. John Adams is now raised above Thomas Jefferson. Forget the Alien and Sedition Acts Adams supported, or his often expressed fear of the democratic masses, or how our history might have been substantially more elitist had Jefferson not become president in what was rightly called "the revolution of 1800." Adams, we are told, was a good and loving man of great character and considerable and consistent intelligence, unlike Jefferson, the arch defender of equality in principle, who had personal flaws, intellectual inconsistencies, and owned slaves. Maybe his flaws were even as bad as Bill Clinton's.

TODAY, THEN, AMERICA ACCEPTS its growing inequality equably. Yet the increase in income and wealth inequality since the late 1970s is striking. In 1979 the top 5 percent of earners made eleven times more than those in the bottom 20 percent. Now they earn nineteen times what the bottom quintile earns. The top 10 percent earn 40 percent of total income in America: They earned only about 30 percent from the 1940s to the late 1970s. We are now back to the income-distribution levels of the 1920s. In terms of wealth—homes and financial assets such as stocks and bonds (less debt)—the top 1 percent have 40 percent of all assets, again about the same as in the 1920s.

Some of the skewing toward the wealthy has been the result of capital gains on stocks during the extraordinary bull market of the late 1990s, which are temporary. If we include only wages, salaries, government payments, rent, dividends, and interest, however, we find that income became highly unequal, anyway. Families in the top 20 percent earned ten and a half times what families in the bottom quintile earned in the 1970s.

Forbes magazine's four hundred richest Americans were almost ten times richer in 2002, on average, even after the market crash, than the four hundred richest were in 1982. The economy grew by only three times over this period, and typical family incomes only doubled. In 1982, when the list was started, it required only $50 million to make it; in 2002, it required $550 million. The average net worth was almost $2.2 billion. Kevin Phillips, author most recently of *Wealth and Democracy*, figures that ten thousand families in 2000, at the height of the market, were worth $65 million. A quarter of a million may have been worth $10 million or more.

The CEOs, of course, ate their cake and had it, too. In the late 1970s, the average CEO made twenty-five times what the average worker made each year. By 1988, that ratio had soared with the stock market and the enormous Reagan tax cuts. The CEO now made nearly one hundred times what the typical worker made. By

2000, with stock options and a bull market like no other, the CEO made five hundred times on average what the typical worker made.

Phillips and others point out that the last twenty years or so are a period much like the late 1800s, the era of the robber barons. But, in fact, there is a disturbing difference. When such fabulous wealth accrued in the past, such as in the late 1880s and the 1920s, the economy grew rapidly. Wages on average rose handsomely, even if unevenly, over these years for most levels of workers. So did the typical family's net worth. Rising revenues enabled the nation to afford a federal government that ultimately minimized worker abuses and established new regulations for trade and markets. A case could at least be made that rising inequality was a price worth paying for rapid economic growth—a case I nevertheless think is wrong. Had incomes been more equal and abuse less prevalent, I believe that the economy would have grown still faster.

Since the rise of inequality in the recent era, however, the economy grew unusually slowly with the exception of the late 1990s. Even including the rise in wages in the late 1990s, average wages in 2002 were still only slightly higher than they were in 1973. Male workers bore the brunt of this decline. As they grew older and more experienced, nearly half of them lost ground over twenty years and another 10 percent made almost no gain—an extraordinary failure unprecedented in American history over so long a period of time. Women, by contrast, experienced fairly rapid wage increases, but they were still earning less than men, often when they were doing the same job. Businesses clearly substituted lower-wage women for men in these years. But this did not explain the decline in the average wage for all workers. And, even with so many spouses working, family income rose at an unusually slow rate. It could no longer be argued that rising inequality was worth the price, as it could have been argued in the late 1800s and the 1920s, because the economy raised the standard of living for all others. In the last quarter century, this was not true.

Arguably, the accrual of individual wealth in this period was as extreme as in the Gilded Age, although comparisons are difficult to draw. By the late 1990s, the great fortunes were surely much larger than they were, comparatively speaking, in the 1920s or 1960s when the American economy as a whole did far better. When we analyze the data further, we find more disheartening news. Average retirement wealth rose over this period, but highly unequally. The economist Edward Wolff calculates that retirement wealth actually fell between 1983 and 1998 for well more than half of America's families. Childhood poverty rates are simply alarming. Every way they can be calculated, whether in absolute terms or by comparison to median or high incomes, a higher proportion of children live in poverty in America than in any other developed nation. Nearly one out of five children grow up in poverty in America, compared to one in twelve in much of Europe. Moreover, the gap between better off and poor children, according to economist Timothy Smeeding, was significantly wider in America than almost everywhere else in comparably advanced nations. Only British children were almost as disadvantaged.

THE PRESSURES OF INEQUALITY are by now quite severe. The strain on working people and on family life, as spouses have gone to work in dramatic numbers, has become significant. VCRs and television sets are cheap, but higher education, health care, public transportation, drugs, housing, and cars have risen faster in price than typical family incomes and in many cases, such as higher education, health care, and drugs, much faster. Life has grown neither calm nor secure for most Americans, by any means. Only in the late 1990s did all levels of workers do well, but they still had not compensated for falling behind in the prior twenty-odd years.

Some argue that Americans did better all along than the data indicated. For a while, some even argued that inequality did not rise, a claim now totally discredited. But the data are clear and, furthermore, anecdotal evidence vastly supports the stagnating economic indicators.

Yet most Americans have accepted slow-growing or stagnating wages and widening inequality with little complaint about the economy, business, or the traditional guarantees of equal opportunity before the law. A key question is: *Why?*

There are a few possible explanations. By the 1970s, America was exhausted by the modern liberal social policies of Presidents Kennedy and Johnson, even though they worked better than was recognized. Welfare programs created dependencies, but poverty was dramatically reduced, racism was seriously circumscribed, good education was made widely available, Medicare was created, and under President Nixon, Social Security was seriously enhanced. Incomes had become much more equal over these early post–World War II decades.

The bigger source of moral exhaustion was probably the Vietnam War, a mostly liberal venture. By the time it ended, the nation seemed tired of government. And the prosecution of the war was not equal. As noted, it fell largely on young working-class men to fight. The educated easily escaped the draft.

But set against this moral political exhaustion, I think it was mostly slow economic growth, high inflation and interest rates, and lost jobs that turned the nation against its long-standing progressive attitudes. The nation had to apportion a pie that was growing much more slowly—that was simply much smaller than Americans had come to expect it would be, based on their history and traditions.

Government was now easily portrayed as the cause of, not the solution to, economically tightened conditions. To many, equality now meant taking from those who worked to give to those who didn't, taking from the working class who were not disposed to higher education to give to those advantaged young people who were, helping people of color at the expense of people who were white. In the past, equality meant that most people's opportunities were expanded. But working people were now suffering, and they needed a scapegoat or two. Business escaped blame partly because government had dominated the previous period. We were tired of government. It did indeed wage an unpopular war and develop expensive new social programs. Moreover, businesspeople were not making fortunes in the 1970s. Profits in general were poor. The stock market stagnated at 1960s levels. There was less obvious cause to direct anger at them.

Ultimately, financially straitened workers did not want to pay more taxes; to the contrary, they wanted to pay less. Beginning in the difficult 1970s, victimized by both high inflation and deep recession, and before Ronald Reagan's large tax cut of 1981, the electorate rewarded politicians who promised tax cuts. Proposition 13, for example, passed in California in 1978. (Californians now pay among the least of any state's citizens for public education per pupil.) A stressed people believed what was easiest to believe and most compatible with low taxes. The economy had stalled in good part because government was too big and people lost their resolve, their work ethic, and their self-reliance—or so they were told, and they were ready to believe the claims. The fight for equality seemed to many to be destructive and financially costly. It was complicated by America's racial composition. With slow growth and higher unemployment, racial antagonism rose in America. Blacks in particular, and the social programs designed to benefit them, could be more easily blamed for economic stagnation.

Finally, as noted, the social sciences gave comfort to the national apathy over inequality and misunderstandings about the consequences of slow economic growth. The pay gap between those who had a college education and those who merely had a high school diploma was large. Even liberals talked about new analytical requirements for workers that many simply would never be able to grasp, even if they went to college. Thus, inequality was said to be a result of natural forces in a more technical and sophisticated economy. Economists even argued that the high unemployment rates—and looser labor markets—of the twenty-five years between 1970 and 1995 were essentially "natural." If government tried to reduce unemployment and tighten labor markets, it would result in self-defeating inflation.

If all these claims were true, a natural response from government might have been to help educate the disadvantaged and provide more benefits to the unemployed. Some economists favored this, and I would still argue it is essential. But laissez-faire economists dominated the era and argued such programs were simply inflationary and created dependencies. Little was done for the poor who almost invariably went to bad schools, subsidies for college did not rise appreciably, and unemployment insurance was rather dramatically reduced since the 1980s, not expanded. The minimum wage was left unchanged until fairly recently, and thus declined substantially in value after inflation.

In fact, the claims of mainstream economists turned out to be exaggerated. In the late 1990s, inequality stopped growing, not because people were more educated, but mostly because labor markets were tight. Apparently, analytical skills and free trade, if influential, were less the cause of income equality than "screening" was. When demand was slack, business hired better-educated people or those with social skills, habits, and backgrounds similar to their own. Similarly, unemployment fell well below the so-called natural rate but it did not generate inflation. And part of the cause of inequality was a new social norm—call it an attitude—for which economists have little room in their models. (With the rise of information and behavioral economics, which are often at odds with mainstream models, this is changing.) The movements toward making businesses mean and lean came at the expense of workers. It became a fashion of sorts to lay off workers and hold wage gains down, a fashion that began with the hostile takeovers of the 1970s, in which companies were bought with enormous loans from willing banks, and then costs were cut drastically, mostly by firing workers, to pay for the debt service. The habit became ingrown and continues in the early 2000s.

And the worker has had few champions in Washington in this era. To the contrary, organized labor was losing power. The influence of corporate money and the rising power of lobbyists had a great deal to do with an agenda that led to reduced regulations, few government protections, and a general drift toward privatization, even of pension plans and potentially Social Security itself, which has long been one of the two or three greatest equalizing social programs in American history. High wage costs were anathema, but high costs of capital were just fine. The most admired company in America until the 2000s, General Electric had aggressively cut its workforce and wage bill but borrowed prodigiously. Its profits grew but its return on capital was mediocre.

America faced a fundamental change in economic circumstances in those years. Growth had slowed and inflation had undermined the normal functioning of the markets. Adjustments were necessary. But the large-scale adoption of private policies that led to declining and stagnating wages and inequality was neither inevitable nor optimal. For all these reasons, America is now more unequal than at any time since the 1920s, and it has happened with hardly any discussion.

A FUNDAMENTAL QUESTION for Americans is whether the inequality in outcomes since the 1980s reflected an inequality in opportunity in these decades. In other words, did it amount to a direct challenge to one of our basic ideals? I think it did. What stands out most is childhood poverty. When one out of five children is so disadvantaged, and another one in five is nearly poor, one simply cannot argue that opportunity is equal in America. The parents of these children are typically at work, they do not get decent childcare, and early education is out of the question. Their standard primary schools are almost always below average. Measures of education quality across America are not as bad as they are often reported to be. But there are huge pockets of inadequate education in poorer and working-class neighborhoods. Some other economies also produce large numbers of poor children. In France, for example, as high a proportion of children are poor as in America. But their significant government social programs raise the lower levels to acceptable standards. Because schools are financed locally in America, poverty and poor education have become a vicious circle. Money matters. As the Nobel Prize–winning economist George Akerlof points out, the evidence is considerable that money spent in these schools has productive results.

Further, as economies become more complex and change in other ways, burdens on people change as well, and they fall on them unequally. Not only the poor, but those in the middle now bear these burdens, and slow-growing incomes for the wide middle of America make opportunity unequal. In recent times, the so-called New Economy of the 1990s placed even more emphasis on education. This economy has created greater need for public childcare because spouses have to go to work. Its demand for worker flexibility means that as workers lose jobs, they also lose pension and health-care benefits. These are all "dis-equalizing" circumstances to which the government should respond but has not.

To the contrary, it has gone energetically in the other direction, creating inequalities rather than ameliorating them. Consider the litany. The rise of defined-contribution pension plans, which supplanted old-style defined-benefits plans, helped corporations reduce their contributions but, it turns out, only the better-off were better off with them. The middle- and lower-income workers did worse. If Social Security is privatized, elderly incomes will become significantly more unequal. The march toward deregulation and privatization—partly, but only partly, necessary—often favored the well-off at the expense of middle- and lower-income workers. The nation in these years steadfastly refused to raise the minimum wage until relatively recently. America did not seriously enforce worker-safety regulations. It did not support laws to enable labor unions to organize. It found no way to provide health insurance for the nearly 20 percent of people who were not covered. It did not strengthen accounting regulations, even when the Securities and Exchange Commission tried to, beaten back by angry legislators who were lectured to by their investment-banking and accounting-industry campaign supporters. CEOs took tens of millions of dollars, workers lost their savings. The government did not adopt new protective regulations, even after the debacle of Long-Term Capital Management. It wholeheartedly supported regulation-free capital flows around the world, even when they were a primary cause of the Asian financial crisis. It reduced the coverage of unemployment insurance significantly. It reduced tax rates dramatically for upper-income workers. In general, as noted, it allowed a financial movement on Wall Street to emphasize job cuts as the best path to profitability; taking on debt was not discouraged. Many economists exalted the restraint on wages but said nothing about overinvestment in high technology and telecommunications and absurdly romantic securities speculation. The Federal Reserve under Alan Greenspan was far more concerned about wage increases than about a stock-market bubble.

Let me be clear that some of these changes were necessary. Profits were probably too low in the 1960s and '70s, wages too high. Some federal programs were poorly thought out. Private business had become more sophisticated and government direction and sometimes even oversight were often no longer necessary. Some social programs will inevitably get more expensive, especially as the population ages, and therefore the nation has to deal with how to pay for them. International competition had toughened, and required leaner and more flexible companies. In general, tax revenues no longer grow as rapidly because the economy grows more slowly, so ultimately we can afford less. But the movement was carried too far, and government's role as a protector of equal opportunity and equal rights was often abandoned. The results showed up in falling wages, slow-growing family incomes, and rising inequality. It is not just the bottom 10 percent who have fared poorly. The lower 50 percent have, and in some ways, even the lower three-quarters are more strained than at any time in the post–World War II era. International competition from low-wage nations, a more sophisticated workplace, and slow growth all contributed to inequality. But government did not perform its traditional role of a counterforce to balance these other factors, and often exacerbated inequality in the name of self-reliance and limiting regulation in general.

WHAT, THEN, IS THE CASE for equality in a democracy? Equal political rights may remain the most important issue. They are an end in themselves. But in practice, fairly equal economic outcomes have helped guarantee equal political rights. Nowhere has this been more true than in the American experience. The original source of political equality was not a simple social contract arrived at through agreement or revolution. Of course, John Locke's ideas mattered, and the European Enlightenment emboldened the Western world and valued the individual and his or her rights. But in America, the primary source of political equality was access to land. It was not an accident that Jefferson promised land to the thousandth generation when he purchased the Louisiana Territory. Land was not an issue of wealth to him but an issue of spreading political power.

Our current acceptance of inequality is dangerous for at least four reasons. First, it is unjust socially and may eventually generate spreading, if unarticulated, discontent, which will seek further scapegoats. Second, contrary to much conventional wisdom, inequality undermines economic growth because it limits the strength of demand, the optimism of a nation, and the capacity for people to educate themselves. Even now, only 60 percent of families own a PC; in contrast, by 1955, 90 percent of families had a television set, which was relatively much more expensive then. Wages were not sufficient to support booming demand in the late 1990s; consumers borrowed at record levels. Contrary to conventional wisdom of the moment, high levels of inequality imply generally low wages, and low-wage economies are generally inimical to growth. They do not create an internal market for goods and services on a sufficient scale to make production efficient. In *Why Economies Grow,* I argue that, historically, growing internal markets are a major source of economic growth, and perhaps the most important source. In fact, almost all economies that have taken off historically, such as those of the Netherlands in the 1600s or Britain in the 1700s, have been more egalitarian than those of their competitors. These domestic markets are themselves often the most important stimulants to capital investment and technological innovation. As British economic historian J. H. Habakkuk argued long ago, low wages do not provide incentives for business to invest in modern equipment or to train and provide private services for their workers. America's South, as economist Gavin Wright has shown time and again, beginning with his book *Old South, New South,* is still dominated by low-wage industries. Slow growth, in turn, invariably hurts lower-level workers more than the rest.

Third, unequal incomes can in themselves mean unequal opportunity. Poor families and even median-income families often cannot afford to live in neighborhoods that will provide their children with a decent education; they cannot get quality childcare when they have to work, and they cannot get adequate health care for the family. Costs of being middle class today—the costs of health care, education, transportation, and housing—have far outrun the incomes of the typical family, not merely those of the poor. Serious inequality of incomes and wealth already reflect unequal opportunity. Today, more than ever before, opportunity means a competitive education, and typically a decent higher education. But America probably has the most unequal education system in the developed world, supported by local tax revenues that reflect the incomes of the community. Vouchers are typical of the current response: They will save a

few and discourage many, and on balance, will lead to more inequality. Those in the bottom half of America also cannot afford the
best health care. They have jobs that do not provide health benefits.
Poor health undermines equality of opportunity as well.

Fourth, inequality can lead to a skewing of political power
toward elite interests. The congressional turn toward deregulation
and lower taxes, many observers argue, is a function of the growing
importance of money in politics. New well-financed think tanks
supported by conservatives spread an ideology about the unimpor-
tance of equality and the dangers of government. Reforms, even of
accounting principles, are beaten back by aggressive lobbyists with
millions of dollars of campaign funds. Rightist foundations spend
tens of millions of dollars to fight ideological battles. Most distressing, the growing numbers of those who do not vote in America are
dominated by the least well off.

In my view, inequality means exclusion, and the nation needs
something like a new social contract that emphasizes both inclusive-
ness and change. New programs should include a higher minimum
wage, a still more expansive earned income tax credit, and serious
savings subsidies for college. Efforts to universalize health care are
critical, yet hardly addressed. Serious public investment must be
directed toward equalizing education locally. Ideally, open discussion of how a high-wage economy can promote rather than impede
growth will begin to change social norms about the expendability of
workers. Campaign-finance reform should be enacted to minimize
the growing political power of rich people and corporations.

The nation must also recognize that times change. Americans
used to look forward, not backward. We built canals, railroads, primary and then high schools, public universities, vast public health
systems to sanitize cities; we regulated business and put down a vast
highway system. In retrospect, we think all this was inevitable, that

the decisions made were obvious. But they were all reactions to change by an open and optimistic society. Now we scorn government responses to change. We look back, unwilling to risk. If we confronted change, we would emphasize new ideas. This means family-friendly policies like flexible hours and high quality day care. In a changing economy, with an increasingly expendable labor force, corporate benefits should be made portable.

A new New Deal? Of sorts, yes. Can we afford it? There are limits. But such programs can enhance economic growth, while reinforcing our long-held beliefs in equality. After a period of soaring incomes for the wealthy, higher progressive rates on very high incomes are entirely in order to pay for part of what we need. The preponderance of economic research suggests high marginal rates do not impede economic growth by undermining incentives for the wealthy.

But none of this is politically possible without a reinvigoration of fundamental principles. Our democracy is no longer working as it should. The influence of moneyed corporations has never been higher. But the most vigorous democracies are essentially about equality—in the case of America, about equality of civil rights and equality of economic opportunity in a complex and changing environment. Democracy is not about making economic outcomes equal. Americans want everyone and anyone to be able to make a fortune. But when outcomes are as skewed as they have been, it is clear that something in the process is badly wrong. Sustaining democracy may now depend on maintaining a vibrant spirit of national equality. If equality—let's call it inclusion, because that is what it is—were again the passion of the people, as it was two centuries ago, we might accomplish what is necessary. I doubt there is any true democracy without such a passion.

PAUL BERMAN

Thirteen Observations on a Very Unlucky Predicament

I.

ON SEPTEMBER 20, 2001, President Bush addressed Congress and described the barely begun war on terror as "the first war of the twenty-first century"—a remark that conjured images of a new tide in world events, a war different from any conflict of the past. This remark has turned out to be reasonably accurate in regard to strictly military matters. The age of barbarian armies stretching to the far horizon and trying to overwhelm by sheer numbers, the age of trench warfare and massed-tank assaults, of indiscriminate carpet bombings and sky-darkening air squadrons—that age does seem to be fading into the past. We have entered an age of miniature units: Highly trained Special Forces versus highly trained underground cells. Pilotless flying drones versus snipers and suicide bombers. Instead of mass war, elite war. This is new, and even now the implications remain far from clear.

But those are military questions. In some other respects, the war on terror does not seem especially different from conflicts of the past. On the contrary, the war has conformed to patterns of conflict all too well known from the twentieth century. We have reason to glance back at the last century, then, to make sure that we understand those patterns. And even further back. For the roots of our current predicament descend deep into the past, both in the Muslim world and in the West.

2.

DURING WHAT IS CALLED the "long nineteenth century"—from the French Revolution in 1789 to the outbreak of World War I in 1914—the Western countries were thought to have discovered the secret of human advancement, the principle that, if allowed to function, would lead to infinite social progress. Science, rational thought, and general education seemed to be leaping ahead. Superstition, ignorance, and illiteracy seemed to be lagging ever further behind. Technology and industry were plainly advancing, wealth was growing, human rights were spreading somewhat, democracy and self-government were growing stronger—at least, in some places, if not everywhere. And the secret behind those many areas of progress— the all-powerful, all-conquering principle of human advancement— seemed visible enough.

It was the recognition that life is not governed by a single all-knowing and all-powerful authority—some force from beyond, a God. It was the tolerant idea that each separate sphere of human activity—science, technology, politics, religion, and private life— should operate independently of the others, without trying to yoke everything under a single guiding hand. It was a belief in the many, instead of the one. It was a faith in the usefulness of freedom of thought and freedom of action—not absolute freedom, but something truer, stronger, and more reliable than absolute freedom, which is relative freedom: a freedom that recognizes the existence of other freedoms, too. Freedom for me, but also for you. The search for truth, but also an open-minded skepticism about the search for truth. This idea was, in the broadest sense, liberalism—liberalism not as a rigid doctrine but as a state of mind, a way of thinking about life and reality.

In the nineteenth century, each new philosopher and political movement proposed new and different ways of organizing society around those liberal principles, and different ways of picturing the expected progress. There were "Whig" ideas of steady, gradual progress, and "positivist" ideas of scientifically led progress. There were left-wing theories of progress achieved through lurches and upheavals, and capitalist theories of benign market equilibriums. Libertarian theories, technocratic management theories, socialist-community theories—dozens, scores, of theories, some of them bristly with facts and figures, others poetic and visionary. Most of those nineteenth-century theories, maybe all of them, had their inconsistencies. Liberal ideas were tethered to illiberal principles, and the combination turned out to be, in decades to come, a serious problem for everyone who tried to put those contradictory and ambiguous theories into practice. But, in the meanwhile, the many nineteenth-century theories conveyed the same general idea.

It was an idea of progress toward ever more freedom, ever more rationality, and ever more wealth. Most of those theories pictured human progress as a universal event, not just confined to Western Europe and North America. And, all over the world, huge numbers of people subscribed to that same belief, even if, in their own regions, progress was hard to see. Even in regions that had fallen under the dark sway of the European empires (or the dark sway of the American empire, which was dark enough, here and there), people tended to believe that progress would ultimately be theirs, and the Western countries' advancement into wealth and freedom would differ from everyone else's only by rushing a few steps ahead. For liberal civilization belonged to the whole of mankind. All over the world in the nineteenth century and into the early years of the twentieth century, hearts pounded with excited anticipation at the achievements to come.

3.

THERE WAS REASON to raise an eyebrow at that idea even in the nineteenth century, and the reason grew weightier and more troubling as the century advanced. It was visible in the strange and astonishing case of King Leopold's campaign in the Congo—the Belgian campaign of destruction against the Congolese. What was the logic behind that slaughter? The Belgians had their reasons. But the reasons didn't add up to much. Ultimately, the Belgians took up murder for murder's sake. There was the case of the Germans in their own colony in Southwest Africa. In 1904, the Germans set up extermination camps in order to wipe out a troublesome ethnic group, the Herero tribe. Such was the white man's burden.

The massacres showed that, even in the days when liberal rationality and human progress seemed to be making their greatest strides, an irrationalist cult of death and murder was already springing up—not among Africans but among Western Europeans. The irrationalist impulse took hold of people in positions of responsibility and power—the captains of civilization, who had the ability to bring about the deaths of millions. The captains of civilization duly acted—and hardly anyone, apart from the victims, sounded a protest. A few noble individuals, no one else. Then came a single terrorist *attentat,* the killing of Archduke Ferdinand at Sarajevo in 1914 (by an admirer of Walt Whitman, no less). And the tides of European irrationality and mass murder went pouring across the European continent itself. Soldiers from the most advanced and civilized of countries slaughtered one another on a factory basis, and kept on doing so, year after year, one Verdun after another.

Each participating country could have explained its own reasoning in World War I—the Germans citing the need to fend off a Russo-French alliance; the French citing the need to defend civilization against the traditional Germanic foe; the British citing the need to preserve the British empire against upstart rivals; and so forth. But, in truth, whatever logic went into that war, sheerest insanity came out of it. The deaths soared upward into statistics too large to be conceivable: nine million soldiers killed, some say ten million, many more wounded. Four years of unceasing death. It was monstrous. Every last thing that people had believed about human advancement, the conviction that progress was inevitable, the satisfied belief that Western Europe and North America had discovered the royal road to wealth and freedom and that everyone else was bound to follow sooner or later, the grandeur of the nineteenth-century optimism—every element in that most marvelous of beliefs tottered and fell. The collapse was shocking to see. No one had predicted such a thing. The many nineteenth-century theories of human behavior couldn't begin to explain it. The theories spoke of rationality; but World War I was an outbreak of irrationality.

4.

New theories therefore arose in Europe. They were left-wing and right-wing, and always extreme. The new theories were accusations, and every one of those accusations pointed a finger at the liberal doctrines of the nineteenth century and at liberal society. The new theories examined the liberal ideas of freedom and progress, the tolerant habit of letting people in different spheres of life go about their business, the faith in the workings of skeptical rational-ism, and the confidence that everyone around the world would eventually benefit from a society organized on liberal principles. And the new theories denounced those several related principles as a horrific lie—a fraud, perpetrated in the interest of a tiny number of people. A menace, a pillage, a crime.

The new antiliberal theories drew on many sources from the past and sometimes even on bits and pieces of the nineteenth-century faith in progress. The new theories were muscular and sat-isfying. They were at one with trends in poetry and the arts. The artistic avant-garde of circa 1910 was antisentimental, antiquaint, primitivist, sophisticated, provocative, violent, anti-ironic, obsessed with the wreckage of ancient myth, and fascinated by the uncon-scious. The new theories expressed the same spirit. The new theo-ries attracted supporters right away. And, in the course of the 1920s and '30s, the new theories mutated with amazing speed into mass movements.

These movements were Lenin's Bolsheviks or Communists (who came to power in Russia in 1917), Mussolini's Fascists (who came to power in Italy in 1922), Hitler's Nazis (who came to power in Germany in 1933), Franco's Spanish Phalange (who staged their coup in Spain in 1936), and so forth throughout Europe—a new movement, sometimes two or three such movements, in each Euro-pean country, and in each country around the world that was influ-enced by European trends. The movements varied hugely. The Communists and the sundry right-wing movements hated one another with a bitter passion—though the Fascists and Nazis also drew influences from the extreme Left. (Mussolini, for instance, was originally a man of the extreme left and modeled his own move-ment on Lenin's.) The movements of the extreme Left and extreme

Right warred against each other with fanatical intensity, and yet sometimes they managed to ally. The Hitler-Stalin Pact of 1939 was, for all its brevity, noticeably warm. Mussolini and the Soviet Union managed to maintain friendly relations, just when you might suppose that friendly relations would have been impossible.

But, whatever their different origins, their varied orientations and mutual hatreds, the sundry new theories and mass movements expressed an identical rage and feeling of disgust at liberalism and at liberal society.

5.

Each of the new theories recounted a story or myth. And the stories and myths were always, in the fundamental shape, the same. They recounted the great ur-myth of the twentieth century.

This myth had a biblical origin, which can be found in the Revelation of St. John the Divine (that is, the Book of the Apocalypse) or even earlier in the Book of Daniel—the apocalyptic myth that was analyzed in the 1950s by Norman Cohn, the historian, and in the 1990s by Andre Glucksmann, the philosopher. According to the Book of the Revelation, there is a people of God. The people of God suffer and are oppressed. The people of God are besieged by satanic forces from abroad, and, at the same time, by insidious forces from within, the evil city dwellers of Babylon. The evil city dwellers worship at the Synagogue of Satan and trade in all manner of goods, and they pollute the people of God with impurities and vileness. The people of God eventually rise up against these oppressors and corrupters, fight a terrible war. It is Armageddon—a war of extermination. Even so, the war does not last long—"one hour," according to St. John. And, afterward, with the foul corrupters eliminated, a perfect society is established, cleansed of all putrifications and impurities from the past. The name of this purified society is the Reign of Christ, and, because it is perfect and uncorrupted, nothing in it will ever require change or create instability, and the reign will last a thousand years: the millennium.

The new antiliberal theories invented many clever vocabularies of their own, which differed radically from one theory to the next; yet, in their different vocabularies, each of the theories presented all of the main elements of the basic myth. There was always a people of God—a special population, endowed with unique virtues, who bore the future of the world on their shoulders and were destined to achieve the millennium. These people were described as the proletariat or the Russian masses (by the Bolsheviks or Communists); as the Italian nation and the children of the Roman wolf (by Mussolini's Fascists); as the Aryan race (by the Nazis); or as the Spanish-speaking Catholics (by the Fascist Phalange). The people of God were always oppressed and polluted by the subversive dwellers in Babylon, who trade commodities from around the world and introduce abominations into social life. These forces of pollution were described as the bourgeoisie and the kulaks (by the Bolsheviks); as the Freemasons, cosmopolitans, and Communists (by the Fascists and Phalangists); and, sooner or later, as the Jews (by the Nazis, and to a lesser degree by the other fascists, and eventually by Stalin, too).

The forces of pollution were aided by all-powerful evil powers from abroad, who pressed down on the people of God. These evil powers from abroad were described as the forces of capitalist encirclement (by the Bolsheviks); as the "pincer" of Soviet and American technology, squeezing the life out of Aryan Germany (by the Nazis); as the combined pressures of Soviet Communism and American culture and technology (by the Fascists); or as the international Jewish conspiracy (again by the Nazis). Yet, no matter how putrid and oppressive was the present age, the reign of God always beckoned in the future.

The reign was pictured as a leap into the remote past, which was also a leap into the imminent future—a return to the Golden Age that was simultaneously the arrival of a radiant tomorrow. The reign was described as the Proletarian Age (by the Bolsheviks); as the resurrected Roman Empire (by the Italian Fascists); as the Third Reich, meaning the resurrected Roman Empire in a slightly different version (by the Nazis); or as the "new Middle Ages" of the Spanish Crusade (by the Spanish Phalange). The new society was always pictured as sleek, modern, forceful, and massive—the sleek modernity that was expressed by massive, clean-looking, neo-Roman architecture (for Mussolini, Hitler, and Stalin).

And yet the new society, for all its embrace of modernity, was going to depart dramatically from the modernity of the liberals. It was going to embody a modernity of a new and superior different sort—a modernity stripped of doubt and skepticism. In the new society, purity was going to reign unchallenged—the purity that was described as unexploited labor (by the Bolsheviks); as Roman grandeur (by the Fascists); as Catholic virtue (by the Phalange); or as the biological purity of Aryan blood (by the Nazis). Instead of the many, there was going to be the one—the single force ruling supreme, cleansed of every abomination. And, in its purity, the new society was going to last a thousand years: a perfect society, without any of the flaws, conflicts, or turmoil that make for change and evolution.

In the new theories, the perfect society was expressed by a monochrome symbol, worn perhaps as a shirt—red for the Bolsheviks, black for the Fascists, brown for the Nazis. And the political structure of that purified, unchanging, eternal perfection was, from one theory to the next, always the same. It was the one-party state (for the Bolsheviks, the Fascists, the Phalange, and the Nazis)—a society whose very structure ruled out any challenge to its own shape and direction, a society that had achieved the final unity of mankind. It was a society of total control—"totalitarian," in Mussolini's word. And in each of those perfect states, the single party was itself monolithic, without factions or internal dissension—a party that represented the purest of the pure, an absolutely centralized party, governed from above. And every one of those parties was going to be ruled by a Leader who was also a symbol.

The Leader was a god. He was a genius. He was an intellectual who wrote works of unspeakable brilliance—works of political theory, works of poetry, or feats of oratory. He was a man of steel. He was the man on horseback who, in his statements and demeanor, was visibly mad, and who, in his madness, incarnated the deepest of all the antiliberal impulses, which was the revolt against rationality. For the Leader embodied a more than human force. He wielded the force of History with a capital *H* (for the Bolsheviks); or the force of God (for the Catholic Fascists); or the force of the biological race (for the Nazis). And, because the Leader exercised a power that was more than human, he was exempt from the rules of moral behavior, and he showed his exemption, therefore his divinelike quality, precisely by acting in ways that were shocking. Massacres were the sign of the Leader's greatness. The Leader's followers loved him not in spite of the massacres, but because of them. Massacres were, in any case, unavoidable. For in each version of the myth, before the millennium could be achieved, there was always going to be the war of Armageddon—the all-exterminating bloodbath. This war, in its global reach and its murderousness, was going to resemble World War I. It was described as the Class War (by the Bolsheviks); as the

Crusade (by the Catholic Fascists); or as the Race War (by the Nazis). But, in each of the versions, it was going to be the final war.

6.

The war of Armageddon was going to be characterized by this, above all: a spirit of transgression. The breaking of all moral codes. A love of death. A fascination with death was, finally, the single greatest appeal of these many antiliberal movements. The fascination drew on a long and distinguished literary tradition, back through the Romantic writers of the nineteenth century. Totalitarianism was, in its fashion, a twentieth-century flower of nineteenth-century verse—an odd thing to consider. The Romantics of the nineteenth century were dandies, though, and the totalitarians of the twentieth century were doers. The doers believed in mass murder and in suicide; and they acted on their belief. Hitler and the top Nazis murdered millions, and in 1945, as the Allied armies closed in, the top Nazis also killed themselves. Stalin oversaw the death of many millions; and, around the world, people rushed to join his party, and hoped to rise within it.

In the Soviet Union, most of the Communists who rose to the top were eventually killed on the orders of Stalin himself. This did not discourage other people from seeking careers in the Communist Party. The late 1930s was the high point of Stalin's murder of his own comrades, in the Moscow Trials; and the late 1930s proved to be the high point of Communism's prestige in the Western countries. In later years, after Stalin's death, Soviet Communism lost its taste for murder and mass death; and masses of people in Western Europe and in the United States lost their taste for Soviet Communism. No matter: Mao picked up where Stalin had left off. Mao killed millions. And, all over the world in the 1960s and early '70s, people chanted Mao's name and waved his Little Red Book. If the Beatles sang a song mocking people who ran around quoting Chairman Mao, it was because, among the Beatles' personal friends and fans, a lot of people were running around quoting Chairman Mao.

One of Franco's generals cried, *"Viva la muerte!"* and, during the Spanish Civil War, Franco's political movement adopted that cry as a slogan. In the antiliberal movements of the twentieth century, everyone, on the Right and the Left alike, eventually adopted that slogan, in one way or another.

The new antiliberal movements that arose after World War I proposed many imaginative programs for human betterment—the achieving of complete efficiency, the total triumph of the state over society, the cleansing of the race, the full victory of Catholic humanism, and so forth—all for the purpose of achieving the final unity of mankind, the reign of purity, the abolition of skepticism and uncertainty, and the creating of an eternal society capable of enduring a millennium. None of those grand-scale programs could ever be realized, though—except in one way. Unity, purity, and eternity were readily at hand, in the form of mass death. And so, each of the antiliberal movements launched massacres, and each movement's popularity duly increased because the ultimate program became visible at last, in the sphere of the dead. Many slogans in the twentieth-century totalitarian movements were unrealizable; but *"Viva la muerte!"* was a realizable slogan.

7.

THE ANTILIBERAL MOVEMENTS OF the twentieth century were paranoid movements. They felt themselves to be under deadly attack from the Babylonian polluters at home and the satanic forces abroad. And so, each one of these movements launched wars in several directions at once—external wars that were indistinguishable from internal purges. The paranoid beliefs of the antiliberal movements were the principal cause of war in the twentieth century—which is not to say that the liberal countries and the European imperialists did not sometimes launch wars of their own.

8.

THE TOTALITARIAN IDEOLOGIES were irrationalist. Fascism was frankly and openly irrationalist. Communists pretended that dialectical materialism, in the Communist version, was rationality itself. But dialectical materialism was, in fact, a mystical doctrine whose true meaning could only be divined by the party chieftains. The appeal of dialectical materialism always rested on the fact that nobody could understand it. The doctrine made people shiver with a sense of mystery—a feeling of intelligence beyond what was intelligible. But this aspect of the totalitarian movements—the devotion to irrationalism—made those movements very difficult for other people to understand.

Liberal-minded thinkers sometimes found it very difficult to believe that great numbers of perfectly intelligent people would join an irrationalist movement; and the liberal-minded thinkers therefore tried their hardest to discover a hidden rationality within those movements. Chamberlain ceded to Hitler at Munich because he wanted to believe that Hitler was expressing reasonable German desires. Chamberlain imagined that Hitler was looking for greater influence in Europe, a reworking of the Treaty of Versailles and its injust provisions, and a few border adjustments in Germany's favor—normal demands of a normal state, even if Hitler's oratory sounded a little demented. But Chamberlain was mistaken. Hitler dwelled on a different plane altogether, and no series of mundane concessions or new arrangements among states was going to satisfy him. Hitler yearned for the Apocalypse, and he knew how to achieve it, too, which was by sending his own soldiers to die, and by setting up his death camps. In order to defeat Nazism, then, liberal-minded thinkers had to confront their own assumptions about the reasonableness of other people. This was not easy to do.

Liberal-minded thinkers had even more trouble understanding Soviet Communism. People tried to believe that Stalin conquered Eastern Europe because he needed a buffer to protect the Soviet Union from Western aggression—that is, he wanted what any normal state might want to achieve, given Russia's history as the victim of German attacks. But Stalin's empire was not a normal state. It was an ideological empire based on irrationalist doctrines, and when, in the age of Gorbachev, the empire finally collapsed, the collapse came about because the Communists themselves had given up on Communism. A decisive number of Communist leaders preferred, by the end, to try to become rich businessmen or mafia chiefs instead of leaders of Bolshevism's imaginary world proletariat. Their new ambitions were of this world; but ambitions of this world could be achieved only by abandoning the Soviet Union and the Soviet empire. And so, the empire collapsed.

9.

IN THE TWENTIETH CENTURY, the totalitarian movements arose as ideological forces, and they were defeated, too, in the field of thought and belief. The war against the Fascist Axis was extremely violent, and the Cold War against Soviet Communism was, at least in Europe, not at all violent (though, with a few chance events, violence could easily have broken out, at the level of nuclear war, no less). Yet both of those wars were fundamentally ideological. Final victory in World War II was not achieved by troops rolling into Berlin. Final victory was achieved by de-Nazification, which took several decades and perhaps in some respects is still going on. De-Nazification began as a purge of officials in German institutions, as administered by the anti-Nazi Allies after the war; but de-Nazification was ultimately a mental process, a purging of Nazi ideas, which was undertaken by the Germans themselves, inside their own heads. Final victory in the Spanish Civil War—the liberal triumph over Franco and Spanish Fascism—came about in the 1970s, when the Fascists themselves began to give up on Fascism. Final victory in the Cold War was achieved when the Communists agreed, of their own free will, to give up on Communist ideology. Victory, in each case, came about when the totalitarians had been convinced of the erroneous nature of their own ideas.

It was not enough merely to defeat those movements militarily or to outcompete them economically—not enough because each of the totalitarian movements was genuinely enormous, with a following of millions of people. No amount of military force or economic pressure could have sufficed to keep those millions of people down, if they had still believed in their own cause. The millions had to change their minds.

10.

ALL OF THE TOTALITARIAN MOVEMENTS of the twentieth century arose in a period of fifteen or twenty years, from 1917 into the 1930s.

The earliest of the movements appeared in Europe and spread from there to other parts of the world. A variant on the European idea arose, however, in the Muslim world—a strictly Muslim totalitarianism, which got under way simultaneously with the European movements, or half a beat later. The Muslim totalitarianism arose in two main versions: Islamism, which was founded in 1928 as the Muslim Brotherhood in Egypt, later on with a different organization in Pakistan, and Baathism, which began as a radical branch of pan-Arabism in the 1920s and '30s and formed its own Arab Baath (Renaissance) Party in 1943.

Muslim totalitarianism followed European totalitarianism in all important particulars. The Book of the Revelation may be a Christian text (and the Book of Daniel a Jewish text), but nothing prevented either Christian or Jewish myth from adopting all kinds of colorful new costumes and labels. The Nazis took the myth of the Apocalypse and dressed it in the Wagnerian costumes of Nordic pagans. The Communists took that same myth and dressed it in the proletarian cap and leather jacket of anticlerical and atheist factory workers. Nothing prevented that same myth from donning Muslim robes.

In the Muslim totalitarianism, there was, then, a people of God. The people of God were described as the Muslims themselves (by the Islamists) or as the Arab nation (by the Baathi). The people of God were being polluted by forces from within. These internal corrupters were described as the Jews, the Zionists, the Communists (for Baathi and Islamists alike), the Freemasons (for the Baathi), and, above all, the Muslim secularists and hypocrites (for the Islamists). The people of God were also under assault by sinister forces from abroad. The sinister forces were described as the Zionists once again, together with the Western imperialists and, in time, the United States. The paranoid element in the Muslim totalitarianism was large, especially the feeling that all of Islam was under assault from Zionists. (I am not the first to observe that a paranoid belief in sinister Jewish conspiracies turns out to be the most widely shared doctrine of the last hundred years around the world.)

And yet, the people of God were eventually going to win. They were going to exterminate the internal corrupters and fend off the external forces of oppression. And they were going to inaugurate the reign of God—the millennium. This was going to be, for the Baathi and Islamists alike, the resurrection of the Muslim Caliphate of the seventh century, from the pristine age of Islam. In Europe, Mussolini and Hitler pictured their proposed resurrection of the Roman Empire in different ways; and, in the Muslim world, the Baathi and the Islamists likewise pictured their proposed resurrection of the Caliphate in different ways. The Baathi pictured the Caliphate as the Arab Empire of long ago, with an emphasis on material power—though with a clear recognition that, in days of yore, Islam was the Caliphate's grand doctrine.

The Islamists reversed these emphases. The Islamists pictured the Caliphate in religious terms, as the restoration of Shariah or Islamic law, though with a clear recognition that Shariah and the Caliphate must wield power in the material world—must rule entire states. Because of these differences, the Baathi are sometimes described as a secular movement, and the Islamists as a strictly religious movement; but neither description is fully accurate. These two movements differ mostly in their emphasis: more worldly in one case, more religious in the other. But the Baathi and Islamists agree in picturing the resurrected Caliphate as worldly and Islamic, both. The differences and similarities between the Baathist and Islamist visions of the Caliphate have meant that, on ideological grounds, the two movements have sometimes gone to war and have sometimes collaborated against their shared enemies. Saddam did not begin by constructing mosques; but then he took to constructing mosques. This did not mean that he had abandoned Baathist doctrine—merely that he shifted his own emphasis, a little.

It has become conventional to suppose that the Islamists, if not the Baathi, are antimodern. But the totalitarianism that arose in the wake of World War I has never been antimodern. Each of the totalitarian movements has wanted to create a modernity of a new and different type, and that is true of Islamism, too. Islamists have never opposed technological advances. On the contrary, Islamists have gloried in the technological and scientific contributions of Islamic civilization in the past, and have sought a renovation of the scientific spirit in a Muslim version of the present age. Islamists want more technology, more science, and more modernity, within their idea of the resurrected Caliphate. The Muslim Brotherhood has for this reason always proved exceptionally attractive to engineers and other technical people in Egypt.

II.

THE ISLAMISTS AND BAATHI looked for an Armageddon, too—in a Muslim version, of course. Armageddon was going to be the giant struggle to resurrect the seventh-century Caliphate—a vast and difficult struggle, global in its implications, an ultimate struggle of good and evil. The Baathi described this struggle as the Arab revolution, and the Islamists as the jihad, or holy war. The Baathi and other pan-Arabists always imagined that, at least in connection to Zionism, the Arab revolution was going to be violent—violent on principle, and not just for pragmatic reasons. This has been one of the main Islamist ideas, too—the idea of anti-Zionist violence as a sacred obligation, incumbent on the devout. Even so, the Islamists have sometimes pictured the rest of their jihad in a peaceful and reformist light, rather the way Communist Parties in the Western countries used to dream of making the Communist revolution in a peaceful and even legal manner. The reform Islamists have represented only one wing of the movement, though. The more radical factions have always favored violent action, sometimes in the most extreme form. And these movements, Baathi and Islamist alike, have acted on their beliefs.

The Muslim totalitarianism has produced great leaders—figures like Ayatollah Khomeini and Osama bin Laden and other people (among the radical Islamists), and Saddam Hussein and other figures (among the Baathi). These leaders have presented themselves precisely in the style of the great leaders of European totalitarianism—leaders who appear to be superhuman, therefore mad, therefore flecked with the divine; leaders who prove their mad and divine quality by administering spectacular massacres. In some places around the Muslim world, the leaders and their movements have acquired a lot of power, too. And, in power, Muslim totalitarianism has likewise followed the European model. The resurrected Caliphate has turned out to be a modern, one-party police state, characterized by neighborhood-watch committees, a thought police, and top-down structures. And Muslim totalitarianism has brought about mass death. The Iran-Iraq War of the 1980s was one of the most macabre wars in all of modern history. Khomeini's version of the seventh century battled against Saddam's version of the seventh century, and "human wave" suicide attacks marched into fields of poison gas and land mines, and a million people were killed. In Algeria, a hundred thousand have been killed in the course of Islamism's uprising. The fighting between the Baathi and the

Islamists in Syria killed tens of thousands. Islamism in the Sudan has brought about the death of between 1.5 and 2 million people. And so forth, from one country to the next.

Mass death did not prove detrimental to these movements, though. The massacres and suicides took place, and the popularity of Islamism and the Baath increased. Nor did those movements try to disguise their bloodiness. The rhetoric of Islamism in its more radical version—a rhetoric of martyrdom and random slaughter—is scarcely to be believed. Venerable holy men speak of blood, charnel houses, and massacres. Islamist kindergarten teachers among the Palestinians instruct their tiny students to commit suicide when they grow older. Islamist preachers advise their followers to commit suicide. Young men parade through the streets dressed in shrouds, as if boasting of their coming suicide. In these respects the rhetoric and iconography of massacre and suicide have gone beyond even Nazism in their glorification of death—though perhaps that is only because Islamism prides itself on its emotional quality, and Nazism prided itself on a scientific coolness. It is true that, for all its rhetoric, Islamism and the Baath have not killed as many people as Nazism. But it would be a mistake to take comfort in that fact. Muslim totalitarianism has killed millions. Besides, the wave is not yet over; and the existence of high-power weapons and of vulnerable nuclear power plants has put Hitlerian achievements within reach of even the tiniest of groups.

12.

LIBERAL-MINDED THINKERS in the Western countries have had trouble understanding Muslim totalitarianism, just as, in the past, liberal-minded thinkers had trouble understanding Nazism, Fascism, Stalinism, Maoism, and other totalitarian movements. The liberal thinkers, in their high-minded respect for other people, have not wanted to believe that irrationalist movements are authentically irrational. The liberal thinkers have asked in an earnest spirit: Aren't these movements ultimately reasonable, even if they seem otherwise? Don't these movements express genuine grievances, and not just paranoid visions of the world? The Muslim totalitarians, Baathi and Islamists alike, have been convinced for many decades that Zionism is plotting to destroy Islam; and, among liberal thinkers in the Western countries, there has been a temptation to imagine that Israel is indeed responsible for the violence of the totalitarian movements. In France, immigrants from Algeria and Morocco have staged violent attacks on French Jews, who are themselves mostly refugees from Algeria and Morocco and other North African countries. And liberal-minded thinkers, reluctant to believe that a strictly doctrinal and irrational hatred is at work, have instinctively regarded the violence as a natural and reasonable response to Israeli policies in still another part of the world, the Middle East, thousands of miles away.

The Muslim totalitarians have emphasized their hostility to the United States—and there has been a temptation likewise to believe that anti-Americanism must similarly reflect genuine grievances against the United States. Yet what has America ever done to, say, Morocco and Algeria—except help liberate those countries from the Nazis? What terrible things has America done to Egypt—apart from siding with Egypt in the Suez crisis of 1956, and pressing for Israel to return the Sinai Peninsula in the days of Jimmy Carter, and bolstering the Egyptian economy with billions of dollars in government aid? There is a temptation to suppose, even so, that, if masses of people in those countries express virulently anti-American attitudes, some reasonable explanation must exist. We should raise a skeptical eyebrow at that supposition. Totalitarianism in the European past always cited grievances, and the grievances were sometimes genuine; but grievances were never the cause of the totalitarian movements. Totalitarianism was not imposed on Russia, Italy, Germany, or Spain from abroad. It sprouted indigenously. The same is true in the Muslim world. A great many countries in the Muslim world are awash in sinister conspiracy theories; but this is not because of sinister conspiracies.

There is another reason why liberal-minded people in the Western countries have failed to pay attention to the totalitarianism of the Muslim world—and this other reason does, in fact, reflect the heritage of Western imperialism. There is a Western reluctance to take seriously the deaths of millions in other parts of the world. From an extremely coldhearted point of view, the Iran-Iraq War appeared to be in the national interest of the United States and of many states around the world. If the totalitarians of Iran and Iraq were slaughtering one another, then they weren't slaughtering anyone else. And so, in the Western countries, liberal-minded people, responding to what seemed to be their own true interest, averted their eyes. The Muslim insanities seemed far away, and it was easy to ignore them. That was a mistake, though. Apocalyptic movements devoted to gigantic massacres do not reliably stay at home.

The difficulty that liberal-minded people have had in understanding totalitarianism explains the intelligence errors in the United States that allowed the September 11 attacks to take place. The CIA, the FBI, the National Security Council, the Pentagon—these bureaucracies simply did not consider it likely or even possible that powerful and supremely wealthy groups of people from the Muslim totalitarian movements would want to stage massacres in the United States. The totalitarians were staging massacres all over the Muslim world, and had been launching violent attacks on

Americans in other parts of the world ever since a suicide attack on the U.S. Marines (and on French forces) in Lebanon in 1983. An Islamist faction tried to demolish the World Trade Center in 1993. Yet, for all the evidence, the authorities in the United States simply could not imagine an attack on American soil—a slaughter committed for slaughter's sake, without any obvious advantage to be gained. The implicit assumption was that no one would want to do such a thing. Nor would anyone in the United States have predicted that, if Arab terrorists did stage a terrible massacre, masses of people all over the Muslim world would attribute the massacre to Israel. But slaughter for slaughter's sake has been a central theme of world history for a long time now; and paranoid conspiracy theories have always been a staple of totalitarian culture.

13.

EACH OF THE TWENTIETH-CENTURY WARS between liberal society and totalitarianism was fundamentally a war of ideas; and the present war is no different. The war on terror is a war of arguments, of textual discussions, of theologies and ideologies—a war in which the terrorist armies will crumble when many millions of people have been persuaded to abandon their conspiracy theories and totalitarian ideas in favor of liberal ideas and habits of thinking. Bush, in the same speech from September 2001, declared that he was going to wage just such a war—a war of ideas. He has not done so. He has demonstrated an instinct for acting coercively, and coercive action has been appropriate at times, given the aggressive and murderous nature of several factions among the Muslim totalitarians. But Bush's instinct for wielding a big stick is oddly accompanied by an instinct for speaking softly, or speaking not at all. Wars against totalitarianism can only be won by speaking loudly, though. Perhaps the president does not believe in the power of oratory. But then, neither has he managed to express the liberal argument by means of eloquent action or force of example. Once upon a time the United States had a Franklin Roosevelt, who knew how to wage a violent war while also waging a war of ideas—knew how to oppose totalitarian movements by offering a liberal alternative, which he expressed in words and in policies, both. The current president's policies speak, instead, of sheer power. He has evoked a world in which each nation will simply have to look out for its own affairs, and devil take the hindmost. At the very least, Bush has not known how to prevent his intentions from appearing in that light. This is a tragedy. It means that America's president has decided to withdraw from the war of ideas. In this one field, he appears to favor unilateral disarmament. The terrorists and totalitarians speak; but Bush does not answer, or does so only fitfully.

The war of ideas will have to go on nonetheless, with or without the White House. Here we run into a serious difficulty, though, and this difficulty reflects yet another heritage of Western imperialism. During earlier wars of liberalism against totalitarianism, it was relatively easy for people with liberal ideas in the Western countries to strike up arguments and debates with the champions of Fascist or Communist totalitarianism. Muslim totalitarianism has the appearance of being more exotic. People find it is easy to suppose that Muslim totalitarianism represents something utterly outside the main intellectual currents of Western society and therefore impervious to argument—a special Muslim barbarism, perhaps, remote from anything in the Western experience.

That is a delusion. The notion that Muslim totalitarian ideas derive from strictly Muslim sources, without reference to the Western intellectual tradition, is itself a Muslim totalitarian idea. We should resist it. The philosophical roots of Muslim totalitarianism trace back in some instances to the same German Romantic philosophical roots that led to the totalitarianism of Europe. The Stalinist, Fascist, and Nazi influences—the influences of Europe, in short—are all too obvious in the Muslim totalitarian movements. But this means that a war of ideas is entirely viable. Liberal-minded people and the Muslim totalitarians do not live on different planets. The war of persuasion is, in fact, what the Muslim totalitarians fear most of all. The whole purpose of totalitarian movements has always been to erect a wall against liberal ideas, and that has certainly been the purpose of the Baathi and Islamists—to erect a wall against ideas from the liberal world precisely because those ideas might well gain ground among Arabs and Muslims.

Where should the war of ideas be waged? Paris and London are the intellectual capitals of the Arab world, and the war should take place there, first of all. The Europeans will have to play their role. The Europeans may not be up to the task. Europe, on its own, has never been able fully to resist totalitarianism in the past. Unfortunately, life has offered Europe a new opportunity—the chance to get it right, this time. But Europe's failures, if they remain failures, will only make America's responsibilities all the greater. There is a responsibility to put up a fight, militarily, and Americans will have to accept it. But there is an even greater responsibility to speak convincingly for liberal ideas, in spite of liberalism's every grievous failing—a responsibility to give the military actions a purpose and meaning. To speak on our own behalf, and on everyone's behalf. To speak among ourselves, and to our enemies. Especially to our enemies. Even if our own government does not know how to do so.

CONTRIBUTORS

PAUL BERMAN is the author of *Terror and Liberalism,* which proposes a theory of the war on terror and totalitarianism. He is also the author of *A Tale of Two Utopias: The Political Journey of the Generation of 1968.* He contributes reviews and essays on politics and literature to *The New Republic, Dissent, New York Times Book Review,* and many other magazines. He is a fellow of the World Policy Institute and of the New York Institute for the Humanities at New York University.

WILLIAM FINNEGAN has been a staff writer at *The New Yorker* since 1987. He has reported from South Africa, Mozambique, Somalia, Sudan, Central America, South America, Sri Lanka, Indonesia, Spain, and the Balkans, as well as from many places in the United States. He has written primarily about politics, war, poverty, race, U.S. foreign policy, and globalization. He is the author of four books: *Crossing the Line, Dateline Soweto, A Complicated War,* and *Cold New World.* He lives in New York City with his wife and daughter.

TODD GITLIN, a professor of journalism and sociology at Columbia University, is the author of ten books, including *The Whole World Is*

Watching; The Sixties: Years of Hope, Days of Rage; Media Unlimited: How the Torrent of Images and Sounds Overwhelms Our Lives; and *Letters to a Young Activist.* He was president of Students for a Democratic Society in 1963–64 and helped organize the first national demonstration against the Vietnam War in 1965. He is a contributing writer to *Mother Jones* and a member of the editorial boards of *Dissent* and *The American Scholar.*

SUSIE LINFIELD is the associate director of the Cultural Reporting and Criticism program at New York University. She writes about culture and politics for a variety of publications, including the *Los Angeles Times Book Review, The Nation, Dissent, Salmagundi,* the *Boston Review,* and the *Washington Post Book World.*

JEFF MADRICK is editor of *Challenge* magazine and contributing economics columnist for the *New York Times.* In addition, he is editor of *Indicators,* a new journal about the quality of life. He is the author of *Taking America, The End of Affluence,* and, most recently, *Why Economies Grow.* He is a regular contributor to the *New York Review of Books,* and has written for a variety of other publications. He is also adjunct professor of humanities at the Cooper Union.

KANAN MAKIYA was born in Baghdad and now teaches at Brandeis University. His books include *Republic of Fear: The Politics of Modern Iraq; The Monument: Art, Vulgarity, and Responsibility in Iraq;* and *Cruelty and Silence: War, Tyranny, Uprising, and the Arab World.* His most recent book, a work of historical fiction, is *The Rock: A Tale of Seventh-Century Jerusalem.*

GEORGE PACKER is the author of two books of nonfiction—*Blood of the Liberals,* which won the 2001 Robert F. Kennedy Book Award, and *The Village of Waiting*—and two novels. A recent Guggenheim Fellow, he is a staff writer at *The New Yorker* and has contributed to the *New York Times Magazine, Dissent, Mother Jones,* and other publications. He lives in Brooklyn, New York.

LAURA SECOR is the staff writer for Ideas, a Sunday section of the *Boston Globe.* She served as deputy editor of *The American Prospect* in 2002 and as managing editor and then senior editor of *Lingua Franca* from 1997 through 2001. Her work has appeared in the *New York Times, Los Angeles Times Book Review, Dissent, Lingua Franca,* and *The Nation,* among other places.

VIJAY SESHADRI was born in India and moved to America in 1959, at the age of five. He is the author of *Wild Kingdom,* a book of poems. His poetry has received many awards and is widely anthologized. His new collection, *The Long Meadow,* will be published in spring 2004. He teaches poetry and directs the graduate nonfiction writing program at Sarah Lawrence College.

MICHAEL TOMASKY is the political columnist for *New York* magazine. He is the author of *Left for Dead,* a history of the intellectual collapse of the American Left since the 1960s, and *Hillary's Turn,* about the 2000 New York Senate race. His work has appeared in numerous publications—the *New York Review of Books, New York Times Book Review, Washington Post, The Nation, Harper's, Dissent, Newsday, GQ,* and many others. He spent the spring semester 2003 as a visiting fellow at the Shorenstein Center on the Press, Politics, and Public Policy at Harvard's Kennedy School of Government. A native of Morgantown, West Virginia, he lives in New York City with his wife.